DANIEL WEBSTER &
THE SUPREME COURT

DANIEL WEBSTER &
THE SUPREME COURT

MAURICE G. BAXTER

*The University of
Massachusetts Press*

1966

PREFACE

This is the story of one man's contribution as a lawyer to the development of the American constitutional system. As the leading attorney of the early nineteenth century, perhaps of the entire history of this nation, Daniel Webster argued a wide range of important cases before the Supreme Court, with profound effects upon law and government. A comparison of his arguments at the bar with the Court's opinions reveals much about the evolution of legal rules and constitutional doctrines laid down by the bench. In some instances the Court borrowed heavily from Webster's briefs, and in others it reacted against them. Whatever the outcome, an awareness of the lawyer's role clarifies the profile of a case—the social setting, the political implications, the legal issues and holdings, the long-term consequences of the decision.

Except for the first two chapters and the last, which are biographical and general, the organization of this book is topical. Each chapter concerns a class of Webster's cases on a given subject or constitutional clause, though internally it has a chronological framework as far as practicable. Such an organization may sacrifice the kind of perspective that a rigorous chronological treatment could afford; but a countervailing advantage is that the reader will more readily see the relationship of cases, often separated by a good many years, on the same basic questions.

A few preliminary remarks may compensate for what is lost by this topical arrangement. Patterns emerge as one looks over Webster's long legal career, for in each of several periods the kind and volume of his work were rather distinctive. During the first of these, the years from 1814 to 1819, the new Congressman from New Hampshire predominantly concerned himself with admiralty cases. The Court decided numerous questions of prize, piracy, and neutral rights. Out of the War of 1812 came controversies relating to trade with the enemy, blockades, and embargoes. The revolt of the Spanish American colonies also caused extensive litigation. Whether a ship was a legitimate privateer or a rapacious freebooter, whether the sailors were subject to American jurisdiction or immune from it in terms of Congressional legislation, and whether citizens of the United States were or were not violating neutrality laws became recurrent issues. Webster gained valuable experience and helped formulate a system of maritime law. But the leadership fell to other attorneys, especially the superb William Pinkney of Maryland.

The second period, roughly 1819 to 1827, represented the height of his practice, coincidental with the golden age of Chief Justice John Marshall's Court. Webster's famous arguments of the *Dartmouth College* case and of *McCulloch* v. *Maryland* brought him to the first rank of the Federal bar. Indeed, after Pinkney's death in 1822 his standing surpassed all others. After several years' absence from Congress, he returned in 1823, thus making more practicable his annual attendance through the entire terms. The following year he argued *Gibbons* v. *Ogden,* the first commerce case in constitutional history. He won the decision and in doing so set forth a classic position for exclusive national power over interstate commerce. The Court did not adopt this position, but in time it would evoke a formula not far removed. *Osborn* v. *Bank of the United States* also came up in 1824, and his corporate client obtained the valuable privilege of access to the Federal courts. Webster's greatest setback, and Marshall's too, was his loss of *Ogden* v. *Saunders* (1827), limiting the operation of the contract clause of the Constitution to *retrospective* state legislation. During this time he participated in most of the leading cases relating to the contract and commerce clauses and to the status of corporations.

Despite his grief at his wife's death early in 1828, the lawyer soon plunged into business at Court. In numbers of cases the next few terms were the peak of his activity, at the very time that Congressional politics demanded so much attention. The national bank now employed him on a regular basis, and other corporations found him to be an effective counsel. Another productive source of income was a series of Florida land claims, which depended upon the construction of the Adams Treaty of 1819. But in the decade after 1827 he argued few important constitutional cases. Two exceptions were *American Insurance Co. v. Canter* (1828), upholding broad Congressional power over the territories, and *Wheaton v. Peters* (1834), rejecting common law protection of copyrights. Webster won the first and lost the second.

From 1837 to 1845 his practice declined, in part because he seemed to lose interest and in part because his political activities interfered. New judges had ascended the bench by the 1837 term, all Jacksonian appointees and foremost among them Chief Justice Roger B. Taney. With the passing of judicial power from the hands of John Marshall to such a Democratic partisan, Webster felt deep despair. "The business of the court is not now great," he wrote, "nor is the court itself what it has been." Taney's opinion in the *Charles River Bridge* case (1837), strictly construing a corporate charter, the contract clause notwithstanding, disappointed and shocked him. Yet there were occasional, surprising successes. For example, Taney and his associates adopted a very generous rule of comity to permit the interstate operations of corporations in the *Alabama Bank Cases* (1839). In the early forties Webster seldom entered the Courtroom, owing to his tenure as Tyler's Secretary of State. Two of the cases he did argue and win were *Groves v. Slaughter* (1841), involving the interstate slave trade, and *Swift v. Tyson* (1842), laying the foundation for a Federal commercial law. Not long after he left the State Department, he unsuccessfully opposed the charitable bequest of Stephen Girard on religious as well as legal grounds. He argued valiantly, but the tide of the law ran against him.

In the final phase (1845–1852) his practice regained

momentum. Over several terms he argued important commerce questions in the *License* and the *Passenger Cases*. Arduously he insisted that the national commerce power was exclusive, a contention that the Court did not wholly accept even though he won the latter cases by a narrow margin. There were also issues concerning the contract clause, such as those posed by *West River Bridge* v. *Dix* (1848). In it Webster's expansive version of the clause did not prevail against the developing doctrine of eminent domain. Friendly to broad judicial power, he was pleased with his victory in the *Lexington* case (1848), which significantly extended Federal admiralty jurisdiction. Paradoxically, however, he contributed to the establishment of limits upon judicial power by the rule of political questions in *Luther* v. *Borden* (1849). Driven on by his insatiable financial needs, the lawyer continued to go into Court often, down to the last months of his life in 1852. He never retired.

Out of the 168 cases that Webster argued in the Supreme Court, he won about half. Twenty-four involved constitutional questions and therefore were especially important because they related to the structure and workings of American government. He won thirteen of these. But the *decisions* rested on constitutional grounds in only fifteen cases, of which he won eight. Not surprisingly Webster fared better in Marshall's Court than in Taney's. In the former, he won six of nine constitutional decisions; in the latter, only two of six. Yet such figures do not adequately measure actual effects. Supreme Court decisions are seldom reducible to the simple expressions of victories or losses, for they usually compromise variant ideas or accommodate opposing interests. A lawyer may "win" a case for a client, but lose some highly valued point of argument. And a "lost" decision may incorporate a fundamental part of the "losing" argument. With a standard of this sort instead of mere numbers, one can better assess the work of Webster the lawyer. The purpose of this study is to do so by examining the extent and nature of his influence upon the decisions of the Supreme Court.

I should like to thank the many persons who assisted me in writing and publishing this book. Though I cannot impose upon the reader by naming all of them, I am particularly indebted to Kent Newmyer for his expert substantive criticism of the manuscript, to the trustees of Dartmouth College for permission to reproduce Webster's portrait, to my colleague Robert Ferrell for his invaluable help in bringing the book to its final published state, and to my wife Cynthia Lewis Baxter for her collaboration at every stage of the enterprise.

Maurice G. Baxter
Indiana University

CONTENTS

	Preface	v
I	Webster the Lawyer	1
II	Court and Counsel	17
III	The Judicial Power	36
IV	The Dartmouth College Case	65
V	The Contract Clause	110
VI	The Rights and Uses of Property	142
VII	The National Bank	169
VIII	The Commerce Clause	195
IX	Constitutional Lawyer in American Politics	227
	Appendix	247
	Bibliography	253
	Index	261

I

WEBSTER THE LAWYER

In the formative years from the end of the War of 1812 through the famous Compromise of 1850, no lawyer had more effect upon the United States Supreme Court, that wondrous engine of national power, than Daniel Webster. The God-like Daniel, the Defender of the Constitution as contemporaries described him, first appeared before the Court in 1814 soon after arrival in Washington as a newly elected Congressman. During the next four decades until his death in 1852 he rarely missed a term and often argued a dozen or more cases each year. The number of his cases and long span of his practice are impressive, but the character and consequences of that practice are more important. The Constitution's physiognomy was indistinct in 1814—the Court had asserted its power to review laws but had interpreted only a few constitutional provisions—and many questions were unexplored, among them interstate commerce, corporate charters, bankruptcy, eminent domain, admiralty jurisdiction, copyright, adaptation of the common law. When Webster argued his last case in 1852, the bench and bar had examined all these issues, several exhaustively, and produced answers that would endure. Webster the lawyer was the chief crystallizing agent, so to speak, in many of the most important decisions. Without his forceful personality and instinct for the confusions and cohesions of the law, without his illumining wit and metaphors and the resounding

I

symbolism of his oratory, without his truly great contributions at the bar, the epochal opinions of the Court might have been very different from what they were.

It is, of course, a truism to say that Webster's extraordinary influence upon the Court was no sudden or easy occurrence. His early years in the hard and humble circumstances of frontier New Hampshire allowed only a modest entrance into his profession. His father, Ebenezer Webster, had pioneered in the upper Merrimack valley in the 1760's. A veteran of the French and Indian War and of the Revolution, the elder Webster was a man of ability. At Salisbury about twenty miles north of Concord he raised a large family and became a respected citizen of the town. In a small, rough frame house surrounded by rocky hills and thick forest, Daniel was born during the wintry month of January, 1782.

Farmer, tavern keeper, member of the state convention ratifying the Constitution in 1788, and lay judge of the Court of Common Pleas, Ebenezer Webster provided for his frail son educational opportunities he himself had never enjoyed. Young Daniel had no interest in farming, nor the physical endurance for it apparently, but did have a driving interest in reading. In 1796, at the age of fourteen, the rustic youth went down to Exeter to Phillips Academy where he studied Latin and Greek to be fitted for college. Next year, still a boy with more promise than training, he entered Dartmouth College over on the Connecticut at Hanover. And in his four years there young Webster emerged as one of the ablest and most popular members of his class. His favorite occupations were reading the Latin classics and English literature and exploiting his remarkable gift of speech. He excelled in rhetoric and declamation, as his ambitious orations and contributions to the press demonstrated. But his tastes were not wholly intellectual, and he loved to roam in solitude through the woods, to hunt, to fish, or to talk for hours with friends.[1]

Immediately after graduation in August, 1801, he entered

---

[1] Webster's "Autobiography," James W. McIntyre (ed.), *The Writings and Speeches of Daniel Webster* (18 vols., Boston, 1903), XVII, 3–13. Hereafter this set of Webster's works is cited as *WS*. Claude M. Fuess, *Daniel Webster* (2 vols., Boston, 1930), I, 5–61.

the law office of his father's neighbor at Salisbury, Thomas W. Thompson. Some years previously this country lawyer had settled near the Webster farm after studies at Harvard. Thompson was a loyal Federalist, an occasional officeholder (later a United States Senator), and trustee of Dartmouth College. He had taken paternal interest in Webster as the young man struggled against discouragement. In Thompson's small two-room office Webster and another "clerk" read law, mainly on their own with sporadic opportunity to question their mentor about some puzzling point.[2] To be sure, such an informal, inefficient arrangement typified legal education, or lack of it, in early America. In all the land there was hardly a law school in the true sense of the term, there were few printed judicial reports of decided cases for the student to read, nor were there American commentaries and textbooks on the law. Available treatises, Coke, Blackstone, Vattel, Burlamaqui, a few others, came from England or the Continent. Though in many states, one of them New Hampshire, county bars required the prospective lawyer to read for three years, admission to practice consisted in the casual step of a sponsor introducing the young attorney to the court.[3]

At even this early date money, later to be such a temptation to Webster, was difficult to come by. Soon after beginning in Thompson's office he learned that his older brother Ezekiel, then a student at Dartmouth, required assistance; and he decided to teach school for a while. So early in 1802 he went to Fryeburg, Maine, to serve as master of the local academy. In spare time he copied deeds for the county register and made a try of continuing preparation for the law by an occasional, half-hearted foray into Blackstone's *Commentaries*.[4] He seems to have preferred to read history and literature. "A 'student at law' I certainly was not," he later recalled, "unless 'Allan Ramsay's Poems' and 'Female Quixotism' will pass for law books."[5]

[2] Samuel P. Lyman, *The Public and Private Life of Daniel Webster* (2 volumes in one, Philadelphia, 1890), I, 259–61; II, 5–9.

[3] John A. Krout and Dixon R. Fox, *The Completion of Independence, 1790–1830*, Vol. V in *A History of American Life* (New York, 1944), 280–90; Elizabeth K. Bauer, *Commentaries on the Constitution, 1790–1860* (New York, 1952), 17–24; Webster to James H. Bingham, Mar. 16 and Sept. 14, 1804, and Thomas W. Thompson to Webster, Oct. 17, 1804, *WS*, XVII, 159–60, 186, 188.

[4] Webster to James H. Bingham, May 18, 1802, *WS*, XVII, 110–11.

[5] Webster to Judah Dana, Dec. 29, 1804, *ibid.*, XVI, 670.

That autumn he returned to Salisbury for renewed work at the law, but despite an intense reading program his spirits sank. He complained of "murdered" Latin and the agonizing perplexities of *Coke on Littleton.* Happening to pick up Espinasse's *Law of Nisi Prius,* he took heart from the plainer writing he found there.[6] On the whole he disliked his reading. He found law books dry, dull, abstract. Seldom did he find inspiration, beauty, the intellectual stimulus that would have made the work something better than drudgery.[7] Besides, he believed most attorneys were sorely tempted to be dishonest or at least careless about their ethical principles, for they dealt with "the very refuse and remnant of mankind." The chances of a large income were slight. Even the very successful lawyer earned only a few thousand dollars a year—ten thousand was an unusual sum indeed— while the fortunate businessman could expect much more because he took greater risks.[8]

For some time Webster had hoped to study in Boston. Early in 1804 Ezekiel went there to become a schoolmaster and urged his brother to join him at this "focus of information," this capital of New England where opportunity abounded.[9] Daniel went and with youthful rashness obtained an interview with one of the leading lawyers, Christopher Gore, who let him into the office as a clerk. A capable Federalist lawyer and politician, Gore recently had returned from London where he had served for several years as a Jay Treaty commissioner. Under Gore's expert guidance Webster now learned more readily than in rural New Hampshire. "He has great amenity of manner," Webster said of Gore, "is easy, accessible, and communicative, and take him all in all, I could not wish a better preceptor."[10] From the summer of 1804 to the next spring Webster read on international, maritime, and common law—Vattel, Abbott, Viner, Bacon; he copied papers, looked up authorities and cases, performed the many tasks Gore assigned to him, learned how to transact the business of a flourishing law office; more important,

[6] "Autobiography," *ibid.,* XVII, 13–14.

[7] See his numerous letters to his Dartmouth classmate, James H. Bingham, *ibid., passim.*

[8] Webster to Cook, Jan. 14, 1803, *ibid.,* 131; Webster's diary, *ibid.,* XV, 179.

[9] Ezekiel Webster to Webster, Apr. 4, 1804, *ibid.,* XVII, 164–65.

[10] Webster to Thomas Merrill, Nov. 30, 1804, *ibid.,* 194.

he attended all sessions of the courts, noticed how lawyers argued, and diligently briefed judicial opinions.[11]

Finally, on a spring day in 1805, Gore escorted Webster into court and introduced him with some complimentary remarks, whereupon the court admitted the twenty-three-year-old protégé to the bar. No doubt Webster had been better prepared than most initiates. He had read basic legal references of the day, had learned a little history and literature, acquired essentials all practitioners had to have. Nevertheless he had shown no sign of unusual dedication to the law.

His prospects were good but not excellent when he headed home to open his first office in the village of Boscawen a few miles south of the family farm. He would have preferred Portsmouth but had to be near his ailing father. Often in letters to former classmates he predicted that his life would drone along in some hamlet; but the very repetition of the remark suggested higher ambitions, and in truth he did aspire to something more as he neared the end of his apprenticeship. On the advice of Gore he declined the clerkship of Hillsborough County Court of Common Pleas, paying fifteen hundred dollars a year. Later he would exaggerate the importance of this decision, for the clerkship need not have damaged his career.[12]

Webster remained at Boscawen for two years, a period neither as profitable nor as inspiring as he wished. The quantity of business sufficed, the attorney complained, but not the quality. Drafting writs, collecting debts, traveling the circuit to neighboring counties kept him employed.[13] Meanwhile he gained a reputation as a keen-witted and eloquent lawyer. In his defense of a prisoner accused of murder he argued against capital punishment and, though losing the case, impressed the court with a moving speech.[14] He was still troubled when he contemplated the legal profession. It was at this time he wrote that the

evil is, that an accursed thirst for money violates everything. We cannot study, because we must pettifog. We learn the low recourse of attorneyism,

11 Fragment of a diary kept while he was in Gore's office, July 17, 1804, to Mar. 5, 1805, ibid., XV, 178–84; "Autobiography," ibid., XVII, 17–20.
12 "Autobiography," ibid., XVII, 20–23; Fuess, Webster, I, 79–84.
13 Webster to James H. Bingham, May 4, 1805, WS, XVII, 206; Webster to Ezekiel Webster, May 12 and 25, Oct. 13, 1805, ibid., XVI, 6–8.
14 Fuess, Webster, I, 89.

when we should learn the conceptions, the reasonings, and the opinions of Cicero and Murray. The love of fame is extinguished; every ardent wish for knowledge repressed; conscience put in jeopardy, and the best feelings of the heart indurated, by the mean, money-catching, abominable practices, which cover with disgrace a part of the modern practitioners of the law. . . . Our profession is good if practised in the spirit of it; it is damnable fraud and iniquity, when its true spirit is supplied by a spirit of mischief-making and money-catching.[15]

He removed to Portsmouth late in 1807, to a hustling maritime center of about five thousand population that invited an enterprising young attorney. Brother Ezekiel, newly admitted to the bar, took over the Boscawen office and looked after the family farm.[16] Within a few months Webster married Grace Fletcher, a school mistress at Salisbury. Now his practice turned more lucrative, and soon his income reached two thousand dollars a year, three to four times what he had made as a country attorney. He spent much time traveling circuit with the Superior Court, which sat at regular terms in the state's five counties. It was no easy life. Travel over poor roads in summer's heat and winter's blizzards tried his stamina; uncomfortable, dirty taverns made him long for comforts of home; the multitude of cases he took on short notice, without access to libraries, tested his ingenuity as much as his knowledge. The genial company of fellow lawyers and judges as they sat around the taproom in evenings provided some compensation. And the crowds, tired of bucolic routine and eager for display of eloquence in the courtroom, exhilarated him.[17]

Fortunately the New Hampshire bar included several highly competent men who inspired young Webster to move ahead in law and politics, and foremost of those attracting him was Jeremiah Mason. When Webster came to Portsmouth, Mason had an established reputation as a learned, resourceful lawyer. This giant of a man spoke plainly and incisively, and from him Webster learned the value of lean, direct statement instead of the floridity so tempting to young attorneys. They were good friends, drawn together by their Federalist convic-

[15] Webster to James H. Bingham, Jan. 19, 1806, *WS*, XVII, 222.
[16] Their father had died in April, 1806.
[17] "Autobiography," *WS*, XVII, 23–27; Fuess, *Webster*, I, 94–121.

tions, but often aligned against each other in the many cases out on circuit. Webster always believed Mason was the best lawyer he ever knew.[18] The chief justice for most of the period from 1802 to 1816 was Jeremiah Smith, an amiable and scholarly judge who materially improved the state's court system.[19] Others on the scene included William Plumer, leader of the Republicans after the War of 1812; George Sullivan, attorney general of New Hampshire for a while; and Ichabod Bartlett, who, like Webster came from Salisbury. All, as lawyers and politicians, would later become involved in the *Dartmouth College* case.

At the end of the War of 1812 Webster yearned for larger fields and thought that New York would have a brighter future than any other city. "Our New England prosperity and importance are passing away," he said. "This is fact. The events of the times, the policy of England, the consequences of our war, and the Ghent Treaty, have bereft us of our commerce, the great source of our wealth."[20] Nevertheless he decided on Boston where he had many friends and where already a financial spurt was accompanying the new factory system of industry. Here he found banks, insurance companies, corporation offices. From 1816 onward, the name of Daniel Webster would be closely associated with Boston. Whatever his interests, he always would keep an office there to receive clients and prepare cases for state and Federal courts. Besides a succession of students, who received even less attention than Thompson had given him, he had assistants and junior partners to carry on during his residence at the capital. Beginning in the 1830's, he also had a small office building at his country estate of Marshfield for occasional use.[21]

At Boston he came under new and broadening influences. Ever since pre-Revolutionary days the Suffolk County bar of Massachusetts had been one of the best in the nation, and a

[18] George S. Hillard, *Memoir and Correspondence of Jeremiah Mason* (Cambridge, 1873); John C. Gray, "Jeremiah Mason," William D. Lewis (ed.)., *Great American Lawyers* (8 vols., Philadelphia, 1907), III, 3–36. See Webster's eulogy of Mason before the Suffolk County Bar, Nov. 14, 1848, *WS,* IV, 177–91.

[19] John H. Morison, *Life of the Hon. Jeremiah Smith* (Boston, 1845); Lynn W. Turner, *William Plumer of New Hampshire, 1759–1850* (Chapel Hill, 1962), 32 and *passim.*

[20] Webster to Ezekiel Webster, Mar. 26, 1816, *WS,* XVII, 256.

[21] Fuess, *Webster,* II, 319.

lineage of outstanding lawyers continued into Webster's time. While he had been in Gore's office, he admired Theophilus Parsons, soon to be the state's chief justice, and the ingenious Samuel Dexter;[22] and now Chief Justice Isaac Parker became his close friend. Parker's successor, Lemuel Shaw, was an associate in the *Charles River Bridge* case in the state court; a luminary of American jurisprudence, Shaw remained on the bench for thirty years. Webster would pride himself for urging the reluctant appointee to take this position.[23] Rufus Choate arrived in 1833 and gained a reputation as a brilliant trial lawyer. Graduate of Dartmouth, once a clerk in William Wirt's office, tireless devotee of the classics, the tall, olive-hued Choate was a striking figure and graceful speaker. He admired Webster unreservedly, and some people thought he needlessly fell under the older man's shadow.[24]

Because Webster won fame as advocate in leading constitutional cases before the Federal Supreme Court, the great variety and volume of his work in other courts have usually received less notice. Actually he spent more time on a much larger number of cases in tribunals outside Washington than in the Supreme Court. He handled every class of case, civil and criminal, law and equity, trial and appellate, from county courts to state superior and Federal district or circuit courts. Added to these were many questions brought to his office for legal advice or written opinion, part of every counselor's business.[25] The sparse surviving records of Webster's trial work indicate his effectiveness as a jury lawyer.[26] One such case was his defense

---

22 *WS*, XVII, 183–84.

23 Peter Harvey, *Reminiscences and Anecdotes of Daniel Webster* (Boston, 1878), 127–28; Leonard W. Levy, *The Law of the Commonwealth and Chief Justice Shaw* (Cambridge, 1956).

24 Claude M. Fuess, *Rufus Choate: The Wizard of the Law* (New York, 1928); Joseph Choate, "Rufus Choate," Lewis (ed.), *Great American Lawyers* III, 531–60; Horace Hagan, *Eight Great American Lawyers* (Oklahoma City, 1923), 142–67.

25 Some of Webster's legal arguments in lower courts are printed in *WS*, XI, 185–216; XV, 268–74; and some legal opinions are in *ibid.*, XV, 275–77, 288–89, 364–72, 410–36. His arguments in the Massachusetts Supreme Court are found in numerous volumes of its reports. In later chapters a few of his cases in lower Federal courts will be discussed where they are pertinent.

26 Several such cases are described by Webster's friend, Peter Harvey, in his *Reminiscences and Anecdotes of Daniel Webster*, but the accounts must be accepted with caution. See also Fuess, *Webster*, II, 312–17.

of the Kenniston brothers, Levi and Laban, indicted for highway robbery of Elijah P. Goodridge. At trial before the Massachusetts Supreme Court in April, 1817, Webster subjected Goodridge to a merciless cross-examination and exposed his wild tales as a clumsy fabrication to conceal a plan of evading his creditors. The lawyer's closing statement to the jury—one of the few of this sort reported in detail—was a model of logic and attention to the record.[27] There is a much fuller report of trials of Frank and Joseph Knapp, also before the state Supreme Court, in 1830. The Knapp brothers were up for the ruthless murder of their uncle, a wealthy, retired ship captain, Joseph White of Salem. Great popular excitement arose because of the prominence of the victim. Fresh from the great nullification debates in the Senate, Webster came in as special prosecutor, probably the only time he so served. It was a difficult case owing to defective statutory provisions on accessories and principals to a murder, keenly disputed rules of evidence, the emotional atmosphere. The Knapps were convicted, though the law was probably stretched a good deal to do "moral" justice. Webster's skill in examining witnesses and addressing the jury was very apparent.[28]

What qualities, one might ask, did Webster have that placed him in a rank so high among American lawyers? Certainly his imposing physical appearance would count heavily. Since oral argument supplied such important ingredients to the judicial process in those days, the physique, dress, bearing, and manner of lawyers materially affected judges as well as crowds. Few members of the bar made a more vivid impression. Broad shouldered, deep chested, solidly built, he suggested strength of character and will. His swarthy complexion and glossy black hair, which had given him the name of Black Dan as a boy, were his obvious marks. And his eyes, unbelievably dark and large, sometimes suggesting sleepy unconcern, flashed and cut without mercy when he was roused. Observers also noticed his bushy eyebrows, equally black, and the enormous crag of a forehead. Often in Court or Congress he dressed in a fashion befitting the patriotic expounder of the Constitution: he would wear a blue

[27] WS, X, 177–93; Harvey, Reminiscences, 97–102.
[28] 26 Mass. 495–519 (1830); John D. Lawson (ed.) American State Trials (17 vols., St. Louis, 1917), VIII, 395–670; WS, XI, 41–105.

coat, its front cut away straight at the waist, ornamented with shining brass buttons and revealing underneath a buff waistcoat and white ruffled shirt; encircling his collar was a wide black stock that heightened the thickness of his neck; altogether, he much resembled Charles James Fox, it was said, at some historic Parliamentary moment.[29]

Undoubtedly the ablest orator of his time and one of the greatest in American history, he used speech with telling effect. As a young man he had shown aptitude, but he was then too flamboyant and ostentatious. Observing others, he realized the importance of clarity and simplicity, and his style began to acquire a terseness which had special value in legal arguments where the subject was likely to be abstruse but where he had to be persuasive. Succinct sentences, repetition of pivotal words or phrases, pithy expressions graced his elocution. But he understood that his listeners must have variety. His speeches expertly mingled the simple with the complex and, though generally incisive, sparkled with literary and historical allusions. A gifted Latin scholar, he spiced his arguments with classical quotations. There was indeed a Websterian format. He commenced in a quiet, almost monotonous tone by stating the facts and questions of a controversy. His voice deepened and took on organ tones as he warmed to the topic. When he reached the crucial part of his case, his delivery attained compelling force, sweeping aside opposing positions as superficial or erroneous, advancing his own points—few and carefully chosen—with emphasis that made them plain. Finally his peroration. Wonderful moment! Here the pace slowed, but sentiment was lofty, punctuated with some of the lawyer's favorite Latin. At the end his auditors felt profoundly moved and nearly as exhausted as the orator.[30]

It would be far from the truth to credit whatever success Webster enjoyed as a lawyer to declamation alone, for the con-

[29] Nathan Sargent, *Public Men and Events* (Philadelphia, 1875), 172; New York *Tribune,* Dec. 27, 1847.

[30] See the perceptive appraisal of Webster's oratory in Fuess, *Webster,* I, 291-93. Gamaliel Bradford thought that it was "undeniable that it was Webster's power of speech that made his greatness." *As God Made Them: Portraits of Some Nineteenth-Century Americans* (Boston, 1929), 15. Many of Webster's arguments in routine cases were of course not so dramatically delivered. For example, see Charles F. Adams (ed.), *Memoirs of John Quincy Adams* (12 vols., Philadelphia, 1875-77), VIII, 536.

tent and organization of his arguments were surely as important as delivery. As a rule he prepared well before he went to court. In many cases at Washington he had briefs and other papers from counsel in lower courts. Often his junior associates at the capital looked up the precedents, searched the commentaries, prepared the writs, bills, or answers. It appears that in most instances, certainly in all important cases, Webster nonetheless took hours for thorough personal study. He was adept in using what others gave him. Then he set down his own brief, normally a full one of many pages, indicating his argument, cases cited, and sometimes key words and phrases.[31] Seldom did he miscalculate which points were crucial, which defensible, which he should abandon. As a whole his *forte* was a clear, logical pattern. This characteristic, as much as any other, marked off his oral presentation from ordinary ones.

Perhaps his most serious weakness was the variability of his interest from one case to another. Those persons who knew him well, especially in later years, believed he was nearly invincible when aroused. If the issue was not large or challenging (or possibly if the fee was negligible) he was no less human than anybody else and gave the case slight attention, yet his range of maximum and minimum application seemed decidedly wider than that of the average lawyer.[32] Occasionally he compensated for disinterest by being pompous. His behavior toward opposing counsel, even the court, might become haughty or patronizing. Usually he released his irritation with biting sarcasm, nothing unique in the legal profession. But Webster normally made a strong effort in behalf of clients and conducted himself with propriety.

His political and economic ideas naturally affected the kind of lawyer he was, and over the years certain clients tended to come to him—notably corporations in commerce and industry. As Webster the politician became the foremost spokesman of conservative nationalism, Webster the lawyer represented those

[31] His brief in *Luther* v. *Borden* (1849) is printed in Lyman, *Webster,* I, 289–300.

[32] Contrast his strong effort in *Vidal* v. *Girard's Executors* (1844) with a weak one in *Wheaton* v. *Peters* (1834), though the latter case actually raised an important legal question.

who opposed policies of economic regulation by the states. Reviewing his legal career, one finds few cases in which he argued the side opposing vested rights or upholding state over national power—even if national power remained dormant, as it usually did. His Federalist-Whig convictions were of course nationalistic. Though the New England Federalist opposed the expansionist agitation of 1812 and voted against a national protective tariff as late as 1824, he always considered his political faith the Federalism of Washington and Hamilton. In response to the new economic climate of his section after 1825, he reversed his position on the tariff; but this reflected his fundamental belief that government must secure the rights of property. In every way possible it must encourage economic development of the nation. All classes of the populace and interests of the economy would benefit, he declared, for there was no necessary conflict between labor and capital, agriculture and business, commerce and manufacturing. Nor did he share the fears of many Jacksonian Democrats that generous charters to corporations or broad interpretations of the patent laws might foster monopolies hostile to the general welfare.[33]

Never known as a lawyer of extraordinary scholarly inclination, Webster had at least an adequate, respectable command of the principal branches of the law. As a young man in Thompson's office he did not fully commit himself to serious study and relieved the tedium of Coke and Blackstone with poetry, history, or literature. The year in Gore's office at Boston deepened his appreciation and understanding of legal writings but did not convert him into a genuine student. After he had practiced a few years, a critic described him with discernment as an excellent speaker not "deep read."[34] Now and then he contributed magazine pieces reviewing a new publication or commenting on a judicial term,[35] but largely confined his reflec-

[33] An excellent analysis of Webster's political and economic ideas is Richard N. Current, *Daniel Webster and the Rise of National Conservatism* (Boston, 1955). See also Vernon L. Parrington, *Main Currents in American Thought* (3 vols., New York, 1927), II, 304–16; Robert L. Carey, *Daniel Webster as an Economist* (New York, 1929).

[34] William Plumer, Jr., "Reminiscences of Daniel Webster," *WS*, XVII, 546.

[35] Review of Volume III of Wheaton's Reports in *North American Review* VIII (Dec., 1818), 69–71; summary of work of 1836 term of the Court, *WS*, XV, 112–13.

tions on the law to practical preparation necessary for arguing a case. His Supreme Court briefs, buttressed with citations to state and Federal decisions and a few special references, were similar in this respect to most other briefs.

Like everyone in the profession of his day, Webster relied heavily upon English authorities. Blackstone's great work continued a staple in the United States far into the nineteenth century. Other writers upon the common law, admiralty jurisprudence, equity, special pleading were standbys; and he constantly used English decisions not only from the colonial period but from current reports. His observations of bench and bar in England reinforced respect for that country's law when he visited there in 1839. "They are vastly better *trained* than we are," he noted, though he thought that the oral arguments were brief and schoolboyish.[36]

With appearance of Chancellor James Kent's *Commentaries* in 1826, Webster and his fellow lawyers for the first time had a reliable guide to American jurisprudence. He and the great New York judge were mutual admirers. The conservative Chancellor often praised Webster's professional attainments, and his political conduct as well.[37] More intimate was Webster's relation with Justice Joseph Story; he profited from the judge's treatises, such as *Commentaries on the Constitution* (1833), and from his close friend's advice and assistance in many ways. Story shared Kent's highly favorable opinion of Webster the lawyer and defender of the Union in the Senate.[38] Webster himself contemplated a commentary on American law and government, but nothing resulted.[39]

A revealing view of Webster's professional career opens from the perspective of his personal finances. Except for the first

[36] Webster to John P. Healey, June 9, 1839. Quoted in Harvey, *Reminiscences,* 116. See also his admiration of Lord Campbell's book on the Lord Chancellors. Webster to Fletcher Webster, Dec. 26, 1848, *WS,* XVI, 509.

[37] Webster to Story, Aug. 9, 1819, Story Papers (Massachusetts Historical Society); Webster to Kent, Apr. 27, 1832, Kent Papers (Library of Congress), V, and other letters in the collection; Kent to Webster, Oct. 10, 1847, Webster Papers (Library of Congress).

[38] See Chapter II.

[39] William Plumer, Jr., to Webster, Feb. 24, 1847, Webster Papers (Lib. Cong.); Edward Everett, *Orations and Speeches on Various Occasions* (4 vols., Boston, 1868), IV, 222.

years when he practiced at Boscawen and Portsmouth, his annual income from fees usually amounted to between ten and fifteen thousand dollars. But figures varied widely: fifteen thousand in 1819; five thousand in 1823; again fifteen thousand in 1827, 1832, and 1844; and twenty-one thousand in 1836, one of the best years for which there is information.[40] His income seems to have been all that anyone in the profession could have expected and far exceeded what most lawyers were receiving.[41] As a rule it was three or four times larger than his salary earned in Congress. Although he represented clients of all sorts, a great many were corporations—insurance companies, railroads, banks, and shipping houses. Some, foremost the Bank of the United States, gave annual retainers to assure his availability when needed. Another steady client was the English banking house of Baring Brothers. Most business came in as cases arose, however, and individual fees ranged from twenty dollars to as much as several thousand.[42] A profitable argument was his last, in the Goodyear rubber case, which brought fifteen thousand.[43] Another was *New Orleans* v. *U.S.* (1836), $7,500, which would have been impressive had not his associate Edward Livingston received around $25,000.[44] Over a long period in the 1820's Webster appeared as counsel for claimants before the Federal commission on Spanish depredations. His five-percent commission totaled about seventy thousand dollars.[45] For *Dartmouth College* v. *Woodward* and *Gibbons* v. *Ogden*, compensation was one thousand dollars each. Sometimes he obtained a bonus when his party won. After *McCulloch* v. *Maryland* the Bank supple-

---

[40] Records of legal earnings, *WS*, XVII, 291–98, 545; Webster to David Sears, Feb. 5, 1844, *ibid.*, XVIII, 183; Harvey, *Reminiscences*, 84–85. His annual records ended each September.

[41] Krout and Fox, *Completion of Independence*, 292. In the last year of his life, William Pinkney earned $21,000. William W. Story (ed.), *Life and Letters of Joseph Story* (2 vols., Boston, 1851), I, 278.

[42] The records for 1819 and 1833 are itemized in *WS*, XVII, 291–98.

[43] *Goodyear* v. *Day*, 10 *Federal Cases* 678 (1852), in the Circuit Court of New Jersey.

[44] Livingston bore the far greater burden of preparing and arguing the case. Memorandum [1836] in Webster Papers (New Hampshire Historical Society).

[45] As a member of Congress in 1824 Webster took the lead in advocating legislation for payment of these claims. Fuess, *Webster*, I, 318; *Senate Executive Document No. 74*, 49 Cong., 1 sess.; Plumer, "Reminiscences," *WS*, XVII, 552; Webster to George Blake, Dec. 20, 1823, *ibid.*, 334; Webster to Fletcher Webster, Dec. 20, 1847, *ibid.*, XVI, 488.

mented his retainer of five hundred dollars with fifteen hundred more.[46] Webster's accounting was rather casual, and he managed his financial affairs so carelessly it is doubtful he knew the exact sums of his receipts and expenditures; but he was not at all philosophical when it occurred to him that he had not received his fees in due course.[47]

Without much question Webster's notorious ineptitude with regard to money was the primary reason he continued to practice law actively throughout his lifetime. It is likely that without this incentive he would have made a much fainter mark on constitutional law. Other men having the income he enjoyed and being as fully engaged in politics would have retired or slowed down. It was not because he did not wish to, but because he could not otherwise maintain his extravagant level of living. Often he complained about the drudgery of going into court when he preferred the leisure and sports of Marshfield or excitements of politics. "To be sure, I should be very glad to be done with the courts," he declared in 1844, "but their atmosphere, if not altogether pleasant, is yet usefully *bracing,* to those whose purses are slender, however it may be with their constitutions."[48] During his latter years he was constantly in financial trouble and seemed driven to heavy practice by what he sadly thought his "singular destiny."[49] Sometimes he blamed peculiar defects of the profession. "After twenty-five years' observation," he lamented, "I can give it as the condensed history of most, if not all, good lawyers, that they lived well and died poor."[50]

However tempting it is to conclude that Webster looked upon his professional labors solely, to use the expression of his

[46] Langdon Cheves to Webster, Apr. 2, 1819, Webster Papers (New Hamp. Hist. Soc.), I.
[47] On the case of *Rhode Island* v. *Massachusetts,* see Webster to John Davis, Apr. 16, 1841, *WS,* XVI, 340–41. For his fees from the Bank of the United States, see Chapter VII.
[48] Webster to Mason, Feb. 6, 1844, *WS,* XVI, 424.
[49] Webster to Samuel P. Lyman, Jan. 15, 1849, *ibid.,* 511. In his correspondence there is plentiful evidence of his constant financial difficulties and their relationship to his law practice. His former law teacher, Christopher Gore, once said that "however much he may justly earn & receive from his Profession, he will never be other than he has been for years in his pecuniary Relations." Gore to Rufus King, June 2, 1822, Charles R. King (ed.), *The Life and Correspondence of Rufus King* (6 vols., New York, 1900), VI, 473. A general discussion of Webster's finances is in Fuess, *Webster,* II, 384–94.
[50] Speech to the bar of Charleston, South Carolina, 1847, *WS,* IV, 88.

early years, as a means of "money catching," the fact is that his attitude was not completely materialistic, for no one could have given so much energy to such a long and busy career without other motives. When he paused to reflect, Webster understood the social and political importance of the law, "that noble profession," he once said, "that sublime science which we all pursue." In a republic like the United States, he believed, a lawyer's service was to maintain its valued institutions. More conservative than creative, this function was indispensable to society, he thought, and deeply satisfying to the lawyer who performed it.[51]

All things considered, Webster deserved his eminent position among American lawyers. His style not unusually colorful or elegant, his learning in special branches of the law not profound, term after term he came to Court as well or better prepared for argument than the rest of the bar. His unexcelled oratory in a day of oral argument, his great power of organization and analysis, the setting in which he practiced before the Supreme Court: such factors explain his lustrous reputation. During Webster's lifetime when the country was first defining the nature of the Constitution, no one his equal in capacity and performance argued so many important cases over such a span of years. Nor has anyone since.

[51] *Ibid.*, 88, 92.

II

COURT AND COUNSEL

On a winter's morning in 1814 Representative Webster left the endless disputes in Congress about the war with England and went down to the Capitol basement to argue a case before the Supreme Court—his first appearance before the highest tribunal of the land. Entering the doorway he looked upon an unpretentious, gloomy room hardly suggesting the Court's increasing importance. The small Courtroom directly beneath the Senate Chamber was neither attractive nor comfortable. A lawyer at the counsel table faced the long bench on a platform near the east wall; three windows behind the bench admitted a dim light; and overhead a low-arched ceiling supported by massive pillars further hindered vision. Along the perimeter of the semicircular room ranged the seats, not nearly enough when an interesting case came up for argument. Women and other favored persons would then sit beside and around the justices or at the attorneys' table, and less fortunate visitors would squeeze into the aisles and corners. At an ordinary session such as this one the few spectators were other lawyers or Congressmen coming in to pass an idle hour.

The seven justices gathered behind the bench and in full view put on their black silk robes. By eleven o'clock they were in their customary places, the Chief Justice in the center, on either side his associates in order of seniority. On or around the platform were other officers—Attorney General, Clerk, Reporter, Marshal. The session began with the Marshal's cry: "Oyez, oyez, oyez! The Supreme Court of the United States is now in session. All persons having business before the Court, will be heard. God save the United States and this honorable Court!"[1]

Presiding was John Marshall. The sociable disposition and unaffected manners, the careless dress, the warm good humor of this great Virginian were well known to friends at Washington and Richmond. In Court he guided proceedings with dignity and patience—with a genius for leadership unmatched in the Court's history to the present day. His personal and judicial attributes seemed, in a way, inconsistent; yet their combination explained his greatness. He was a successful chief justice because he was able to understand those with whom he served. His strength lay in the way he and his associates arrived at decisions. Marshall was always anxious to maintain the unity of his Court.[2] Whenever possible, he delivered the Court's opinion; and so in thirty-four years on the bench nearly half the 1106 opinions were his. Of sixty-two constitutional decisions, thirty-six were his.[3] Many opinions represented concession by all members of the Court, including the Chief Justice.[4] Because he could usually

[1] Fuller information about the Courtroom is in the following, from which the above description has been taken: Charles Warren, *The Supreme Court in United States History* (3 vols., Boston, 1923), I, 457–61; Oliver H. Smith, *Early Indiana Trials and Sketches* (Cincinnati, 1858), 137–39; George Van Santvoord, *Sketches of the Lives and Judicial Services of the Chief-Justices of the Supreme Court of the United States* (New York, 1854), 459–60. Damage to the Capitol, caused by the British raid of 1814, forced the Court to hold its sessions in other quarters for the terms, 1815–18.

[2] Jefferson attributed Marshall's power to his opportunistic craftiness, but this was a partisan view. Albert J. Beveridge, *The Life of John Marshall* (4 vols., Boston, 1916–19), IV, 80–95, emphasizes the importance of Marshall's personality and especially his comradeship with his fellow judges at their Washington boarding house. The latter explanation seems too superficial.

[3] Henry Hitchcock, "Constitutional Development in the United States as Influenced by Chief-Justice Marshall," in Thomas M. Cooley et al., *Constitutional History of the United States as Seen in the Development of American Law* (New York, 1890), 56–57.

[4] See Bushrod Washington's opinion in *Ogden* v. *Saunders,* 12 Wheaton 263–64 (1827), and Johnson's, *ibid.,* 272–73, commenting on the Court's compromise in *Sturges* v. *Crowninshield* (1819). In *Mason* v. *Haile,* 12 Wheaton 379 (1827), Washington said, "It has never been my habit to deliver dissenting opinions in cases where it has been my misfortune to differ from those which have been pronounced by a majority of the Court." In *Inglis* v. *Trustees of Sailor's Snug Harbor,* 3 Peters 145 (1830), Story said, "It is not without reluctance, that I deviate from my usual practice of submitting in silence to the decisions of my brethren, when I dissent

form a consensus or remained silent when he could not, Marshall dissented in only eight cases and in just one constitutional case.[5] Soon after Webster began to practice before the Court, the United States concluded a peace treaty with England, and some of the sectionalism, so bothersome before 1815, diminished as a mood of high nationalism swept the political scene. The Marshall Court now announced its boldest constitutional decisions, upholding national sovereignty by restricting state powers. Marshall's doctrines harmonized with the day. It is perhaps an exaggeration to say that the country thus came round to Marshall's view. Unquestionably these few years, the Era of Good Feelings, offered the Chief Justice a splendid opportunity to build a constitutional law consonant with his nationalism.

It took some time, perhaps, for Webster to make an impression on the Court and its Chief Justice, yet an impression he surely made. Though Marshall was always guarded in comments about politics and personalities, it is clear his opinion of Webster as politician and as lawyer was entirely favorable. In 1834, a year before his death, Marshall wrote to Story endorsing his associate's article in the *New England Magazine* which lauded Webster as a statesman. It was lamentable, he observed, that so many politicians either talked nullification or supported President Andrew Jackson's usurpations and did not measure up to the high standards set by the great constitutional lawyer.[6] Marshall also wrote Webster in approval of the Senator's speeches for renewing the national bank's charter (after he had extensively discussed the question, he apologized for betraying himself "into the politics of the day").[7] In Court Marshall came to an enormous admiration of Webster's professional abilities. His opinions are replete with references to the attorney's argumentative eloquence, exhaustiveness, and logic. In *Gibbons* v.

---

from them." See also Donald G. Morgan, *Justice William Johnson: The First Dissenter* (Columbia, So. Car., 1954).

[5] In apologetically filing a dissent, Marshall once said: "I should now, as is my custom, when I have the misfortune to differ from this Court, acquiesce silently in its opinion." *Bank of U.S.* v. *Dandridge*, 12 Wheaton 90 (1827).

[6] [Joseph Story], "Statesmen—Their Rareness and Importance. Daniel Webster," *New England Magazine*, VII (Aug., 1834), 89–104; Marshall to Story, Oct. 6, 1834, William W. Story (ed.), *Life and Letters of Joseph Story* (2 vols., Boston, 1851), II, 172–73.

[7] Marshall to Webster, June 16, 1832, *WS*, XVII, 518–19.

Ogden the Chief Justice referred approvingly to the attorney's contention that such commerce as Congress left unregulated was meant to be free. He said this even though he did not determine the question on that basis. In *Johnson* v. *McIntosh* Marshall found no difficulty deciding the case against Webster's client, yet he carefully wrote a full opinion because, he said, counsel's argument had been so elaborate.[8] In *Ogden* v. *Saunders* he completely adopted Webster's points for his sole dissent in a constitutional case.[9]

Webster reciprocated the admiration. His first term in Court he was struck by the intellect and character of the Chief Justice.[10] Esteem grew to veneration, and after Marshall's death Webster could not mention the Virginian's name or decisions without recalling his pre-eminent judicial qualities.[11] With the passage of time Marshall seemed to symbolize for Webster the Constitution itself.

In considering the forces that impinged upon the thought of Webster the constitutional lawyer, one must mention, in addition to Marshall, the Chief Justice's eminent colleague Joseph Story. During his many years on the bench this jurist-scholar surpassed even Marshall in nationalistic, conservative ideas. Story's sensitive facial expressions, amiable disposition, and studious habits revealed a man of rare qualities. Possessing amazing resources of intellect and industry, he might have been one of the outstanding politicians of his day if he had continued his career as state legislator and Congressman. Or if he had never served in the Court, his illustrious accomplishments as a Harvard law professor and prolific author of legal treatises would have entitled him to a place in history. His learned three-volume *Commentaries on the Constitution* plainly speaks his attachment to vested rights, English common law, and national power.[12]

---

[8] 8 Wheaton 604–05 (1823).

[9] The Court Reporter, Richard Peters, wrote to Marshall on March 20, 1830, and said that if he continued to report arguments of counsel, he would be compelled to publish two volumes for that term instead of one. Marshall replied that the arguments ought to be included and thought it "advisable to give us two." This was done. 3 Peters iii–iv (1830).

[10] Webster to Ezekiel Webster, Mar. 28, 1814, *WS*, XVII, 243–44.

[11] See Story (ed.), *Story*, II, 506.

[12] Elizabeth K. Bauer, *Commentaries on the Constitution, 1790–1860* (New York, 1952). The true measure of Story's contributions to the formation of Ameri-

The friendship of Webster and Story was a source of deep satisfaction to both. They spent much time together, talked for hours on end about common interests, lent books to one another, corresponded on a variety of subjects.[13] There were times when Story posted his personal letters under Webster's Congressional frank.[14] At every opportunity each was certain to praise the other. The Story and Webster families traveled to Niagara Falls for a six-week holiday in the summer of 1826.[15] A year or so later Grace Fletcher Webster died, and to Webster's letters expressing grief at this dark moment the Justice responded with sympathy and counsel that only an intimate friend could offer.[16] In turn Webster felt free to urge Story not to overwork in his many pursuits. "I beg this of you," wrote the lawyer, "out of the depths of my regard & affection. *For all our sakes spare yourself.*"[17] On political issues Story and Webster agreed completely. Nominally a Jeffersonian Republican before appointment to the Court, the Justice identified himself as an independent but was in fact Federalist, National Republican, and Whig in all he thought about politics. And he thought about politics a good deal.[18] Understandably Webster appeared to Story the very model of a constructive statesman. As early as 1821 after the two men had served as delegates to a state constitutional convention, Story predicted his friend would surely rise to the presidency.[19] Years later Story wrote an anonymous

---

can law awaits a long-needed competent biography. William W. Story (ed.), *Life and Letters of Joseph Story* (2 vols., Boston, 1851) is useful only as a convenient printing of some of Story's correspondence. Several valuable essays on Story have been recently published, such as Henry S. Commager, "Mr. Justice Story," in Arthur N. Holcombe et al., *Gaspar G. Bacon Lectures on the Constitution of the United States* (Boston, 1953), and R. Kent Newmyer, "Joseph Story and the War of 1812: A Judicial Nationalist," *Historian,* XXVI (Aug., 1964), 486–501.

[13] The Story Papers at the Massachusetts Historical Society contain many items showing this relationship.

[14] Story to Charles Sumner, Feb. 6, 1833, and Jan. 24, 1834, Sumner Papers (Harvard University).

[15] Story (ed.), *Story,* I, 449–80.

[16] Numerous letters during January and February, 1828, Story Papers (Lib. Cong.).

[17] Webster to Story, Sept. 18, 1830, *Proceedings of the Massachusetts Historical Society,* Second Series, Vol. XIV (1900–01), 408.

[18] See R. Kent Newmyer, "A Note on the Whig Politics of Justice Joseph Story," *Mississippi Valley Historical Review,* XLVIII (Dec., 1961), 480–91.

[19] Story to Jeremiah Mason, Jan. 21, 1821, *Story* (ed.), Story, I, 395–96.

article commending Webster in every particular of his career and denying any inconsistency in his positions, on the Union, national bank, or tariff.[20]

Countless times Story advised Webster the politician. The Judge drafted judiciary and bankruptcy bills, a criminal code, and other proposals which Webster sponsored in Congress; and during the Missouri debates Webster, though not in Congress, probably received help from Story in drawing a memorial against the extension of slavery.[21] At the height of the national bank controversy in 1833, Story composed a long paper opposing removal of the government's deposits from the bank, an argument Webster restated in the Senate.[22] While Webster was President John Tyler's Secretary of State (1841–43), he often called on his learned friend for counsel, especially on problems arising from the negotiations with Lord Ashburton over the northeastern boundary.[23] "Mr. Webster was in the habit of drawing from that deep and copious well of [Story's] legal knowledge, whenever his own bucket was dry," Theodore Parker once declared. With a mixture of classical allusion and plain Yankee humor Parker said Story was "the Jupiter Pluvius from whom Mr. Webster often sought to elicit peculiar thunder for his speeches, and private rain for his own public tanks of law."[24] Despite animosity toward the compromiser of 1850, the abolitionist Parker was close to the truth. But he as well as others also believed Webster selfishly had refused to acknowledge professional indebtedness to Story, even after Story's death in 1845. The Justice's son and biographer William W. Story had unsuccessfully requested permission from Webster to publish correspondence that would reveal this relationship.[25] Why Webster refused is difficult to say. Perhaps to safeguard his own reputation. Or to protect what he thought was the confidential charac-

---

20 [Story], "Statesmen," *New Eng. Mag.*, VII (Aug., 1834), 89–104.

21 Webster to Story, Dec. 4, 1819, Story Papers (Mass. Hist. Soc.); "Memorial" printed in *WS*, XV, 55–74.

22 Story to Webster, Dec. 25, 1833, Story (ed.), *Story*, II, 155–58.

23 Correspondence printed in *WS*, XVI, 363–65, 367–70. See also Webster to Edward Everett, Apr. 20, 1836, Everett Papers (Massachusetts Historical Society).

24 Theodore Parker, *Additional Speeches, Addresses, and Occasional Sermons* (2 vols., Boston, 1855), I, 170.

25 W. W. Story to Webster, May 20, 1846, Webster Papers (New Hampshire Historical Society); Story (ed.), *Story*, II, 408.

ter of the letters. Yet he never hesitated to praise the remarkable achievements of the Justice as a commentator, teacher, and jurist. One of the many occasions he did so was a meeting of the Suffolk County Bar to which he delivered a touching eulogy of his deceased friend.[26]

On matters of law and administration of justice, as in politics and personal affairs, Webster and Story thought as one. Both men had exalted ideas about the role of the judiciary in American government, both deeply respected the common law, both admired the exhaustive and flowery arguments of counsel typical of that day. Story asserted that as a constitutional lawyer Webster had "no compeer." To Chief Justice Marshall, he continued, "Mr. Webster seems silently to appeal in all his constitutional arguments, as one able to comprehend and analyze them, and with a consciousness, that what he asserts, can scarcely fail to receive his decisive approbation."[27] Story's accounts of several Webster arguments show the favorable effects they had upon him too.[28] With the death of Marshall in 1835 and the coming of five new members to the Court at about this time,[29] Webster and Story despaired of the future. "Judge Story arrived last Evening, in good health, but bad spirits," Webster observed. "He thinks the Supreme Court is *gone,* & I think so, too; and almost everything is gone, or seems rapidly going."[30] Often during the next decade they exchanged complaints and misgivings about new currents of constitutional law. What would be left of the old?

Webster thought Roger B. Taney's appointment as chief justice a catastrophe for the proper explication of the Constitution and did his very best to keep the Jacksonian Democrat off the Court. In the sessions of 1834 and 1835 the Senate haggled over Jackson's nominations of Taney, first as an associate justice

---

26 *WS,* III, 295–302.

27 [Story], "Statesmen," *New Eng. Mag.,* VII (Aug., 1834), 103.

28 Story's recollections in Webster Papers (Library of Congress), XII, 18009–15, from which George Ticknor drew a portion of his review of the 1830 edition of Webster's speeches, *American Quarterly Review,* IX (June, 1831), 420–57.

29 Congress increased the number of justices from seven to nine by the Judiciary Act of 1837. New members of the Court were: James M. Wayne (1835); Philip P. Barbour and Roger B. Taney (1836); John Catron and John McKinley (1837).

30 Webster to Caroline Webster, Jan. 10, 1836, *WS, XVI,* 264.

and then as chief justice. It would have been strange indeed for Webster to have acquiesced in these nominations, for Taney had been too involved in politics. As one of the President's closest advisers and as acting Secretary of the Treasury, Taney had removed the government's deposits from the Bank of the United States in the face of violent protests by Webster. More than any other person, he symbolized to Webster all that was most dangerous in Jacksonianism. He was the "pliant instrument" of Andrew Jackson, said the Senator. Webster had found the Bank to be a "profitable client" and was its "pliant instrument," retorted Taney.[31] So on the last day of the Senate session, March 3, 1835, in fact past midnight and the deadline for adjournment, while President Jackson sat waiting in a nearby room, Webster moved to postpone indefinitely Taney's nomination as associate justice. The motion carried twenty-four to twenty-one, and old Jackson stalked out of the Capitol in a rage.[32] The President was not the kind of man to surrender; he felt compelled to try again, and this time for a greater prize—the chief justiceship, vacated by Marshall's death. In December, 1835, Jackson nominated Taney. Led by Webster, some Whigs again opposed, seeking delay until Congress should pass a new judiciary act to redraw circuits. But the administration's pressure was too great;[33] Taney now had support from a few Whigs and very helpfully the backing of the Baltimore bar; and over the opposition of Webster, Clay, Calhoun, and a handful of irreconcilables the Senate confirmed Jackson's pliant instrument.[34]

That dispiriting March day in 1836 was a moment Webster could not soon forget. This jesuitical and cunning judge,

31 Samuel Tyler, *Memoir of Roger Brooke Taney* (Baltimore, 1872), 233–34; Carl B. Swisher, *Roger B. Taney* (New York, 1936), 287–88, 300–03; *Niles' Register*, XLVII (Oct. 18, 1834), 106–07; Bernard C. Steiner, "Taney's Correspondence with Van Buren," *Maryland Historical Magazine*, VII (Dec., 1913), 305–06.

32 *Journal of the Executive Proceedings of the Senate* (Washington 1887), IV, 459, 463, 465, 484; Swisher, *Taney*, 311–14; Thomas H. Benton, *Thirty Years' View* (2 vols., New York, 1883), I, 598. The vacancy was the place of Gabriel Duval. Interestingly, Marshall approved the appointment as associate justice. Tyler, *Taney*, 242.

33 The goal was to combine Virginia and Maryland in one circuit so that either Taney or the recently nominated Philip P. Barbour of Virginia would be ineligible.

34 *Senate Journal*, IV, 499, 505, 520–22; Swisher, *Taney*, 316–23; Warren, *Sup. Ct. in U.S. Hist.*, II, 284–92.

the Senator predicted, would corrupt the office of chief justice to protect friends and punish enemies. He never changed his mind about the undesirability of the appointment, though others, such as Clay, were less adamant as time passed.[35] Webster seems to have recognized Taney's ability and went so far as to deny that the Chief Justice's Catholicism was objectionable, but never uttered one word directly praising him. Unceasingly he criticized the new Court for overturning the rights of property and diminishing national power. History has not judged Taney so severely.

What sort of man was this antagonist of Webster? Tall, thin, harsh-featured, the Jacksonian judge presented far from a pleasing appearance. Taney filled out the ugly image his enemies created of him: bony hands, irregular teeth yellowed by heavy cigar-smoking, his figure carelessly clothed and stooped. Even so, here was an unusual person with many qualities of a great jurist. Upon closer inspection the observer, whatever his bias, discovered that the Chief Justice had a razor-sharp intellect and a thorough knowledge of the law (as well as party politics). Indeed he was informed about an endless number of things, highly gifted in oral and written expression, altogether capable of the responsible office he held. Taney's lineage was traceable through several generations in plantation Maryland. Conservative, upper-class, as a young man he became a staunch Federalist and served in the state legislature; but during the War of 1812 he broke with his party because he disapproved opposition to the war by its mercantile segment, and in the 1820's he energetically supported Jackson. It was understandable that the President selected Taney as attorney general when the Calhounites in the cabinet departed in 1831. It was a good choice not merely on political grounds but in consideration of professional competence. Taney's credentials as a lawyer were excellent—a flourishing practice at the Baltimore bar then distinguished for its brilliant membership, several years as state attorney general, extensive experience before the Federal Supreme Court. Nevertheless Taney became known primarily for his role in the Bank

[35] Webster to Jeremiah Mason, Feb. 3, 1837, Webster Papers (New Hampshire Historical Society); Bernard C. Steiner, *Life of Roger Brooke Taney* (Baltimore, 1922), 182.

War. Advocacy of the presidential veto that killed the "monster," removal of government deposits from the Bank, Senate rejection of his nomination to the Treasury and later to the Court as an associate justice, all these enveloped him in controversy. Yet Jackson finally had his way, and Taney became Chief Justice.[36]

The departures taken by the Taney Court were not to be so extreme as Webster feared. If the new Chief Justice and his colleagues were attentive to states' rights, they recognized that the nation had substantial powers. And within its legitimate sphere national power was supreme, as Article VI of the Constitution said it was. On some questions, notably commerce, the Court fashioned an accommodation of state and national powers corresponding to the interests and needs of both levels of government. Taney's was no radical court in any sense. What the Jacksonians objected to was special privilege or monopoly, not business enterprise itself. It did not regard property rights so lightly as Webster predicted. Although the contract clause of the Constitution so broadly construed by Marshall was sometimes offset by the rule of strict construction of corporate charters, the states' police power, and the doctrine of eminent domain, vested rights were still secure.

Judicial review likewise did not become so weak and useless as Taney's critics foresaw. Undeniably there was a new tendency to invoke more often the old rule that in doubtful cases the greatest deference was due the legislative branch. Quite logically Taney's Court developed the doctrine of "political questions." But on the whole the Court continued to occupy a very important, though not supreme, position in American government.[37] Possibly the characteristic of the Taney Court that disturbed Webster as much as any was that it discarded the mask

[36] Swisher, *Taney*; Swisher, "Mr. Chief Justice Taney," in Allison Dunham and Philip B. Kurland (eds.), *Mr. Justice* (Chicago, 1956), 203–30.

[37] Charles G. Haines and Foster H. Sherwood in their book, *The Role of the Supreme Court in American Government and Politics, 1835–1864* (Berkeley, 1957), 287–336, maintain that Taney's Court continued to follow Marshall's path toward "judicial supremacy" in American government, despite some evidence of judicial restraint. Such an interpretation does not accurately assess the many political and social forces acting upon the Court or making the Court's decisions less than final in public affairs.

of judicial unanimity. Unlike Marshall, the new Chief Justice made no effort to conceal divergencies about issues admitting many answers. More concurring and more dissenting opinions deprived the Court of its monolithic appearance. This Taney did not regret, for it revealed the several lines of reasoning by which justices arrived at their conclusions. To Webster, accustomed to Marshall, it meant absence of a "strong and leading mind" at the helm.[38]

Webster's colleagues at the bar—as well as judges on the bench—of course influenced his career as a constitutional lawyer. What, one might ask, were his colleagues like? Throughout these years many capable lawyers helped the Court break new ground. Often they determined the direction the Court took, since from them the justices obtained cues in developing precedent-setting legal rules. In comparison with counsel in other periods these men were peculiarly well-prepared for such a function. Many, like Webster, had political experience applicable to questions before the bench. Many more contributed from their study of scarce or obscure reports and commentaries. And— interesting to the latter-day observer—most of them, owing to the latitude the Court permitted, argued their cases with an eloquence and fulness rarely displayed afterward.

During Webster's early Washington years the most eminent lawyer was William Pinkney, then at the zenith of his distinguished legal career. A native of Maryland, he had been in England almost continuously from 1796 to 1811 as Jay Treaty commissioner and American minister, had been Attorney General three years, and then turned to flourishing private practice until his sudden death in 1822.[39] Whenever Pinkney appeared in a case the result was memorable. Into the crowded chamber strode this magnificent figure, clothed in most elaborate fashion—ruffled shirt, tailored blue coat, spotless amber gloves. Intolerant of mediocrity, he often offended other attorneys but constantly

---

[38] Of course Webster believed that Story had a "strong and leading" mind. Webster to Franklin Haven, Dec. 28, 1847, *WS*, XVI, 488–89.

[39] Horace Hagan, *Eight Great American Lawyers* (Oklahoma City, 1923), 21–56; Henry Wheaton, *Some Account of the Life, Writings, and Speeches of William Pinkney* (Philadelphia, 1826), 177–89; William W. Story (ed.), *The Miscellaneous Writings of Joseph Story* (Boston, 1852), 794–99; William Pinkney, *The Life of William Pinkney* (New York, 1853).

excited the marvel of spectators. He had all the skill a situation invited. Learned in every branch of the law, he was particularly adept in prize and other maritime cases where he could apply his diplomatic experience.[40] After impatiently waiting to speak, he would argue with a swift flow of polished language. Unlike Webster, he did not need some special circumstance to arouse him. As a rival said facetiously, "he could get into his tragical tone in discussing the construction of an act of Congress."[41] He never neglected the ladies who came in taffeta droves to listen and to see. His arguments were sometimes as much legal bouquets for their enjoyment as they were briefs for judicial consideration. Once he remarked "he would not weary the court, by going thro a long list of cases to prove his argument, as it would not only be fatiguing to them, but inimical to the laws of good taste, *which on the present occasion,* (bowing low) he wished to obey."[42]

The Attorney General from 1817 to 1829 was William Wirt, a more modest if capable person, possessing qualities and professional capacity to make important the office he held so long. Virginia aristocrat, once a young Jeffersonian, biographer of Patrick Henry, he captivated his audiences with wit and smooth talk.[43] Though his practice in the Court covered a period less than half of Webster's,[44] he argued as many cases; and during his time at the capital he appeared in nearly every important constitutional case. Webster's associate in *McCulloch* v. *Maryland* and *Gibbons* v. *Ogden,* he opposed the Massachuetts attorney in *Dartmouth College* v. *Woodward, Cohens* v. *Virginia,* and *Ogden* v. *Saunders.* He also argued *Brown* v. *Maryland*

40 For eight years, as Jay Treaty commissioner, he sat on a tribunal deciding maritime claims. As the minister to Britain, 1806–11, his primary concern was to maintain American maritime rights as a neutral during the Napoleonic wars.

41 William Wirt to Francis W. Gilmer, Apr. 1, 1816, John P. Kennedy, *Memoirs of the Life of William Wirt* (Philadelphia, 1860), 358.

42 Margaret Bayard Smith, *The First Forty Years of Washington Society* (edited by Gaillard Hunt, New York, 1906), 96. See also George Ticknor, *Life, Letters, and Journals* (2 vols., Boston, 1876), I, 39–41; Edward G. Parker, *Reminiscences of Rufus Choate* (New York, 1860), 31.

43 He was born in Maryland, lived as a young man in Virginia, and retired to Baltimore in 1829 after his service as Attorney General. One of his early professional tasks was to act as one of the prosecutors in the treason trial of Aaron Burr at Richmond in 1807.

44 The years 1816 to 1832.

and the *Cherokee* cases. In his last years Wirt grew more conservative and ran for president as an Anti-Mason against Jackson in 1832, but he was basically a National Republican.[45]

There was also the exiled Irish patriot, Thomas A. Emmet of New York, brother of the martyred Robert Emmet, himself imprisoned for participation in the United Irish movement
in 1798. In America his fortunes rose rapidly. As one of the
ablest members of the talent-filled New York bar, he came into
the Supreme Court to argue his first case in 1815. He clashed
head-on with Pinkney. Protesting what seemed an arrogant personal attack, he responded with a warmth of feeling that ex-
ploded like internal combustion.[46] Through the next decade he
handled many cases, notably against Webster in *Gibbons* v.
Ogden on behalf of long-standing clients, the Fulton-Livingston
steamboat interests.[47] One day in 1827 while arguing a case
against Webster in New York, he suffered a stroke, collapsed,
and died.[48]

Among other prominent attorneys during the twenties
was the gifted Reporter, Henry Wheaton, who not only reported
the Court's decisions with accuracy and learned comment but
often appeared as counsel. He was Webster's associate in the
important bankruptcy suit of *Ogden* v. *Saunders*.[49] The brilliant
Philadelphia lawyer, Joseph Hopkinson, was active too; in the
Dartmouth College case Hopkinson was Webster's colleague,
but at next term he delivered decidedly the strongest argument
against the constitutionality of the national bank in *McCulloch*
v. *Maryland*. After 1828 he served as Federal district judge.
One of the great lawyers of this early period, the arch-Federalist
Robert Goodloe Harper, practiced until his death in 1825.
Probably Harper's best argument had been a successful defense
of Justice Samuel Chase against the Jeffersonians in the Senate

---

[45] Joseph C. Burke, "William Wirt: Attorney General and Constitutional
Lawyer," Ph.D. Dissertation (Indiana University, 1965); Hagan, *Eight Lawyers*,
57–84; Kennedy, *Wirt;* Warren, *Sup. Ct. in U.S. Hist.*, II, 154.

[46] Story to William Sampson, Feb. 27, 1829. Story (ed.), *Story*, I, 566–70.

[47] Hagan, *Eight Lawyers*, 85–141; Thomas A. Emmet, *Memoir of Thomas
Addis and Robert Emmet* (2 vols., New York, 1915).

[48] The case was later heard by the Supreme Court. *Inglis* v. *Trustees of
Sailor's Snug Harbor*, 3 Peters 99 (1830).

[49] See the discussion of *Wheaton* v. *Peters* (1834) in Chapter VI.

impeachment trial of 1805. A list of his cases includes *Fletcher* v. *Peck* and *Osborn* v. *Bank of U.S.*—in the latter he opposed Webster.

Chronologically, the Court practices of several other men paralleled Webster's. Henry Clay, better known in politics, accepted cases as time and inclination permitted. As Webster's associate in *Osborn* v. *Bank of U.S.* and *Groves* v. *Slaughter,* he exhibited more than ordinary ability. David B. Ogden of New York, never interested in politics but a tireless counselor, appeared with or against Webster thirty-two times, as in *Ogden* v. *Saunders, American Insurance Co.* v. *Canter,* and the *Passenger Cases.*[50] A perennial figure was the durable though unspectacular Walter Jones. In part because he so long served as United States Attorney for the District of Columbia and in part because he lived in Washington most of his life, Jones had nearly twice as many cases as anyone else, a total of 317 between 1801 and 1850.[51] John Sergeant of Philadelphia was also busy, frequently as standing counsel for the national bank.[52] Webster was Sergeant's colleague in some of these cases.

The Supreme Court bar of the early nineteenth century was fairly homogeneous. Due to difficulty of travel, most attorneys came from nearby cities or, as in the case of Jones, from Washington itself. Many were from Baltimore. In his dozen years as attorney general Wirt carried on an extensive practice there as well as in the capital. In the thirties Reverdy Johnson of Maryland arrived on the scene and after Webster's death was the acknowledged leader of the bar. Some men, such as Joseph Hopkinson, were Philadelphians who could conveniently attend the annual terms of the Court. Others, such as Ogden and Emmet, came from New York since it was not too far for

[50] Near the end of his life Ogden had a quarrel with Webster and broke off their long-standing friendship. Webster to Richard M. Blatchford, Jan. 22, 1849, *WS,* XVIII, 292–93.

[51] Russell L. Caldwell, "The Influence of the Federal Bar upon the Interpretation of the Constitution by the Supreme Court under John Marshall," Ph.D. Dissertation (University of Southern California, 1948), 198, 255. Jones opposed Webster in *McCulloch* v. *Maryland* and was his associate in the *Girard Will* case.

[52] Other outstanding lawyers, whose names will appear in later chapters, were John Whipple of Rhode Island, Richard S. Coxe of Washington, Horace Binney of Philadelphia, and William H. Winder of Maryland.

attendance each year. After 1830 more New Englanders appeared—from Boston and elsewhere—and geography was a
lesser influence as the nation's transportation improved.[53]

Many were Congressmen and therefore in Washington
when the Court sat. They could supplement their incomes hand-
somely by work in the judicial chamber downstairs from the
House and Senate. Frequently a solon of serious mien ducked
into the lower chamber, so to speak, for a lucrative hour or two.
After all, should not those who made laws help interpret them?
Webster's dual career as lawyer and legislator was typical of a
legislative generation capable of dividing energies between the
two roles. In this period a Clay or Sergeant could easily move
up and down, from one level of the Capitol to the other. Later
when duties of Congressmen increased and Court terms length-
ened, such division was impossible. Clients or constituents may
have sometimes received less than full value of their services; at
any rate, the practical knowledge these men brought to their
professional labors assisted the Court on constitutional questions
reaching deep into American politics. When Pinkney delivered
his classic argument in *McCulloch* v. *Maryland,* he drew on his
own experience as well as law books.[54]

Having similar backgrounds, counselors felt an attraction
of comradeship peculiar to these still-simple times. Now and
then they met as a body to transact business of common interest,
a sort of *corps judiciaire.* The occasion might be the death of a
fellow lawyer or one of the justices, and the assembled bar
adopted resolutions of grief after hearing a suitable eulogy.
Their relations were normally less formal, as groups gathered in
the lobby to hear the latest gossip or to speculate about an anticipated decision. Attorneys often knew beforehand how the
Court would vote. Such information, supposedly confined to the
judges, filtered out of the Court's conferences. There were social
events, dinner parties, receptions, where they built friendships
with associates and with the justices. In fact, one newspaperman

---

[53] Charles Warren, *A History of the American Bar* (Boston, 1911), 366–71,
408–13.

[54] Henry Wheaton, "Life of William Pinkney," in Jared Sparks (ed.), *The
Library of American Biography* (New York, 1840), VI, 36.

reported that Washington's social season began with the opening of the Court's term.[55]

There was a persistent belief that these lawyers shared
attitudes and purposes as well as friendship. Notwithstanding
their attachment to political parties with different and changing
appearances, it was said they all belonged to a unified conservative class. "Lawyers, as a body," Tocqueville would declare,
"form the most powerful, if not the only, counterpoise to the
democratic element." The effect, he thought, was to neutralize
"the vices inherent in popular government," to check the passions and impetuosity of the people. By staunch adherence to
the common law they showed their preference for security instead of innovation, tradition instead of new ideas. So concluded
the estimable French traveler.[56] Allowing for extravagance of
this analysis, one feels its force. These men who practiced before
the Supreme Court had drunk from the same cup, one might say,
when they learned their profession. Drawing up their briefs for
a case, they understandably turned to the same legal rules and
authorities, with the result that they did indeed perform a conservative function in society whatever political party they represented.

These men were great speakers—no conservatism marred
their rhetoric. Emphasis upon oral presentation gave attorneys
broader latitude than they have today when printed briefs usually
predominate.[57] It is true that long before Webster came to Washington, the judges had required counsel to supply "the material
points" of a controversy; and in 1821 they ruled they must have
printed briefs in all cases, though the rule was not always enforced. By 1832 they were insisting that attorneys comply. Next
term the Court announced that parties could submit cases upon
printed briefs alone, without oral argument, and occasionally
this happened.[58] Such instances were rare and did not involve
questions of deep or general interest, for the bench, the bar, and
the public placed high value upon appearance in Court where

[55] Warren, *Sup. Ct. in U.S. Hist.*, I, 471–72, 474 n. 1.
[56] George E. Probst, *The Happy Republic: A Reader in Tocqueville's
America* (New York, 1962), 476–77, 482–83.
[57] Today each side has only one hour for oral argument.
[58] Rules of the Supreme Court at front of 1 Peters (1828).

lawyers could present cases fully and, with luck, persuasively. Until the close of Webster's career the Court imposed no limit upon the length of arguments. Remarkable era of talk! In leading cases it was not unusual for a lawyer to speak for two or even three days and for all the arguments to consume a week or more. Pinkney's three-day oration in *McCulloch* v. *Maryland* was one of the great speeches in constitutional history. Webster's argument in the *Girard Will* case (1844) was equally long, and his opponent Horace Binney was just as expansive. Compared to others, Webster was not verbose—indeed he grumbled over the extended speeches of counsel. As judicial business mounted and the docket carried over cases term after term, sentiment against unlimited argument grew, and at last in 1849 the Court adopted a rule restricting each lawyer to two hours.[59] This must have seemed severe to veterans of the bar like Webster, though it was overdue relief for the justices.

Oral argument naturally tempted counsel to transcend dry-crusted citations of precedent into more exciting altitudes of eloquence. Wirt, grounded in literature as well as law, fascinated his listeners with classical allusions and poetical quotations, all laced with disarming humor. Webster's moving peroration in the *Dartmouth College* case—"It is, Sir, as I have said, a small college"—will never be forgotten (nor would it, by a modern-day judge, be forgiven). Strictly, such flights ought not to have influenced the administration of justice, but no doubt they did. Marshall, Story, and their associates did not conceal admiration of these performances and seemed to expect them for an adequate hearing of an interesting case.[60]

It is not difficult to see why oratory was often as significant as learning, if not more so. The dual role of lawyers at the bar and in politics was a principal reason. Accustomed to interminable speeches in Congress, these political war horses could not change their pace when they went to Court. But in both instances they exemplified the standards of their times, for this was the golden age of American oratory. As college students

[59] 7 Howard v.
[60] Story highly praised Webster's eloquence in the *Girard Will* case (1844), but he and the majority decided against the lawyer's clients.

they had attended rhetoric classes, read the Greek and Latin orations, joined debating societies. Back home they had attracted public attention by ability to talk at county circuit court, political canvasses, barbecues, Fourth-of-July festivals.[61]

In the Supreme Court the attorneys were fulfilling the expectations of everyone. Into the judicial chamber pressed crowds hungering for finished elocution. The cause was not altogether important. In a routine case Henry Clay drew a throng of spectators one day in 1848 because it was said that this was his farewell appearance—but like a prima donna's farewell it was not his last. An observer reported that the admiring audience collected two hours before Court opened, and many people stood during his indifferent argument of three hours. Squeezed into the small room, enduring near-suffocating heat, they were deeply impressed when Clay told them he had never before seen such a brilliant and elegant assembly (including fashionably dressed ladies), even in the English Parliament or the Court of King's Bench.[62] About this time Webster filled the Courtroom and disappointed others who could not get inside when he argued the *Lexington* steamboat case. The public was more interested in the tragic maritime disaster involved in the case than in the intricate question of admiralty law it posed.

Neither bench nor bar felt as restrained by jurisdictional limits as would its modern counterpart. In their elaborations lawyers wandered far beyond the record. Judges did not always insist, as they do nowadays, that counsel establish jurisdiction at the threshold of the case. In the well-known lottery case of *Cohens* v. *Virginia,* turning upon a jurisdictional pivot, Chief Justice Marshall could have decided at the outset that the Congressional statute affecting the District of Columbia was not a "law of the United States," in the usual sense, and that therefore his court had no authority to hear the appeal. Instead he asserted jurisdiction in the first hearing and only in the second

---

[61] Roscoe Pound, *The Spirit of the Common Law* (Boston, 1921), 124–25, 137, suggests that the free rein given to lawyers' arguments is traceable to frontier modes of thought in early America and interfered with fair judicial procedure.

[62] John P. Frank, *Justice Daniel Dissenting: A Biography of Peter V. Daniel, 1784–1860* (Cambridge, 1964), 239. The "observer" was Justice Daniel.

hearing held this was not a *national* measure.[63] Other illustrations of laxity come to mind: the proliferation of argument and opinion on the commerce power in *Groves* v. *Slaughter* despite a much narrower question at issue; the first decision in *Ogden* v. *Saunders,* controversial as it was, on the basis of an incomplete record of facts; Wirt's argument on the patent clause in *Gibbons* v. *Ogden* even though both state and Federal courts ignored the point; and unchecked exploration of the state's power of eminent domain in the *Charles River Bridge* case in the face of the obvious fact that the state had not pretended to exercise the power.[64]

And so the lawyers powerfully influenced the Court: these years were a formative era of constitutional law, to some extent of other branches of law as well, and counsel enjoyed the freedom of pioneers.[65] Penetrating the unmapped wilderness of social and legal problems, they defined issues, uncovered precedents, suggested promising rules of decision. The Court, and the public too, was willing for them to do so. A dual status as lawyers and politicians strengthened their ability to cut paths through the legal thickets of their time.

[63] Jurisdiction was upheld at the first hearing on the ground that there was a national question, involving a law of the United States as required by the Judiciary Act of 1789. But at the second hearing the Court ruled that the Congressional law did not extend beyond the boundaries of the District of Columbia. Webster appeared in the second but not the first hearing.

[64] The reasoning in support of these generalizations will appear as the cases are discussed in later chapters.

[65] Some experts on early legal history say that the "formative era" preceded the nineteenth century.

III

THE JUDICIAL POWER

Webster left no room for doubt about his view of the Supreme Court's role. Unswervingly he believed the Court was the best possible balance wheel of the constitutional system. "It is," he asserted, "the expounder of fundamental principles of government; it is the appointed umpire on questions of the profoundest interest and most enduring consequences between conflicting sovereignties."[1] Occupying the sensitive place that it does, it faces complaint and attack, he observed; yet "the Constitution without it would be no constitution; the government no government."[2]

He had boundless faith in judicial power. Administration of justice by learned and virtuous judges, he said, "makes every one feel safe in life, liberty, and property."[3] But the judiciary must be independent of shifting legislative whims. As a delegate to the Massachusetts constitutional convention of 1820, he attacked a proposal to make judges removable by governor and council upon address of the legislature. English and colonial history showed, he warned, that subservient judges falter in defense of fundamental liberties.[4] Furthermore, detailed statu-

1 Speech at Savannah, 1847, *WS,* IV, 100–01.
2 Speech in House of Representatives, Jan. 25, 1826, *ibid.,* V, 176.
3 Speech at Charleston, 1847, *ibid.,* IV, 89.
4 *Ibid.,* V, 26–32.

tory codes can unduly restrict courts. Legislative enactments, however extensive, cannot meet all eventualities in specific cases coming before judges. So he would turn to the common law, that great body of judge-made law handed down through the centuries. Out of the wisdom of jurisprudence—from the opinions of a Lord Mansfield or the commentaries of a Blackstone—must come capacity to determine cases according to highly variable circumstances. He felt no hesitancy about broad application of the common law because it might result in uncertain and partial decisions. Resort to well-established legal precedents ensured the rule of law and not, as some people feared, the rule of men.[5]

In the familiar rule of judicial self-restraint he saw little value. Judges had the duty of deciding the validity of statutes, and they must not evade it by deferring to legislators. This assumption underlay many of his legal arguments, and its most explicit statement appeared in his state-court brief of the *Charles River Bridge* case. Legislatures often pass bills of doubtful constitutionality because they know that courts, qualified for the task, will determine the question.[6] Webster would assign little responsibility to either the law-making or executive branches to interpret the Constitution. Ideas of this sort suggested judicial supremacy.

Like most of his contemporaries, he believed there were universal laws of natural justice anterior to positive, man-made law. "Written constitutions sanctify and confirm great principles," he said, "but the latter are prior in existence to the former."[7] In numerous cases he appealed to natural law as sufficient ground to invalidate legislation. Perhaps the best example is the *Dartmouth College* case. Another is *Ogden* v. *Saunders,* in which he insisted that laws of nature, always superior to human laws, create a contractual obligation and therefore make it immune from statutory impairment.[8]

[5] Review of the third volume of Wheaton's *Reports* in *North American Review,* VIII (Dec., 1818), 63–68, reprinted in *WS,* XV, 45–52.

[6] *WS,* XV, 347, 363.

[7] *Ibid.,* IV, 90.

[8] In this part of his argument he was relying upon natural law, exclusive of the contract clause of the Constitution, and was contending that the obligation of contracts rested upon the principles of natural justice rather than upon legislative statutes. See Chapter VI.

Foremost among these first principles, he thought, was the right to hold property. During this period the Court solidly established the doctrine of vested rights. Once a person acquires property, according to this doctrine, a right is vested and cannot be arbitrarily divested. The legal and philosophical idea was of course not new, but judges now integrated it into the evolving constitutional law. Interestingly the rationale of vested rights became closely associated with separation of powers between legislative and judicial departments. A legislature could vest rights, such as corporate franchises, but could not divest them. Legislative repeal or alteration of corporate charters was not only unwise policy, it was an unconstitutional invasion of the judicial sphere. Cases of private right like this, Webster declared, lay outside legislative competence. The "law of the land" or "due process of law" demanded that the property holder have a fair trial in the circumstances and with legal protection that a politically minded legislature could never afford. Webster and all other exponents of the doctrine trusted courts more than other branches to protect these valued rights.[9]

In Webster's time the Court defined and expanded its jurisdiction in several ways. The nation as a whole accepted, and bench and bar seldom questioned, judicial review. Story and Marshall affirmed the right of appeal from state courts; and so a means of invalidating unconstitutional state legislation was available.[10] Protests from Virginia or Kentucky or some other dissatisfied state followed several decisions, but proposals in Congress to restrict appeals were ineffectual. Although the Court did not declare a national statute invalid, it stood ready to do so.[11] Through the years, judicial power grew also because the contract and commerce clauses acquired fuller meaning. In many other kinds of cases, such as those involving corporate parties

[9] For a revealing example of Webster's position, see his argument in behalf of the Boston and Lowell Railroad before a committee of the Massachusetts legislature, Jan. 20, 1845. *WS*, XV, 373–401.

[10] *Martin* v. *Hunter's Lessee*, 1 Wheaton 304 (1816); *Cohens* v. *Virginia*, 6 Wheaton 264 (1821). Webster did not argue either of these cases on jurisdictional grounds, but the Court assigned him to represent Virginia in the *Cohens* case after jurisdiction had been affirmed and the state had withdrawn her counsel. For the hearing of the case on the merits, see 6 Wheaton 430.

[11] No Congressional statute was invalidated between *Marbury* v. *Madison* (1803) and *Dred Scott* v. *Sandford* (1857).

and those having some relation to treaties, the Federal judiciary assumed ever broadening responsibility vis-à-vis state tribunals.

One area of jurisdictional development was admiralty law. Maritime commerce, an important economic interest in the early nineteenth century, raised many legal questions; and problems stemming from the War of 1812 and relations with revolutionary Latin America gave special interest to this branch of law. In the first fifteen years of Webster's Supreme Court practice, about a third of his work was admiralty cases.[12] Article III of the Constitution simply confers upon national courts jurisdiction in "all cases of admiralty and maritime jurisdiction," and provisions of the judiciary acts were equally brief and general.[13] From these sources Federal judges had little guidance. It was necessary to draw on English and colonial jurisprudence, to adapt old rules, sometimes to innovate.

In his first major admiralty case, *U.S. v. Bevans* (1818), Webster argued against Federal jurisdiction, and even the nationalistic Marshall found it impossible to take cognizance in the absence of statutory authority. In Federal Circuit Court a marine, William Bevans, had been convicted of murder aboard a United States naval vessel at anchor in Boston harbor. Questions were certified to the Supreme Court concerning jurisdiction over offenses in such a location. Did the Federal court have jurisdiction under the Congressional Crimes Act of 1790? Or did the local courts have cognizance since the ship was within a state's territorial boundaries? The answer depended on construction of Article III in the Constitution and of the Federal statute, as well as the principles of admiralty law. Opposing Henry Wheaton and Attorney General William Wirt, both formidable antagonists, Webster appeared in behalf of Bevans to challenge Federal jurisdiction. Marshall's opinion followed Webster's interpretation of the act of 1790, which did not specifically grant the Federal courts jurisdiction over crimes on ships in harbors and bays but only on the high seas. The Chief Justice referred approvingly to the lawyer's argument that Congress in these cases had constitutional power, if it saw fit, to

12 See Appendix for list of cases.
13 Original jurisdiction was granted to the district courts, and appeals could be taken to the circuit courts and finally to the Supreme Court.

confer admiralty jurisdiction upon the circuit courts but had not done so. The state, with jurisdiction coextensive with its territory, therefore must take cognizance. Notwithstanding his praise of Webster's learned exposition of English admiralty law, Marshall did not cite any cases or commentaries the lawyer had relied on—or any at all, for that matter.[14]

A large amount of the Court's business in the decade after 1815 reflected events in Latin America where, one by one, the Spanish and Portuguese colonies were making good their independence. A way in which these new nations fought the mother countries was to commission private vessels to prey on shipping. Repeatedly this affected the United States, for many vessels flying the flags of her neighbors to the south were built in American yards, manned by American citizens, supplied out of American ports. There were violations of the neutrality laws of 1794 and 1817 forbidding such activity; and there were depredations, complained the Spanish government, prohibited by the Pinckney Treaty of 1795. A hesitant policy of recognizing the new Latin American republics compounded the difficulty. For a long time the United States did not even acknowledge the legal status of some of the revolutionary wars.[15] Privateers of these countries were vulnerable to the charge of piracy, a crime under a statute of 1790 or its amendment of 1819. Besides, a swarm of freebooters and mutineers sailed the seas without commissions from any government, recognized or not. All this embarrassed relations with Spain, particularly during the sensitive negotiations to purchase Florida. At home, complex cases of international law flowed into the courts, which with the help of the bar had to adapt old rules to new questions.[16]

In several cases Spanish consuls filed claims to recover ships and cargoes taken as prizes by privateers, but on the whole they fared poorly. Representing a consul in the *Divina Pastora* (1819), Webster argued that a privateer commissioned by the

---

[14] 3 Wheaton 336–91 (1818).

[15] The neutrality law of 1817 and presidential proclamations recognized the existence of civil war between Spain and some of her colonies—not all of them being covered at first. The United States formally recognized the independence of some of the new nations in 1822, but not all of them until 1826.

[16] Charles Warren, *The Supreme Court in United States History* (3 vols., Boston, 1823), II, 27–38.

United Provinces of the Rio de la Plata had violated the neutrality laws and the Pinckney Treaty. Chief Justice Marshall did not reject the appeal, inasmuch as he remanded it to the lower court for further proceedings; but on the basic issue he held prizes lawful if capturing vessels carried commissions from governments recognized as belligerents by Congress and the President.[17] Nevertheless captors must not compromise the neutrality of the United States, as the Court found in the case of the *Santissima Trinidad* (1822). Again appearing for a Spanish consul, Webster proved that a public vessel of the United Provinces had been illegally manned and supplied at Baltimore.[18]

Rightful prizes were one thing, but piracy something else. Murder, robbery, other piratical acts on the high seas were punishable under the laws of 1790 and 1819.[19] At the 1820 term the Supreme Court at last handed down a series of decisions virtually putting an end to this thriving crime. Lower courts had convicted about fifty men of piracy and sentenced them to death. For argument on questions certified to the Supreme Court, the Chief Justice appointed Webster and William H. Winder to represent the defendants in absence of regular counsel. On the other side was Wirt, who asked for broad application of the laws. Whether Webster made much of an effort is unknown, but he did insist that the language of the statutes punishing piracy "as determined by the law of nations" was too vague. Unconvinced by this reasoning, the Court upheld the convictions; and some of Webster's hapless clients were executed.[20]

Webster also had maritime cases in the lower Federal courts. One that deserves notice, since it concerned the thorny question of the foreign slave trade, is *U.S.* v. *La Jeune Eugénie*.[21]

---

[17] 4 Wheaton 52–65; Webster to William Sullivan, Feb. 27 and Mar. 13, 1818, *WS*, XVI, 41, and XVII, 272. The Court followed its recent decision in *U.S.* v. *Palmer*, 3 Wheaton 610 (1818).

[18] 7 Wheaton 282–355 (1822). Story also doubted that the master of the vessel, an American, had actually expatriated himself as he alleged.

[19] In *U. S.* v. *Palmer* (1818) the Court had held that the piracy statute of 1790 did not apply to persons on the high seas who were not citizens of the United States. Congress then enacted the law of 1819 punishing piracy committed by any persons whatsoever. See Warren, *Sup. Ct. in U. S. Hist.*, II, 38–39.

[20] *U.S.* v. *The Pirates*, 5 Wheaton 184–206 (1820). Webster's unreported argument was similar to the one he made in *U.S.* v. *Smith*, ibid., 156–57. See also *U.S.* v. *Holmes*, ibid., 412, and *U.S.* v. *Klintock*, ibid., 144.

[21] 26 *Federal Cases* 832–51 (1822).

It involved the colorful naval officer Robert F. Stockton, always a stormy figure from early service against the Barbary pirates to command of California operations in the Mexican War. As a young lieutenant commanding the *U.S.S. Alligator,* Stockton in the spring of 1821 was cruising off the West African coast where he had just negotiated a territorial concession for the new free-Negro state of Liberia. The antislavery-minded officer espied a suspicious looking schooner, *La Jeune Eugénie,* apparently equipped for transporting slaves. He seized the vessel and sent it to Boston for libel in the United States District Court.[22] The district judge quickly moved the case up to Justice Story's Circuit Court. The question would have been simple if the *Eugénie* had been American, for Congress years before had prohibited the slave trade. But two Frenchmen owned the vessel. Did the slave trade violate international law? Could an American prize court invoke such a rule if it existed? Or could a court of this country enforce the laws of France against the trade?

Webster's argument was an animated attack on slave traffic, his main purpose to show this trade illicit under international law.[23] This "barbarous, unauthorized, private, piratical warfare, carried on against the Africans," was contrary to the law of nature, which is a part of the law of nations, he declared. The practice "instigated and encouraged the most atrocious crimes and barbarities," and most civilized nations had forbidden it by municipal law, treaties, conventions. So this court, he concluded, ought to consider the trade a violation of international law. At the following term (May, 1822) Justice Story decided the case on much the same grounds urged by Webster.[24] He condemned the *Eugénie* because her owners had violated both French ordinances and international law. Relying upon the latter, Story faced a recent English opinion by Lord Stowell holding the law of nations did not prohibit the slave trade.[25] Webster

[22] Commodore Robert Stockton, father of the young officer, wrote to Webster and expressed the hope that the lawyer "could get Robert out of this scrape." But, he continued, "he ought to know that as long as the General Govt. is under absolute Southern influence there can be no bona fide wish to put an end to the slave trade." Letter of Nov. 5, 1821, *WS,* XV, 278–79 n. 2.

[23] *Ibid.,* 279–81. He also contended that the ship was not really French but that, if it were, the Court should condemn the vessel for violating French law.

[24] 26 *Federal Cases* 840–51 (1822).

[25] *Le Louis,* 2 Dodson 210.

was aware of this English case, criticized it in a private letter to Story, but did not cite it in argument.[26] Story did discuss it, partly to distinguish the present question and partly to deny the soundness of Stowell's decision. Three years later in the *Antelope* Case, Chief Justice Marshall, speaking for the Supreme Court, adopted the opposite position, holding that the law of nations, as Lord Stowell had said, did not forbid the slave traffic because throughout history many nations had considered it legal. Story silently acquiesced.[27]

Responding to recurrent pressures, the Court during the 1840's edged up to an explicit enlargement of national admiralty jurisdiction, and a leading case in which Webster was counsel was *New Jersey Steam Navigation Company* v. *Merchants' Bank* (1848), otherwise known as the *Lexington* case. It arose out of a terrible steamboat disaster, one of the most shocking during a time of many such accidents, with heavy loss of life among the vessel's passengers. Representing a Boston bank whose shipment of money went down with the burning steamboat, Webster successfully contended for an expanded Federal cognizance.

Early in the evening of January 13, 1840, in Long Island Sound about fifty miles out of New York enroute to Providence, the steamboat *Lexington* caught fire. Ignited by sparks from the smokepipe and feeding rapidly on dozens of bales of cotton stowed nearby, the fire enveloped the whole ship. In the panic of the moment, everything went wrong. The suction hoses for the fire engine were missing, heaving lines for fire buckets could not be found, the vessel swung out of control after the steering ropes burned, the unnerved captain joined crew and passengers in a rush for the scarce lifeboats, and finally all but two of the 140 persons on board perished. Among the losses was a crate of gold and silver coin amounting to eighteen thousand dollars, shipped by the Merchants' Bank of Boston. The bank's agent, William F. Harndon, had a contract with the New Jersey Steam Navigation Company, owners of the *Lexington,* for a regular

[26] Webster declared, "I very much fear my Lord Stowell has missed a figure. However, I suppose, as usual, he has given plausible reasons." Webster to Story, Sept. 24, 1821, *WS*, XVII, 316.

[27] 10 Wheaton 66 (1825). Marshall also held that the courts of the United States cannot enforce the laws of foreign nations.

daily shipment of one crate on the boat between New York and Providence. Despite a clause in Harndon's contract stipulating shipment exclusively at his own risk, the Merchants' Bank brought suit against the steamboat company for gross negligence as a common carrier. The action was a libel originally filed in the Federal District Court in Rhode Island, sitting as a court of admiralty. Hearing the case on appeal from a *pro forma* decree, the Circuit Court decided for the bank and awarded damages.[28]

In review of these proceedings the Supreme Court had to decide several difficult questions. First, had the District Court possessed admiralty jurisdiction in a case of a contract performed on the sea but made on *land?* An affirmative answer would expand the ancient English rule that admiralty courts had cognizance only over contracts made as well as performed on the high seas or within the ebb and flow of the tide—and thus outside the jurisdiction of other courts. Second, even though its contract was with Harndon, was the steamboat company liable to the bank? Third, was the steamboat company responsible for the bank's losses notwithstanding the contract's proviso that Harndon assumed entire risk?

Typical of many cases of the 1840's, *New Jersey Steam Navigation Company* v. *Merchants' Bank* came on slowly at Washington. The record arrived soon after the circuit decision of 1843, but counsel did not argue until four years later. Alive to interests of his client, the Merchants' Bank, Webster was sorely disappointed with the delay. He hoped in vain that the case would come up on the docket at the 1846 term and relayed his estimate of the prospects to the bank's president in Boston, Franklin Haven.[29] Naturally he felt misgivings about the disposition of the jurisdictional question. "In regard to this," he wrote, "we shall feel the loss of Judge [Story]."[30] The Justice, who had recently died, had been an acknowledged expert on admiralty law and had sat on the circuit bench in the cause.

[28] 6 Howard 345–54 (1848); Traveller, *A Letter to the Hon. Daniel Webster on the Causes of the Destruction of the Steamer Lexington as Discovered in the Testimony before the Coroner's Jury in New York* (Boston, 1840).

[29] Webster to Franklin Haven, Dec. 21 and 26, 1845, *WS*, XVI, 438–39.

[30] Webster to Haven, Jan. 16, 1846, Webster Papers (Harvard). See also letter of Jan. 28, *ibid*.

Lawyers on both sides examined the case intensively. Counsel for the steamboat company were Samuel Ames and John Whipple. As expected, they sought reversal of the lower court's decision primarily on the ground that this was not a proper admiralty suit; but they canvassed the merits of the case too, even challenging the factual findings of deficient equipment and unskilled handling of the *Lexington*. For the Merchants' Bank a Rhode Island attorney, Richard W. Greene, concentrated on jurisdiction and foreshadowed what his associate Webster would say with greater force.[31] A newspaper reporter heard Webster's first argument on February 1 and 2, 1847, took short-hand notes, and fortunately rescued one of the lawyer's best performances from oblivion. The two-day effort, apparently reported verbatim, was an effective mixture of emotion and reason, oratory and solid legal discourse, historical allusion and topical comment.[32]

In an introduction calculated to win the attention and sympathy of his audience, Webster remarked how news of the *Lexington* disaster had shocked him. In January 14, 1840, he recalled, he had been at Stonington in Connecticut, intending to board the steamboat, and had learned it had burned and sunk the previous night with horrifying loss of life. This was not the only instance of such tragedies which came to his mind. He mentioned other accidents, collisions, fires, sinkings—all he had barely escaped by mere chance. His audience, male and female, must have sighed as he related his dangerous life. To the attorney the meaning of all this was plain: passenger safety was a serious problem for the whole nation. "I speak here," he declared expansively, "for the people of the United States, who commit their lives to the care of steamboat owners and navigators." It was good, he thought, that the question now came before this court for full consideration.

On the jurisdictional issue, coming down from the plane of oratory, Webster's objective was to show that America had long since developed an admiralty law much broader than that of

---

[31] 6 Howard 354–76 (1848).

[32] Printed in the Washington *National Era,* Feb. 4 and 11, 1847. The Bank, through Webster, paid the reporter for his services. Webster to Haven, Mar. 18, 1847, *WS,* XVI, 471. 6 Howard 377–78 (1848) lists Webster's points briefly and includes changes he made for the second argument in January, 1848.

England. From the fourteenth century onward, he admitted, the jurisdiction of the English Court of Admiralty was narrow. The only civil cases of contract cognizable by that court related to seamen's wages and bottomry bonds, but not affreightment such as the present case. Jealous common law judges had imposed these strict limits on the Court of Admiralty, he reminded his listeners, as a consequence of sustained rivalry between the two jurisdictions. Why was there rivalry? The reason was not so much a desire by defenders of the common law to safeguard trial by jury (not enjoyed in civil cases of admiralty) as it was judicial hunger for "profits of jurisdiction," answered Webster. Be that as it may, he continued, *American* vice-admiralty courts had possessed jurisdiction over other subjects, especially revenue cases from the Navigation Acts, as early as the reign of Charles II. True, the patriots of the Revolutionary era were aroused against these courts during the controversy with the mother country; but, he contended, they were opposing the Parliamentary revenue measures enforced by the courts rather than the form of judicial proceedings employed.

Regardless of the extent of admiralty jurisdiction in England and in the colonies, Webster went on, the decisive point of reference had to be the Constitution. Article III, section 2, provided that the judicial power of the United States shall extend to "all cases of admiralty and maritime jurisdiction," a brief provision leaving much for interpretation. The attorney seized on the word "all" in his advocacy of broad jurisdiction. He thought it noteworthy that the authors of the Constitution, many the same men who led the colonies into the Revolution, attached no qualifications to this grant of power, despite the controversy concerning British Vice-admiralty courts. Contrary to opposing counsel's contention that this constitutional clause ought to be interpreted with reference to English common law and admiralty rules, Webster maintained that the general and theoretical writers of the Continent, such as Grotius, were better authorities. Continental admiralty law was far more extensive than England's and should be the measure of American jurisdiction.[33] Webster urged the Court to follow Justice Story's

[33] From Webster's point of view, both Coke's and Blackstone's commentaries, though definitive on the common law, reflected the partisanship of common law

Conflict of Laws and his disposition of this very case of the *Lexington* on the circuit.[34] The lawyer found another exposition of the Constitution in the Judiciary Act of 1789, granting the Federal district courts "exclusive original cognizance of all civil cases of admiralty and maritime jurisdiction," again with no restrictive provisions. Indeed the law departed from the English rule because it also empowered these American admiralty courts to hear revenue cases.[35]

Webster was quite aware of the inconclusive precedents and writings on this question of admiralty jurisdiction since adoption of the Constitution.[36] Chancellor James Kent and Nathan Dane both had objected to admiralty courts trying revenue cases without jury trial, even though the Court had upheld that procedure. Nevertheless, Webster pointed out, Dane in his celebrated *Abridgment* assumed that American admiralty jurisdiction derived from the *Constitution* and not English common law. One of the judges asked, "What page and volume of Dale's did you mention?" "*Dane,* I said, may it please the Court, not *Dale,*" snapped the irritated attorney. "The Royal Dane . . . one Nathan Dane."[37] It was a piece of Websterian audacity—but apparently he got away with it. Then he painstakingly

judges in the long rivalry with the admiralty courts. On this subject they gave little attention to the law of nations, the basis of the maritime law expounded by the Continental authors. See Blackstone, *Commentaries,* III, 69, 106–07, and IV, 368, for the rules against which Webster was arguing.

34 Webster said that Story "has given to this country, to Europe and the world a treatise on public law, worthy to be the production of Grotius; worthy to be the companion of him who owns the Institutes; a work which may be called the GREAT BOOK of the age; which is cited by the most learned on both sides the water, and endeared to Judicatures here and elsewhere. The Court will understand that I allude to . . . his admirable work, 'The Conflict of Laws.' " New York *Tribune,* Feb. 4, 1847.

Nevertheless, in an opinion for the Court in the case of *The Thomas Jefferson,* 10 Wheaton 428 (1825), Story had followed the English rule of limiting admiralty jurisdiction to waters within the ebb and flow of the tide. And in his *Commentaries on the Constitution* (3 vols., Boston, 1833), III, sections 1657–1667, Story had generally applied English doctrine in defining admiralty jurisdiction of the national judiciary. Specifically, he had omitted contracts of affreightment, such as the one involved in the *Lexington* case, when he listed contracts within admiralty jurisdiction.

35 On the other hand, the act revived the same kind of jurisdiction in revenue cases once exercised by the English vice-admiralty courts in the *colonies. U.S. Statutes at Large,* I, 77.

36 See *The Vengeance,* 3 Dallas 297 (1796), and *The Schooner Betsey,* 4 Cranch 443 (1808), as well as *The Thomas Jefferson,* cited above.

37 New York *Tribune,* Feb. 5, 1847.

showed that the Constitution guaranteed jury trial in all criminal
cases, even in admiralty, and allowed it in civil cases, should
Congress see fit so to provide.[38] In fact Congress had provided
jury trial for civil cases in a statute of 1845 extending admiralty
jurisdiction over inland lakes and connecting rivers. This statute
was convincing support for Webster's version of broad jurisdiction because it abandoned altogether the English territorial
limit of the ebb and flow of the tide.[39] Finally, there were some
judicial decisions upon which Webster could lean, though in
truth there were others more helpful to his opponents.[40]

The heart of the argument was that the Constitution
established the admiralty jurisdiction to which his client had
resorted. Forget the English rule that only contracts made as
well as performed on the sea were admiralty cases, Webster
asked, and adopt a more sound standard of drawing jurisdictional boundaries. That standard would be subject matter. If the
contract, here one of affreightment between bank and steamboat
company, concerned maritime services, then the case lay within
cognizance of the District Court of Rhode Island sitting in
admiralty. There was no valid objection, he said, simply because
parties made the contract upon the land. This high tribunal was
not only empowered but bound in duty to say what constituted
proper contract cases in admiralty within the meaning of the
Constitution.

Both Webster and Greene looked into the merits of the
case, though less thoroughly than the jurisdictional question.
Although the New Jersey Steam Navigation Company signed
the contract with William Harndon, the other party to the
agreement was actually the Merchants' Bank, they insisted, for
Harndon was merely the bank's agent. The steamboat company
could not evade responsibility by this device, nor could it evade
usual responsibilities of all common carriers by stipulating in the
contract that Harndon shipped his crate of money at his own

[38] Sixth Amendment for criminal cases. In civil cases at *common law*, the
Seventh Amendment guarantees the right of jury trial. Webster's reasoning was
that in the absence of a provision to the contrary, Congress could grant the right
in civil cases in *admiralty* as well.

[39] *U.S. Statutes at Large*, V, 726–27.

[40] Justice Washington on circuit, *Davis* v. *Brig Seneca, 21 Federal Cases*
1081 (1829); *Peyroux* v. *Howard*, 7 Peters 324 (1844); and other cases cited in
Nelson's opinion below.

risk. The law of negligence held, and they found little difficulty demonstrating gross negligence in the steamboat's operation on the fateful evening of the fire. In full magisterial cadence, Webster concluded by asking, "Is there any one here who feels that he ought to discharge this company from a just, stern, inflexible, unrelenting severity of judicial administration?"[41]

In February, 1847, after completion of argument, the Court was unprepared to decide the *Lexington* case and ordered it over to next term for reargument. Webster was highly displeased. "The second argument," he complained to President Franklin Haven of the bank, "appears to me a very useless labor. . . . I shall be obliged to listen to other counsel, & take notes for five days at least, before time for doing the argument will arrive."[42] Still, during the year between the Court's two hearings of the *Lexington* case the impatient Webster had reason for confidence. At the 1847 term Justice James M. Wayne delivered the majority opinion in a companion case, *Waring* v. *Clarke,* opening the gates to a broad expanse of admiralty jurisdiction and making it more likely Webster would win. "The grant of admiralty power of the courts of the United States," Wayne said, "was not intended to be limited or to be interpreted by what were cases of admiralty jurisdiction in England when the constitution was adopted."[43]

Here the question concerned territorial limits of admiralty jurisdiction over torts. There had been a collision of two steamboats on the Mississippi, ninety-five miles above New Orleans and considerably farther from open sea. Yet by stretching words Wayne held the tort had been committed within ebb and flow of the tide—one requisite for admiralty jurisdiction according to the English rule through the centuries. But he found another requisite inapplicable in America when he concluded that torts within geographical boundaries of the common law courts ("within a county," *infra corpus comitatus,* in legal terms) were cognizable also as admiralty cases in the United States, though not in England. In this country, therefore, admiralty jurisdiction ran farther inland, at least as far as the tide

---

[41] Washington *National Era,* Feb. 11, 1847.
[42] Dec. 28, 1847, *WS*, XVI, 488-89.
[43] 5 Howard 459 (1847). The whole report of the case is at pages 441-504.

had any effect on the rivers and bays. Even this might well not be the end, for English practice, abandoned in one particular, could be abandoned altogether.

Always aware of the Court's numerical divisions, Webster could plainly see, in the months after *Waring* v. *Clarke* and before reargument of the *Lexington* case, that he had to bring around only one justice, probably John Catron, to have the minimal majority of five. Counting three other judges who concurred with Wayne, there were four who would go beyond the constricted boundaries of English admiralty law. Catron concurred in a separate opinion, taking a very cautious step that did not commit him either way on the large jurisdictional question.[44] The other three justices who participated seemed determined to follow the English rule. Levi Woodbury, joined by Peter V. Daniel and Robert C. Grier, dissented in an elaborate opinion attacking Wayne's position at every point.[45]

In early January, 1848, counsel reargued *New Jersey Steamboat Company* v. *Merchants' Bank* over an eight-day period. Webster retraced his earlier route and emphasized new points as well. Understandably he gave prominence to *Waring* v. *Clarke,* which might control this case.[46] He also contended that if the loss of the *Lexington*'s cargo were considered a *tort* instead of a breach of contract, such a wrong committed on the sea was manifestly an admiralty case. Perhaps this would provide maneuverability for some justices who objected to admiralty jurisdiction over contracts made upon land.[47] Whereas earlier he had worried about the outcome and had been reluctant to reargue, he now felt more cheerful. Before his second argument he had gloomily predicted "much division and diversity" because

[44] Catron thought that since the action of the case was *in rem* (a libel of property rather than persons) and since a remedy was unavailable at common law or equity, an admiralty court must afford the remedy. But he did not wish to be committed "to any views beyond those arising on the precise case before the court." *Ibid.,* 466–67. Later, just before the decision in the *Lexington* case, Webster wrote to Haven that "the Judges were waiting [to decide the case] for the restored health of Judge Catron who has been absent from the bench, for a week, thro ill health." Jan. 23, 1848, Webster Papers (Harvard).

[45] 5 Howard 467–503. One justice, probably McKinley, did not sit in the case.

[46] See 6 Howard 377–78 (1848).

[47] A tort is a wrongful act, other than a breach of contract, for which a civil action lies. In this case, therefore, Harndon's contract with the steamboat company would not be relevant. See opinions by Woodbury and Catron below, taking this position.

"the Court wants a strong and leading mind."[48] Afterward he told President Haven he was glad the cause was reargued. "I think we gained by it; and now begin to feel a good deal of hope about the result."[49] There was more delay until the ill Catron returned, and meanwhile Webster talked to some judges about the prospects. "All is safe," he reported to Haven, "keep the peace for 3 or 4 days, and you will hear of the Lexington. Meantime, we must say nothing."[50]

The prediction was correct. Justice Samuel Nelson, speaking for himself and three other justices, delivered a majority opinion wholly favorable to the bank.[51] Accepting arguments of Webster and Greene on the merits, Nelson held the steamboat company liable to the bank, not merely to Harndon, who only acted as the bank's agent. And the company could not escape responsibility for gross negligence, such as proved here, by stipulation in the contract.[52] Nelson's treatment of the jurisdictional question was not as thorough as Wayne's in *Waring* v. *Clarke* nor as Webster's in argument, but it followed that argument's outline. The article in the Constitution on judicial power, the Judiciary Act of 1789, and the recently enacted statute of 1845 concerning inland lakes were the sources of Nelson's holding that American admiralty jurisdiction was broader than the English.[53] The Justice placed more emphasis on earlier Supreme Court cases (though strangely he barely cited *Waring* v. *Clarke*) than Webster had, but took less notice of the English and colonial background. Nelson seemed anxious to show that the Court was not reversing its previous decisions, but actually his opinion set out in a new direction.

An infirmity of the decision was that the majority disagreed among themselves. Nelson had three other judges with him, but Woodbury and Catron concurred on more orthodox lines. These two concurring justices thought the wrong inflicted

---

[48] Webster to Haven, Dec. 28, 1847, *WS*, XVI, 488–89.

[49] Jan. 8, 1848, *ibid.*, 489.

[50] Webster to Haven, Feb. 3, 1848, Webster Papers (Harvard).

[51] 6 Howard 378–92 (1848). The concurring justices were Taney, McLean, and Wayne.

[52] The carrier had not complied with the Federal steamboat safety law of 1838. *U.S. Statutes at Large*, V, 304–06.

[53] The subject matter of the contract, not the location where it was made, was the guiding consideration. *Ibid.*, 387–92.

by the steamboat company was a tort on the sea, making it irrelevant whether contracts like this one were cognizable by admiralty.[54] Nevertheless the trend was clearly toward the nationalistic interpretation voiced by Webster, and this was what disturbed that dedicated friend of states' rights, Justice Peter V. Daniel, who vented his alarm in a lively dissent.[55] A few years later the Taney Court would say that Congress could expand national admiralty jurisdiction very nearly as it saw fit—a power it would possess from that day on.[56]

Although the tendency under both Marshall and Taney was to increase judicial power, the Court discovered limits to what it could do. Even in cases where parties qualified and where the subject seemed appropriate in terms of the Constitution and judiciary acts of Congress, the question might still arise whether the issue was justiciable. Ought not some matters be left to another branch or level of government? Over the years the Court constructed a formula known as the doctrine of political questions. Paradoxically Marshall laid the foundation for this serviceable rule; and Webster, firm supporter of judicial power though he was, contributed to the rule's development. One is less surprised to find Taney giving a fuller and more familiar statement of the doctrine, the antecedents of which went back at least three decades.

An interesting antecedent was *U.S.* v. *Palmer* (1818), the leading maritime case of the post-1815 decade, where the issue was whether the national piracy act of 1790 applied to citizens of the new Latin American republics. Marshall held the law did not operate upon such persons if the President or Congress recognized their nations or classified their revolutions as

---

[54] Catron's opinion, 6 Howard 394–95 (1848) ; Woodbury's, *ibid.*, 418–37.

[55] *Ibid.*, 395–418. Grier concurred with Daniel, and McKinley was absent. Of course this particular case could have come to the Federal courts as a civil case at common law since the parties were citizens of different states. In this sense, it was not necessarily a matter of national versus state jurisdiction.

[56] *Genesee Chief* v. *Fitzhugh*, 12 Howard 443 (1852). Taney's opinion upheld the validity of the Congressional statute of 1845, which conferred admiralty jurisdiction upon the Federal district courts in cases involving commerce on the inland lakes and connecting waters. Recognizing that the United States possessed a vast system of inland waters and thus differed from England in this respect, Taney rejected the tidewater and other traditional limits of the English rules. In 1891, the Court held that Federal admiralty jurisdiction extended to "all public navigable lakes and rivers." *In re Garnett*, 141 *U.S.* 1.

civil wars. The Court, he said, would follow the policy-making branches of the government.[57]

Again in *Foster and Elam* v. *Neilson* (1829) Marshall deferred to policy. This was one of several suits based upon land claims in former Spanish Florida, in which Webster appeared as high-paid counsel for claimants.[58] The plaintiffs, represented by Webster and Richard S. Coxe, stated that in 1811 they had purchased from the Spanish government a large tract of land thirty miles east of the Mississippi. The question was whether this part of West Florida had then been Spanish or American. Webster and Coxe exhaustively discussed all treaties of the United States, France, and Spain from 1763 to 1819 relating to the area in order to prove Spanish sovereignty and the property rights of their clients. Coxe's argument, more far-reaching than Webster's, developed a crucial point: he urged the Court to exercise independent judgment on the issue of sovereignty instead of following declarations of presidents or Congress. His opponent, Walter Jones, concentrated on that aspect and contended that the question was "political," which Congress had settled by legislation governing West Florida from 1804 onward.[59] Jones convinced Marshall.[60] In a rare demonstration of judicial self-restraint the Chief Justice held "it is the province of the Court to conform its decisions to the will of the legislature, if that will has been clearly expressed." Controversies between this nation and others were delicate matters into which judges ought not unnecessarily intrude.[61] Claims of Foster and Elam were therefore inadmissible because they were inconsistent with American foreign policy.

[57] 3 Wheaton 610. See the previous discussion of the prize and piracy cases at that time. Webster did not participate in the *Palmer* case.

[58] Other cases were *U.S.* v. *Arredondo,* 6 Peters 431 (1832), and *Mitchel* v. *U.S.,* 9 Peters 711 (1835) and 15 Peters 52 (1841).

[59] 2 Peters 256–99 (1829). President Jefferson insisted that the area had been ceded to the United States in 1803, but attempted to purchase it from Spain in the following years. In 1810 Congress had extended American law over part of the region; and in 1813 the remainder, as far as the Perdido, was taken as a result of military operations.

[60] *Ibid.,* 299–317.

[61] *Ibid.,* 307. It is possible that Marshall was expressing a nationalistic and expansionist point of view quite as much as a deference to the other branches of the government.

It should be emphasized that Webster was here on the side urging the Court not to defer to Congress.

There was the possibility of applying the doctrine of political questions to cases between two states if they involved sensitive zones of sovereignty. This was a central issue in *Rhode Island* v. *Massachusetts* (1838–46), originating from a protracted boundary dispute between the two states. Webster now spoke for judicial restraint as he represented his state against claims of her neighbor. His argument against jurisdiction did not prevail, for the Court decided it could hear the case. Massachusetts eventually won on the merits; but the Court established a precedent that it could entertain such suits, tortuously worked out a procedure, and handed down a final decree. For the first time in history it fully exercised its power to determine a case brought by one state against another.

As counsel for Massachusetts Webster was involved in this intricate case as early as the 1832 term. Rhode Island filed a bill in equity asking restoration of a strip of territory along the Massachusetts border amounting to about a hundred square miles. The colonial charters of the early seventeenth century had vaguely defined the boundary as an east-west line three miles south of the Charles River. A survey in 1642 had fixed a boundary measured from the southernmost tributary of the Charles. After a time Rhode Island had challenged the validity of the line and contended that the charters referred to the main channel of the river, some distance farther north. In 1719 the Rhode Island assembly had agreed to a new boundary run by a commission, but had soon retracted its agreement. For the next century the question had been disputed and negotiated without satisfaction to Rhode Islanders, and now the little state requested the Supreme Court to secure to her the jurisdiction and sovereignty to which she felt entitled.[62]

Six years passed while the preliminaries crept forward. In response to subpoena, Webster appeared for Massachusetts and filed a plea and an answer, to which the Rhode Island attorneys made a replication.[63] Constitutionally, the Court reached

---

[62] A valuable description of the background and progress of the case is in Charles G. Haines and Foster H. Sherwood, *The Role of the Supreme Court in American Government and Politics, 1835–1864* (Berkeley, 1957), 245–86.

[63] *Rhode Island* v. *Massachusetts,* 12 Peters 657–69 (1838); Theron Metcalf to Webster, Feb. 10, 1835, Webster Papers (New Hamp. Hist. Soc.); Webster to Metcalf, Feb. 14, 1835, *WS,* XVI, 253–54.

the most important stage of the litigation in 1838 when it heard argument on Webster's motion to dismiss the bill for want of jurisdiction. Webster did not make an oral argument, but his associate, James T. Austin, Attorney General of Massachusetts, did. Though the Constitution, Article III, conferred jurisdiction upon the Court in cases between states, Austin said, it did not mean *all* such cases but only those for which there was a rule of law applicable by the Court. Inasmuch as the Judiciary Act of 1789 did not provide a rule or a procedure, Austin continued, the Court could not hear the case. The Constitution was not self-executing in this respect without Congressional legislation.[64] Besides, he concluded, the subject matter of the suit was not justiciable because the plaintiff was asking for a judicial determination of a "political" question, the extent of the sovereign rights of a state government.[65]

Justice Henry Baldwin delivered a lengthy opinion dismissing the motion and entirely accepting the argument by counsel for Rhode Island.[66] Baldwin found no difficulty in deriving the Court's "undoubted jurisdiction" either from the Constitution or the Judiciary Act. The language was general, concerning causes in which two states were parties; and since no exception was made, none was intended. Furthermore Baldwin thought that since the Articles of Confederation had provided for a practical means of settling disputes between states, surely the Constitution would be no less effective. Indeed the Court had previously entertained, but had not decided, controversies of this kind.[67] Nor did this case raise a political question, Baldwin held, because drawing a boundary line was simply a question of fact susceptible to judicial inquiry. Once the boundary was drawn,

[64] His position was that the Eleventh Amendment overruled Chief Justice Jay's holding in *Chisholm* v. *Georgia,* 2 Dallas 419 (1793), that the Constitution, Article III, was self-executing (without Congressional legislation) in permitting suits against a state without its consent.

[65] Austin's argument is in 12 Peters 669–86 (1838).

[66] *Ibid.,* 714–51. Hazard's argument for Rhode Island is in *ibid.,* 687–714. Baldwin spoke for himself and five other justices. Barbour concurred in the decision but not in Baldwin's reasoning. Story did not sit, and Taney dissented.

[67] Article IX, paragraph 2, of the Articles of Confederation provided for special courts to determine boundary controversies between states. Several disputes were heard, and one of them was decided. Under the Constitution, the Supreme Court heard *New York* v. *Connecticut,* 4 Dallas 1 (1799) and *New Jersey* v. *New York,* 5 Peters 283 (1831). See Haines and Sherwood, *Role of Sup. Ct., 1835–1864,* 246–61.

sovereignty was "coextensive" with it. As the only dissenter, Chief Justice Taney protested that though controversies concerning states' "property in soil" were proper judicial questions, "contests for rights of sovereignty and jurisdiction between states over any particular territory" were not.[68]

After Baldwin delivered his opinion, Webster asked permission for Massachusetts to withdraw her plea and even her appearance in Court. His state, the lawyer explained, had appeared and filed a plea merely to challenge jurisdiction but certainly not to admit the validity of the proceedings. He seemed disturbed by a passage in Baldwin's opinion pointing to the appearance of Massachusetts as evidence that the Court could enforce an order to her. If the appearance had given this erroneous impression, Webster contended, it was a mistake. Still, it is puzzling why Massachusetts filed a plea as if to argue the merits rather than objecting on jurisdictional grounds at the threshold. At least to some judges this may have been tacit admission of jurisdiction. Justice Smith Thompson now ruled on Webster's motion. Insisting that the state had not prejudiced her cause by appearing and pleading, Thompson announced Massachusetts was free to withdraw if she wished. Later she did withdraw her plea but elected to continue her appearance.[69]

More twists and turns followed. At each of the next three terms, 1839–1841, the Court grappled with the problem of how to conduct proceedings. Taney suggested that Massachusetts file a demurrer, which would admit the truth of the facts alleged by Rhode Island and bring to issue the questions of law. This Webster did, but it proved a misstep: the two states did not agree at all about the facts. So another tack was necessary.[70] Absences and vacancies on the bench also delayed a final hearing. For part of this period Webster was secretary of state and yet was not unmindful of fees, which seemed to be coming in too slowly. Altogether he was unhappy, displeased with the rulings,

---

[68] 12 Peters 752–54 (1838).

[69] Ibid., 755–61.

[70] 13 Peters 23–25 (1839); 14 Peters 210–81 (1840); 15 Peters 233–74 (1841). John Quincy Adams heard Whipple's argument for Rhode Island at the 1841 term and wrote, "He was harping upon an alleged *mistake,* by Commissioners who settled the question a hundred and twenty-two years ago. The pleader is worthy of the cause." Charles F. Adams (ed.), *Memoirs of John Quincy Adams* (12 vols., Philadelphia, 1877), X, 440.

dissatisfied with his associate Austin, uncertain about the outcome.[71]

Rhode Island v. Massachusetts was heard on its merits
in 1846; and Webster with a new partner, the silver-tongued
Rufus Choate, won.[72] Rhode Island's counsel maintained that
she had a just claim to the disputed territory on the basis of
colonial charters, that in the early eighteenth century the Massachusetts commissioners had deceived her, and that she had vainly
sought a boundary readjustment over many years. Disappointingly, the text of Choate's argument, for that matter of the other
lawyers, does not survive. Enough is known to say it was an
eloquent speech, commanding the attention of an audience that
admired its cogency and ornate imagery. The original charters
were admittedly vague about the boundary, Choate said, as
indefinite as a line "beginning at a hive of bees in swarming
time and running thence to a hundred foxes with firebrands tied
to their tails."[73] But in 1719 the Rhode Island assembly had
agreed to the boundary run by the commission, and since then
Massachusetts had a clear right founded on many years of possession.[74] Through Justice John McLean the Court dismissed
the claims of Rhode Island substantially on these grounds. Early
agreements by the colonies and especially the length of time
during which Massachusetts had governed the area were decisive.
Brushing aside the objection to the Court's jurisdiction, McLean
answered mechanically that "we do nothing more than ascertain
the true boundary, and the territory up to that line on either
side necessarily falls within the proper jurisdiction."[75] To this
view Taney reiterated his strong objections. The question was not
justiciable, declared the dissenting Chief Justice, because it
required determination of the states' political jurisdiction.[76]

Taney's opinion was, in a sense, vindicated in this particular controversy, for despite her victory in court Massachusetts

[71] Webster to Edward Everett, Feb. 16, 1839, Everett Papers (Mass. Hist.
Soc.); Webster to John Davis, Apr. 16 and May 29, 1841, WS, XVI, 341.
[72] 4 Howard 591.
[73] Everett P. Wheeler, Daniel Webster: The Expounder of the Constitution
(New York, 1905), 130.
[74] Samuel G. Brown, The Works of Rufus Choate with a Memoir of His Life
(2 vols., Boston, 1862), I, 109-10; Claude M. Fuess, Rufus Choate: The Wizard
of the Law (New York, 1928), 159-61; Warren, Sup. Ct. in U. S. Hist., II, 424-25.
[75] 4 Howard 628 and whole opinion, pages 628-39.
[76] Ibid., 639-40. Taney was the only dissenter.

later consented to readjust the boundary, established ultimately in 1883.[77] But the case became a significant precedent. In the late nineteenth century the Court settled a good many other state boundary disagreements, and in more recent times has decided various questions to the benefit of interstate relations.[78] Always such matters have been sensitive ones calling for the same blend of caution and sense of duty the judges displayed in this instance.

There were some kinds of issues the Court would not determine. One was how a state should rewrite her constitution, a question posed in *Luther* v. *Borden* (1849). This case resulted from an angry political controversy in Rhode Island during the early forties known as the "Dorr Rebellion." Taney, now speaking for a majority, gave a durable definition of the doctrine of political questions.

Long-standing dissatisfaction of many Rhode Islanders with their constitution reached a climax in 1842. That document was basically its original colonial charter of 1663, retained as the state's fundamental law after the Revolution but increasingly out of joint with a changing society. As the economy industrialized, as more laborers came to the factories, and as urban towns grew more rapidly than rural areas, the charter was subject to complaint on two principal counts: legislative representation was not apportioned among the towns equitably, and the freehold requirement for voting disqualified most industrial workers since they owned no real estate. Thomas Wilson Dorr, upper-class industrialist and crusader for various causes, led a movement for constitutional reform that failed to shake the existing government's determination to maintain the status quo. So early in 1842 the Dorrites called a convention, unauthorized by the "charter" assembly, to draft a more broadly based constitution and to submit it to the people. This was done by March. Meanwhile the assembly was bestirred to draw a new constitution, which also extended the suffrage to all adult white male citizens but was rejected by the voters. During the next three months conditions in Rhode Island were uneasy and explosive. There were two rival governments: one, headed by Governor Samuel W.

---

[77] Haines and Sherwood, *Role of Sup. Ct., 1835–1864*, 274–77.

[78] William C. Coleman, "The State as a Defendant under the Federal Constitution; the Virginia-West Virginia Debt Controversy," *Harvard Law Review*, XXI (1917), 210–45.

King, adhered to the old charter; and the other, led by Dorr, proclaimed its authority in the name of the people. A Dorrite legislature met briefly in early May in defiance of laws passed by the charter assembly declaring officeholding in such bodies to be treasonous. Later Dorr and a small force made a disorganized attempt to seize the state arsenal at Providence. The failure of their cannon to fire symbolized the futility of the whole movement. In late June the bloodless "rebellion" collapsed near the village of Chepachet where a Dorrite aggregation had collected but dwindled away even before the excited charter militia decided to move on them.[79]

Webster, now secretary of state, watched these events anxiously and advised President Tyler on a response to them. Four times Governor King dispatched nervous requests to the President for Federal intervention, and each time Tyler refused to send troops because he hoped that the state itself could act effectively. Although the United States Constitution obligated the national government to protect states from domestic violence and Congressional legislation authorized the President to use armed force for this purpose upon proper application by a state, the states-rights Tyler repeatedly made it clear he would not intervene unless it was absolutely necessary.[80] Before the President sent off his first reply to King, he asked Webster for advice; and the Secretary seems to have counseled utmost caution then and throughout the affair. He talked with representatives from both sides in Rhode Island and at one point asked a friend to report to Washington on the local situation. Most Whigs at the capital shared his views favoring the charter government, but many Democrats did not.[81]

[79] Arthur M. Mowry, *The Dorr War; or the Constitutional Struggle in Rhode Island* (Providence, 1901), 18–222; Peter J. Coleman, *Transformation of Rhode Island, 1790–1860* (Providence, 1963), 254–94; Joseph Brennan, *Social Conditions in Industrial Rhode Island: 1820–1860* (Washington, 1940), 1–146; Jacob Frieze, *Facts Involved in the Rhode Island Controversy with Some Views upon the Rights of Both Parties* (Boston, 1842).

[80] The correspondence between Tyler and King is in James D. Richardson (ed.), *A Compilation of the Messages and Papers of the Presidents, 1789–1897* (10 vols., Washington, 1896–99), IV, 284–307.

[81] *Ibid.*, 290–92, 300–01; Tyler to Webster, undated note [Apr., 1842], Webster Papers (Lib. Cong.); Webster to John Whipple, May 9, 1842, *WS*, XVIII, 127; Webster to Tyler, Apr. 18, 1844, *ibid.*, 190; *House Reports Nos. 546 and 581*, 28 Cong., 1 sess.

Out of this turmoil arose a case, now appealed to the
Supreme Court, seeking a judicial answer to the question of
which Rhode Island government had been legal. Before dawn on
June 29, 1842, at the town of Warren a squad of militia, under
the authority of martial law declared by the charter assembly,
forcibly entered and searched the house of Martin Luther, a
shoemaker and local Dorrite leader. Luther had fled across the
Massachusetts line two days earlier. Some months later he
returned to the state, was tried and convicted by the state court
for participating in an insurrection. Meanwhile he himself filed
a suit to contest the legality of these proceedings. He contended
that Borden and other militiamen had wrongfully entered his
house because the charter assembly authorizing martial law
could no longer legislate. The question was whether the People's
Constitution or the old charter had been the legitimate frame of
government.[82]

Owing to absences and vacancies on the bench, the Court
did not hear *Luther* v. *Borden* until January 1848. Even then
only six justices sat.[83] Spectators crowded into the Courtroom to
hear arguments, lasting six days, by Benjamin F. Hallett and
Attorney General Nathan Clifford for Luther and by John
Whipple and Webster for Borden, thus for the charter government. There was still much interest in this novel case despite
the length of time elapsing since the Dorr controversy.

The interest was not alone in the unusual occurrences in
Rhode Island but in the broad range of questions concerning
general constitutional principles. For three days Hallett, armed
with a mass of documents and papers, sought to prove that a
majority of the adult male citizens had approved the Dorr constitution, that they had done this legally and peaceably, and that
the whole movement had been consistent with the fundamental
political ideas and practices of America.[84] The sovereign people

---

[82] 7 Howard 2 (1849); Mowry, *Dorr War*, 231–32; Mahlen H. Hellerich,
"The Luther Cases in the Lower Courts," *Rhode Island History*, XI (Apr., 1952),
36–38. The case was brought in the Federal Circuit Court of Justice Story. He
and the district judge, John Pitman, both prior to and during their hearing of the
case made it clear that they thought the Dorrite movement was very dangerous.
Story (ed.) *Story*, II, 416, 418–19; Story to Webster, Apr. 26, 1842, Webster Papers
(New Hamp. Hist. Soc.).

[83] Catron, Daniel, and McKinley were absent.

[84] 7 Howard 3–19 (1849) prints the plaintiff's bill of exceptions to the conduct
of the trial in the court below. It summarizes the 150 pages of documentary evidence

institute governments, Hallett said, and they also have a right to alter them. The notion that legislative sanction is a prerequisite to change, he declared, is an "anti-republican doctrine."[85]

Webster and Whipple had to meet head-on this issue as to the character of popular government.[86] Of course the people are the source of all political power in the United States, said Webster, and anyone believing otherwise is worse than Don Quixote, confusing phantoms with reality. But being sovereign, the people delegate powers to governments, some to the states and some to the nation. Legislative power is so delegated because people find it more practical to exercise the power through representatives instead of acting themselves. Such a system depends on fair administration of suffrage laws providing for the time, place, and manner of voting to prevent force or fraud. Qualifications for voters are necessary. Some functions, notably the revision of constitutions, require special safeguards against undue haste, inflammable emotions, shifting popular majorities—against the very excesses committed by the Dorrites. In short, the people have found it wise to limit themselves.[87]

After discoursing on the nature of popular government Webster turned to the specific questions arising in *Luther* v. *Borden*. First, he maintained, whether the old charter or the Dorr constitution was the legitimate fundamental law of Rhode Island was not a proper judicial question for the Court to decide. It was true, he said, that the Federal Constitution guaranteed the states a republican form of government and protected them against insurrections and domestic violence. But Congress enacted laws authorizing the President to use military force, upon application by the states; consequently it was an executive, not

concerning the Dorrite movemnt which the plaintiff had sought unsuccessfully to introduce at the trial. These documents, including resolutions of conventions, long rolls of voters' names, and census lists, are in the MS. record of the case in the Clerk's files, National Archives.

85 7 Howard 19–26 (1849); New York *Courier and Enquirer,* Jan. 26 and 27, 1848.

86 Whipple's argument paralleled Webster's on the question of how governments and constitutions are changed, but it was much more conservative in defending the old frame of Rhode Island government, including the freehold suffrage now abandoned even by the law-and-order party. Webster and Whipple, *The Rhode-Island Question* (Providence, 1848), 3–34. The argument is adequately summarized in 7 Howard 27–29 (1849).

87 Webster's argument is briefly reported in 7 Howard 29–34, but much more fully in *WS,* XI, 217–42.

judicial, power to determine when and how to act. This President Tyler had done. Basically, however, the decision had to come from the existing state legislature (in this case, the charter assembly), for it was the only body competent to authenticate political proceedings and constitutional revisions.[88] The lawyer laid heavy emphasis upon Chief Justice Job Durfee's charge to the jury in the state treason trial of Dorr. The Rhode Island judge had held the judiciary could not inquire into the legitimacy of a constitution because this was a *political* decision the legislature must make. Here was precisely the position Tyler had taken in 1842, said Webster.

The attorney added a few final points. Even if one admitted all that the plaintiff had offered as proof in this cause, the Rhode Island courts had found his acts and those of his Dorrite associates criminal, Webster observed. And it was a well-known rule that the Supreme Court must follow the construction and application of state law by the state courts. The fact was, continued Webster, the Dorrites had not established a going government. Their legislature met for only two days, they elected officers who performed no duties, they had no administrative system and no judiciary. "All was patriotism, and all was paper; and with patriotism and with paper it went out on the 4th of May, admitting itself to be, as all must regard it, a contemptible *sham!*"[89]

Webster's peroration carried conviction and feeling. It had been well, he thought, to examine these fundamental questions of politics. Out of the Rhode Island agitation only good would emerge. "It will purify the political atmosphere from some of its noxious mists," he predicted, "and I hope it will clear men's minds from unfounded notions and dangerous delusions." The charter government perhaps ought to have revised the constitution sooner than it did, conceded the lawyer; but compared to other states, Rhode Island had not been alone in her hesitancy to abandon a freehold qualification. Even Dorr's con-

[88] When they are in session, the state legislatures also have the initiative in applying to the national government for protection against domestic violence. Constitution, Article IV, section 4. Tyler applied this provision quite strictly to withhold intervention when Governor King requested it on one occasion without reference to his legislature, then in session. Tyler to King, June 25, 1842, Richardson (ed.), *Messages and Papers,* IV, 303–04.

[89] *WS,* XI, 240.

stitution, he remarked, included a property requirement for voting tax levies. True principles of popular government lie between extremes of despotism and anarchy, and happily the people had so far safely passed this political strait which was as treacherous as the course betwen Scylla and Charybdis. Prudence and wisdom, Webster warned, would ever be needed to avoid these perils in the years ahead.[90]

To those listening in the packed courtroom and to others reading newspaper accounts, the argument had been fascinating. It was the "event of the day," wrote young Henry J. Raymond of the New York *Courier and Enquirer*.[91] If Democratic reporters thought otherwise, Raymond as a Whig found Webster's exposition instructive and inspiring. At the lawyer's request, Raymond took careful notes, wrote the argument out in full that night, submitted it to the pleased Webster early next morning, sent it to New York to be printed in the *Enquirer*—one of the most reliable reports of a Supreme Court argument by Webster that survives.[92]

Next term, in early January, 1849, Taney delivered the majority opinion in favor of Webster's client.[93] Questions concerning constitutional alterations, the Chief Justice ruled, were "political" and not judicial. Accepting Webster's principal contention here, he deferred to the Rhode Island court. That tribunal in turn had deferred to the charter assembly as to which constitution was legitimate. Courts do not make laws, Taney said, but must act under laws enacted by legislatures. So Chief Justice Durfee had decided in the Dorr treason case, and now the Federal Court must follow the state tribunal's construction of state law. Furthermore, there was Article IV, section 4, of the United States Constitution guaranteeing to the states a re-

---

[90] *Ibid.*, 241–42.

[91] Issue of Jan. 29, 1848.

[92] New York *Courier and Enquirer*, Jan. 31, 1848, from which the text in *WS*, XI, 217–42, and in the pamphlet, *The Rhode-Island Question* (Providence, 1848), are taken verbatim. The brief from which Webster spoke is printed in Samuel P. Lyman, *The Public and Private Life of Daniel Webster* (2 vols., Philadelphia, 1890), I, 289–300. For an account of the reporting see Ernest F. Brown, *Raymond of the Times* (New York, 1951), 58–60.

[93] 7 Howard 34–48 (1849). Justice Woodbury dissented on one point, the declaration of martial law by the state which he thought invaded the sphere of national power and was unwarranted by the local circumstances. Webster, Story, and Taney gave little attention to the point. 7 Howard 48–88 (1849).

publican government and protecting them against insurrections. As Webster had showed, Congress had adopted statutes authorizing the President to act against such domestic disorder, and Tyler had prepared to do this in 1842. What Federal power there was lay with the legislative and executive branches.

Altogether, Taney's opinion was a cogent statement of limitations upon judicial power. The doctrine of "political questions," involving the essentials of federalism and separation of powers, would be a significant concept of constitutional law from that day to this. Occasionally, one suspects, expediency more than principle influenced judges to say that some highly charged questions were not justiciable.[94] And this may have been true in *Luther* v. *Borden* where the practical-minded Taney understood the disarrangements which might result from a decision that all acts of the charter assembly and operations of the Rhode Island government in 1842 had been invalid. But this is simply to say that all doctrines have practical sources.

Notwithstanding the peculiar interest and occasional relevance of the Court's self-imposed limitations, the overriding fact concerning judicial power of that day is that it expanded greatly. There were very few instances where judges found themselves incompetent to decide a question because it was too politically sensitive. Taking the whole list of Webster's cases as typical of judicial business from 1814 to 1852 (which would be a defensible technique), one is struck by the boldness and the vigor not only of Marshall's Court but of Taney's as well. Urged on by such counsel as Webster and responding to its environment, the Court assumed an ever larger burden of interpreting the Constitution and expounding various branches of the law. The field of admiralty law is a good if unspectacular example of what was happening. Webster the lawyer had much to do with this development in many other fields too.

[94] Oliver P. Field, "The Doctrine of Political Questions in the Federal Courts," *Minnesota Law Review*, VIII (May, 1924), 485–513; Charles G. Post, *The Supreme Court and Political Questions* (Baltimore, 1936). A recent instance of changing judicial ideas is *Baker* v. *Carr*, 82 Sup. Ct. Reporter 691–780 (1962), wherein the Court held that the subject of state legislative apportionment is justiciable. The several majority and minority opinions in this case attempted, at some length, to establish their consistency with or distinguish the question from *Luther* v. *Borden*.

IV

THE DARTMOUTH COLLEGE CASE

Webster's first well-known case in the Supreme Court was *Dartmouth College* v. *Woodward,* argued in March, 1818, and decided the following February. It became the case, above all others, associated with his name. Indeed one can scarcely mention the controversy without recalling the advocate whose inspired oratory rescued the small New England college from an unwelcome reconstruction. After so skillfully representing his alma mater, Webster immediately entered the first rank of the bar. This advancement of his professional standing was of course far more important than his fee, substantial though it was. Apart from the effects it had upon Webster's personal career, the case profoundly influenced American constitutional law.

A brief excursion into Dartmouth's history indicates the circumstances underlying the suit. In the 1740's Eleazar Wheelock, a young minister at Lebanon, Connecticut, became much interested in the cause of Indian education. His enthusiasm sprang from the environment of the Great Awakening, a religious revival currently sweeping through the colonies. Wheelock trained several youths as missionaries to their own people. He carried on his work with the assistance of generous gifts, enabling him to organize Moor's Indian Charity School in 1754. Wishing to expand the project, he sent a former student and a fellow pastor to England and Scotland in 1765 to solicit contributions. They obtained a large sum of money from numerous small subscriptions of the lower classes, as well as from gifts by the King and some of the nobility. One of the benefactors was Lord Dartmouth, president of the Board of Trade, who headed a board of trustees in England to supervise application of the funds.[1]

In the spring of 1769 Wheelock selected a new site for the school up the Connecticut River at Hanover, New Hampshire, after considering several places that competed in promising donations. The colony itself granted a township and added more lands in later years. Local assistance was very liberal, to the extent that Wheelock personally received some lands.[2] Governor John Wentworth issued a royal charter incorporating Dartmouth College "for the education and instruction of youth of the Indian tribes . . . and also of English youth and any others." As "founder" and president, Wheelock could nominate his successor. A board of twelve trustees, separate from the English body, secured ample rights and privileges to administer the College. This self-perpetuating board shared broad authority with the president.[3]

Soon it became clear that this was not the kind of school the English trustees had envisioned. Dartmouth was essentially a college for white youths, although a few Indians and missionary students usually attended. A protest from the English trust compelled the American board to draw a line of separation between the College and Moor's Indian Charity School. The board at a meeting in Hanover on October 22, 1770, disclaimed any responsibility for Moor's School, and the President faithfully pledged the English fund to it alone. Thus, though Wheelock was the head of both the College and Moor's School, the American trustees would supervise the former and the English trustees, the latter. In practice, however, Wheelock's drafts on the English fund, exhausted by 1775, paid for clearing lands, constructing buildings, and doing many things that benefited the College as well as Moor's School. Furthermore, Wheelock so intermingled his personal finances with those of both College and School that the distinction was meaningless. He diverted the

---

[1] Leon B. Richardson, *History of Dartmouth College* (2 vols., Hanover, N. H., 1932), I, 13–63.

[2] *Ibid.*, 79–84, 90–97, 216.

[3] A copy of the charter is in 4 Wheaton 519–37.

English donations in order to support a new American college, quite outside the original design. But Wheelock always believed that he was promoting Indian education, despite the limited success he achieved, and probably did not intend to misapply the English contributions.[4]

In 1779 the presidency devolved upon the founder's son, John Wheelock. A strong-willed autocrat, he directed the College's affairs for many years without interference by the trustees, who subserviently acquiesced to his every decision. But after 1793, new independent-minded trustees brought this one-man administration under stricter scrutiny and increasingly challenged Wheelock. By 1809 the President's opponents, now a majority of the board, endangered his dynastic position. Meanwhile Wheelock had waged war with the congregation of the Hanover church, principally concerning an appointment to the pastorate. Apparently he opposed the selection of the new theological professor as the minister primarily because the dominance he had long enjoyed was slipping and not because he differed with him on doctrinal matters. Nevertheless the Hanover church did adopt Congregationalism as a result of the dispute, and Wheelock with a small band of followers from Hartford, Vermont, remained Presbyterian. Wheelock appealed to the trustees for support in the quarrel. Finding them unfriendly, he decided to carry his cause to the people of the state and to their political representatives.[5]

Anonymously, but in a style that identified his authorship, the President published a pamphlet entitled *Sketches of the History of Dartmouth College and Moor's Charity School, with a Particular Account of Some Late Remarkable Proceedings of the Board of Trustees from the Year 1779 to the Year 1815.* He hoped to arouse the public against an alleged sectarian movement by the trustees subverting popular liberties; and to amplify the warning, Wheelock's friend Elijah Parish, a reactionary minister of Byfield, Massachusetts, circulated *A Candid Analytical Review of the Sketches.*[6] Copies of these tracts went to the members of the New Hampshire legislature, before whom Wheelock

[4] Richardson, *Dart. Coll.,* I, 112–18, 144–45, 187–89.
[5] *Ibid.,* 288–303; John K. Lord, *A History of Dartmouth College: 1815–1909* (Concord, N. H., 1913), 1–61.
[6] Richardson, *Dart. Coll.,* I, 303–06.

appeared with a petition for an investigation of the controversy. A committee did visit the campus in August, 1815, but carefully reported facts generally unfavorable to Wheelock's side.[7]

A few weeks before the committee came to Hanover, the President had requested Webster to serve as counsel in legal proceedings that might arise. On general terms the lawyer had assented. Wheelock dispatched a letter to Webster on August 5, asking for his professional assistance before the legislative committee, and enclosed twenty dollars with the assurance of further remuneration.[8] Webster, then being absent from home, did not read Wheelock's letter until after the committee's inquiry of August 16–18 and did not attend. It seemed to the President that Webster's friends among the trustees had influenced him to break his promise. The truth was that the attorney had not anticipated the political turn that the affair took; and had he received the letter in time, he would not have felt obligated to align himself against the trustees outside of court. Characteristically, Webster neglected to return the twenty dollars.[9]

The trustees counterattacked by removing Wheelock from office, by appointing Francis Brown as president, and by publishing a spirited pamphlet, *A Vindication of the Official Conduct of the Trustees of Dartmouth College*. The immediate advantage to the trustees in evicting Wheelock was of course control of the College, which proved very helpful in the protracted struggle that followed. Yet it eliminated the last slim possibility of compromise, if there had been any at all, and strengthened Wheelock's determination to win by resort to state politics. And in spite of their efforts to propagandize their version, the trustees unhappily discovered that many people believed the "venerable" Wheelock was a martyr, persecuted by his bigoted foes.[10]

The politicians thoroughly ventilated the issue in the

[7] *Ibid.*, 307–09.

[8] Wheelock's letter is said to have been later acquired by Kenyon College, Ohio, and was printed in full in the Cincinnati *Gazette*. A clipping of this newspaper (with no date indicated) is in the Webster Papers (Library of Congress), I, 15555a.

[9] Webster to Mr. [Josiah] D[unham], Aug. 25, 1815, *WS*, XVII, 251–53; Lord, *Dart. Coll.*, 69–71.

[10] William G. North, "The Political Background of the Dartmouth College Case," *New England Quarterly*, XVIII (June, 1945), 194–96.

campaign of early 1816. Through necessity, owing to the prominence of Trustees Thomas W. Thompson (a United States senator), Timothy Farrar, and Charles Marsh in the Federalist party, Wheelock joined hands with the Republicans. Isaac Hill, partisan editor of the *New Hampshire Patriot,* warned his readers against a Federalist, Congregationalist plot to dominate the state. The anti-trustee groups seemed unbothered by the incongruity of Wheelock, a confirmed Federalist and a severe Calvinist, seeking aid from the Jeffersonian Republicans, who were then advocating religious toleration. Whether the College question was decisive is unclear, but the declining Federalists lost the legislature and the governorship to the Republicans by a large margin.

The new governor was William Plumer, an ex-Federalist converted to Republicanism in the days of the Embargo. Self-educated, rationalistic, and liberal, Plumer was a remarkable figure. Advocating restrictions upon corporate privileges, complete freedom of individual conscience, and an improved educational system, he saw the Dartmouth College controversy as an opportunity to translate these ideas into worthwhile reforms. A college, he thought, ought to be responsive to public needs, free of sectarian domination, and committed to a broad curriculum for the practical education of its students. He did not wish simply to restore John Wheelock to his former office nor to punish his enemies.[11] The Governor experienced much more satisfaction from a letter by Thomas Jefferson praising his "sound" and "truly republican" principles[12] than from a calculated visit by Elijah Parish, who, Plumer thought, was a "man of strong passions, governed by feeling more than reason."[13] Few others on either side looked at the matter on such an idealistic plane.

In response to Plumer's recommendations, the New Hampshire legislature enacted the law of June 27, 1816, materially revising the College charter.[14] The statute changed the

---

[11] Lynn W. Turner, *William Plumer of New Hampshire, 1759–1850* (Chapel Hill, 1962), 233–39, 245–46, 303–04; William Plumer, Jr., *Life of William Plumer* (Boston, 1856), 439–40 and *passim.*

[12] Jefferson to Plumer, July 21, 1816, H. A. Washington (ed.), *The Writings of Thomas Jefferson* (9 vols., New York, 1853–55), VII, 18–19.

[13] Plumer, *Plumer,* 434.

[14] *Laws of New Hampshire* (Concord, 1920), VIII, 505–08. The statute represented the views of Wheelock's relatives and partisans who had energetically

corporation's name to Dartmouth University, in which additional colleges and an institute could be organized. It increased the number of trustees from twelve to twenty-one and created a board of twenty-five overseers to confirm or disapprove proceedings of the trustees. The new officers, initially appointed by the governor and council, were to report annually on the status of the University. And the governor had to inspect the University at least once every five years. After most of the old trustees refused to attend meetings of the new board, two statutes were passed in December to quash this opposition.[15] One provision reduced the requisite quorum from eleven to nine. The effect of the measures was to change the College to a state institution, at least for the time being. But the legislators appropriated no money to support the University.

Early next year the new trustees were able to transact business without the dissenters and then removed them from office. The board also dismissed President Brown to make way for the restoration of Wheelock. In spite of his victory, Wheelock was so ill he could not resume his duties; therefore his son-in-law, William Allen, served temporarily until June, 1817, and after Wheelock's death succeeded in his own right.[16] From the outset the old trustees had decided to resist these innovations. After the adoption of the first law, they protested that it violated both state and national constitutions, that it deprived them of their vested rights and privileges, and that the prosperous condition of the College needed no improvement.[17] The College, administered by Brown and the old trustees, continued instruction in make-shift quarters at Hanover, since it had been evicted from classrooms and dormitories. Nearly all the students remained loyal to the College, while the newly organized University maintained a struggling existence during the legal battles that ensued.

lobbied at Concord quite as much as it did the recommendations of the governor. Webster and other Federalists had also lobbied but with less success. Turner, *Plumer*, 246–54.

[15] *Laws of New Hampshire*, VIII, 555–56, 584.

[16] Richardson, *Dart. Coll.*, I, 323–25.

[17] Timothy Farrar, *Report of the Case of the Trustees of Dartmouth College against William H. Woodward* (Portsmouth, N. H., 1819), 385–88. These arguments presaged those to be subsequently advanced in the attorneys' briefs in the courts.

The determination of the College trustees to resist the state laws gradually led into a specific strategy. They dismissed Secretary-treasurer William H. Woodward, Wheelock's nephew and probably one of the authors of the New Hampshire legislation; and he soon became secretary-treasurer of the University. On February 8, 1817, they initiated a suit against Woodward to recover the College charter, records, and seal, which that officer had taken with him to his new position. An unusual aspect of the case was that it was brought in the county Court of Common Pleas, of which Woodward was the chief justice.[18] Consequently, there was no trial or verdict of the ordinary kind; but a statement of facts, agreed upon by the parties in the form of a special verdict, went directly up to the state Superior Court. This part of the record merely recited the terms of the original charter of 1769 and the statutes of June and December, 1816. The jury prayed for the Court's advice on the constitutionality of these laws.[19]

The three justices of the Superior Court were talented and competent men. As dependable Republicans, they had recently been appointed by Governor Plumer after the legislature had reorganized the judicial system for familiar partisan purposes.[20] William M. Richardson, a Harvard graduate, ex-Congressman and United States district attorney, remained chief justice for twenty-two years and contributed significantly to the systematization of New Hampshire law.[21] Justice Samuel Bell, graduate of Dartmouth, later governor and senator, was prominent in public affairs.[22] Justice Levi Woodbury, twenty-seven-year-old prodigy, became a well-known figure in American politics for the next thirty-five years as governor, senator, cabinet member, and associate justice of the United States Supreme Court.[23] Selected as a trustee of Dartmouth University, Wood-

[18] Richardson, *Dart. Coll.*, I, 326–27; John M. Shirley, *The Dartmouth College Causes and the Supreme Court of the United States* (St. Louis, 1879), 2, 116–18.

[19] 4 Wheaton 518–51.

[20] Plumer, *Plumer*, 443–48.

[21] Charles H. Bell, *Life of William M. Richardson, LL.D., Late Chief Justice of the Superior Court in New Hampshire* (Concord, 1839).

[22] Charles H. Bell, *The Bench and Bar of New Hampshire* (Boston, 1894), 79–81.

[23] *Ibid.*, 81–84; Charles L. Woodbury (ed.), *Writings of Levi Woodbury, LL.D.: Political, Judicial and Literary. Now First Selected and Arranged* (3 vols.,

bury had resigned from the board prior to the suit and apparently participated in the decision.[24]

The state court heard arguments of counsel at Haverhill in May and again at Exeter in September. Representing the College were Jeremiah Mason and Jeremiah Smith, joined in the second argument by Webster. State Attorney General George Sullivan and Ichabod Bartlett were Woodward's attorneys. The report of what the lawyers said is uncommonly full, since a book recording the briefs and opinions in both state and national courts was later published.[25]

Robust, six-foot-six Jeremiah Mason, now a Federalist Senator, was never better in his many years as the state's leading lawyer.[26] By his penetrating study of the case, Mason laid the foundation for Webster's later argument in the Supreme Court.[27] He emphasized the theory of separation of powers to show that these laws were not within the scope of legislative power. Corporate rights and privileges, he said, were property forfeitable only by judicial trial. If Dartmouth College were a public corporation, like counties and cities, the legislature could regulate it; but in fact, it was an eleemosynary, private corporation to carry out the will of the donors. In supporting this point, Mason cited English cases, Montesquieu, the *Federalist,* and some American precedents; yet, basically, he appealed to natural jus-

Boston, 1852). For Woodbury's friendship with Plumer and his opposition to the old College trustees, see Woodbury to Plumer, Aug. 7, 1816, and Jan. 18, 1817, Plumer Papers (New Hampshire State Library).

24 The docket entry states that Woodbury did not sit in the case. 65 New Hampshire Reports (Parsons, 1888–89) 624–25 n. 1. Shirley, *Dart. Coll. Causes,* 149–51, also says this, but there are other indications to the contrary. Woodbury wrote to Plumer, September 19, 1817, that the case had been elaborately argued by counsel and "We have had, however, more language than *light*—Apprehend an opinion may be given before the term closes; though possibly not till our arrival at Plymouth." Plumer Papers (N. H. State Lib.). Furthermore, William Plumer, Jr., reported to his father on October 4, 1817, that Chief Justice Richardson had told him that each of the three justices would deliver an opinion. Only the Chief Justice did so, but it would seem that Woodbury sat in the case. *Ibid.*

25 Timothy Farrar, *Report of the Case of the Trustees of Dartmouth College against William H. Woodward* (Portsmouth, N. H., 1819). Webster's argument in the state court is not included.

26 George S. Hillard, *Memoir and Correspondence of Jeremiah Mason* (Cambridge, 1873).

27 Two manuscript drafts of Mason's brief, together with his notes on the arguments of opposing attorneys, are in "Briefs in the Dartmouth College Case," Dartmouth College Archives. A printed version is in 65 New Hampshire Reports, 473–502.

tice for some protection against legislative tyranny. He next referred to several sections of the state constitution which forbade what had been done, particularly Article Fifteen providing that "no subject shall be arrested, imprisoned, despoiled, or deprived of his property, immunities, or privileges, put out of the protection of the law, exiled or deprived of his life, liberty, or estate; but by the judgment of his peers, or the law of the land." Derived from Magna Charta, which originally limited royal power, this article materially restricted the legislature's authority in American state government, Mason declared. Similar to "due process" in the Fifth Amendment of the national Constitution applying to Congress, the "law of the land" clause would thus prevent special legislation against private rights and guarantee fair judicial trial.[28]

Rather briefly Mason also argued that the state laws violated the contract clause of the Federal Constitution. The charter of 1769 had created an obligation of the King to the College trustees, which the legislature subsequently assumed and could not now impair. *Fletcher* v. *Peck* (1810) had decided that a state land grant to individuals was a contract; and so grants of land, franchises, and privileges to *corporations* were likewise contracts. Mason concluded by warning that such laws as these would destroy all "literary and charitable" institutions.

Jeremiah Smith, former chief justice of this Superior Court, supplemented Mason's points in a learned, copious argument. He gave extensive consideration to the legal nature of corporations, the question he believed to be "all important to a correct decision of this cause." Corporations might be divided, he said, into two classes, civil and eleemosynary. Counties, cities, and the English universities were civil; and hospitals, schools, and colleges were eleemosynary, charitable institutions founded by donors through benefactions. The *first* benefactors, according to Smith, had the right of visitation, a right to supervise eleemosynary corporations. Though the King and New Hampshire later made gifts of land to Dartmouth College, the first donors were the English contributors, who had vested the right of

---

[28] Edward S. Corwin, "The Doctrine of Due Process of Law before the Civil War," *Harvard Law Review,* XXIV (1911), 366–85, 460–95, discusses early English and American developments of the concept here set forth by Mason.

visitation in the president. Upon the death of Eleazar Wheelock, this right devolved upon the American trustees.[29] Smith's research into the common law was thorough, and his reasoning from it seemed credible.

A reprint or even a summary of Webster's argument in the state court is not extant. He did not join Mason and Smith until shortly before the October term at Exeter and consequently depended upon their organization of the case for his one-hour effort.[30] Yet he deeply moved his listeners, in the words of one correspondent, "by the genius and eloquence of his soul, of sublime sentiment and feeling."[31] Upon hearing reports of Webster's performance, Woodward sarcastically remarked, "D. W. drowned the whole audience in their common tears—and among the rest [,] tears of repentance were shed by zealous advocates of the laws."[32] In a stirring conclusion, Webster compared Caesar's murder at the Senate with his alma mater's betrayal by her trusted sons.[33] These were the seeds of the lawyer's famous peroration in the Federal Supreme Court.

Woodward's counsel, George Sullivan and Ichabod Bartlett, capably defended the validity of the state laws creating Dartmouth University. This corporation, they insisted, was not a private but a public institution, regardless of who were the original donors. In their view, the purpose or the extensiveness of the object for establishing a corporation determined its nature. Dartmouth College received a charter to promote education for the public good; and so the people of New Hampshire, instead of the trustees, held a "beneficial interest" in its property. Nor did the trustees hold legal title to that property, since it was vested in the corporation as a whole. Inasmuch as the legislation had neither destroyed the corporation nor altered its purpose, it had not deprived any rights. Sullivan and Bartlett tried to refute plaintiffs' arguments not only on this point relating to the common law but also on others concerning the state and national constitutions. Generally they spoke for state legisla-

29 65 New Hampshire Reports, 524–63.
30 Webster to Mason, Sept. 4, 1817, WS, XVII, 265–66.
31 Charles Warren, "An Historical Note on the Dartmouth College Case," American Law Review, XLVI (Sept.–Oct., 1912), 668, quoting the Salem Gazette.
32 Woodward to Plumer, Oct. 2, 1817, Plumer Papers (N. H. State Lib.).
33 Shirley, Dart. Coll. Causes, 186.

tive power, acting in the public interest, and saw a similarity between it and the omnipotence of Parliament, as distinguished from the King, whom the common law admittedly limited. If the contract clause of the United States Constitution were unjustifiably stretched to protect corporate charters, they concluded, that provision must not prevent the legislature from nourishing knowledge and virtue by regulating a public corporation.[34]

Sharing the confidence of the University side, Governor Plumer predicted a favorable decision "not from any intimation I have had, from any one, but from my own opinion of the merits of the cause."[35] On the other hand, Webster pessimistically observed, "It would be a queer thing if Govr P's Court should refuse to execute his Laws. I am afraid there is no great hope of their disobedience to the powers that made them."[36] Both parties, for their own reasons, desired prompt disposition of the case to end the troublesome competition of the two struggling schools at Hanover, but the Court did not announce judgment until the next term at Plymouth on November 6, 1817.

Accepting Sullivan's argument that Dartmouth was a public corporation, Chief Justice Richardson wrote an opinion that rested almost entirely on this point.[37] Corporations are either private or public, he said, according to the beneficial interests in their franchises and property. Private corporations, such as canal, turnpike, banking, and insurance companies, are created by individuals for their own benefit. "*Publick* corporations," he continued, "are those, which are created for publick purposes, and whose property is devoted to the objects for which they are created. The corporators have no private beneficial interest, either in their franchises or their property."[38] By this standard, the judge classified Dartmouth as a public corporation. The trustees, having no beneficial interest, could therefore maintain no property rights under either the state or the national constitu-

---

[34] Sullivan's argument can be found in 65 New Hampshire Reports 502–24; Bartlett's, in *ibid.*, 563–93.

[35] Plumer to Woodward, Sept. 27 and Oct. 11, 1817, Plumer Papers (Lib. Cong.). Note that some Plumer papers are deposited in the New Hampshire State Library, and others are in the Library of Congress.

[36] Webster to Mason, June 28, 1817, *WS*, XVI, 38–39.

[37] The opinion is printed in 65 New Hampshire Reports 624–43.

[38] *Ibid.*, 628.

tion. The legislature must have power to supervise and improve
public institutions in the public interest.

Richardson then rejected Mason's contention that the
statutes of 1816 violated the New Hampshire constitutional provision shielding an individual's life, liberty, and estate by the
"law of the land." In New Hampshire, said the Chief Justice,
"all statutes, not repugnant to any other clauses in the constitution, seem always to have been considered as 'the law of the
land,' within the meaning of this clause." The opposite principle
"would probably make our whole statute book a dead letter."[39]
Legislative enactments were accordingly as valid as judicial proceedings.

The contract clause of the United States Constitution
caused Richardson little difficulty. He distinguished the present
case from previous ones on the ground that it involved no private
rights. The clause was not intended, he held, "to limit the power
of the states, in relation to their own publick officers and servants,
or to their own civil institutions."[40] It is noteworthy that the
Chief Justice did not deny that *some* corporate charters were
contracts within the meaning of Article I, section 10, but he did
assert that *this* charter of Dartmouth's was no such contract
obligating the state not to impair it.[41]

A few weeks after the New Hampshire Court's decision,
the College began an appeal to the Supreme Court. On Christmas Day, 1817, a messenger left for Washington with the record
of the case.[42] Neither Mason nor Smith wished to go to the
capital for the February term, and therefore principal responsibility of representing the plaintiffs fell upon Webster. Since he
was no longer a Congressman, he had no other reason to make
the trip except business in Court. So he wished to fix his fee before consenting. "I think I would undertake, for a thousand
dollars, to go to Washington, and argue the case, and get Mr.
Hopkinson's assistance also," Webster informed President

[39] *Ibid.*, 638–39.
[40] *Ibid.*, 639.
[41] See Horace H. Hagan, "The Dartmouth College Case," *Georgetown Law
Journal,* XIX (May, 1931), 415.
[42] Lord, *Dart. Coll.*, 140–41.

Brown. "I doubt whether I could do it for a much less sum."[43] Brown agreed to this proposal, and Joseph Hopkinson of Philadelphia became Webster's associate.

Wisely, Webster recognized the value of depending heavily upon the well-constructed briefs of Mason and Smith. In December, he dispatched letters to the two men, requesting that they send him their notes and a copy of Judge Richardson's opinion.[44] To Smith he remarked that "every one knows I can only be the reciter of the argument made by you."[45] Despite his urgings, however, he did not receive the materials until January, shortly before he left for Washington. Prior to his departure he conferred with Mason, whose brief he intended to follow closely, though he supplemented it with Smith's research into the common law rules on charitable corporations.[46]

Hopkinson readily accepted the offer to participate in the case and felt sure justice was on the College's side.[47] This Pennsylvania lawyer-politician, then forty-eight, was at the height of an active career, marked by such accomplishments as writing the popular "Hail Columbia" and defending Justice Samuel Chase in the impeachment trial of 1805. The studious Hopkinson was a graceful orator and a seasoned lawyer. Though he had appeared before the Supreme Court only a few times previously, he lent strength to the plaintiffs' hopes of success,

[43] Webster to Brown, Nov. 15, 1817, quoted in *ibid.*, 138. Hopkinson later received five hundred dollars, not paid out of Webster's thousand-dollar fee.

[44] Webster to Mason, Dec. 8, 1817, *WS*, XVI, 39.

[45] Webster to Smith, Dec. 8, 1817, *ibid.*, XVII, 268.

[46] Webster to Smith, Jan. 9, 1818, *ibid.*, 268–69; Webster to Mason, Jan. 9, 1818, and Jan. [no day indicated], 1818, *ibid.*, 269–71. A comparison of the manuscript drafts of the arguments by Webster and Mason in the "Briefs in the Dartmouth College Case," Dartmouth College Archives, shows a close similarity between the two. See also W. S. G. Noyes, "Webster's Debt to Mason in the Dartmouth College Case," *American Law Review* (May–June, 1894), 359–67. An editorial note to the above accuses Webster of "plagiarism." Albert J. Beveridge, *The Life of John Marshall*, IV, 250, says Webster "privately admitted" borrowing from Mason, "although he never publicly gave his associate credit." Such acknowledgments as he made directly were in correspondence with Smith, March 14, 1818, *WS*, XVII, 276–77, and with Jacob McGaw, July 27, 1818, Claude H. Van Tyne (ed.), *The Letters of Daniel Webster* (New York, 1902), 77. An important point that these writers neglect is Webster's active role in publishing Farrar's *Report of the Case . . . of Dartmouth College. . . .* Webster was fully aware of the proof this book would publicly give of the similarity between the arguments. Webster to Mason, April 10, 1819, *WS*, XVI, 48. See discussion below.

[47] Hopkinson to Webster, Nov. 20, 1817, quoted in Lord, *Dart. Coll.*, 139.

the more so because his confirmed Federalism recommended him
to Chief Justice Marshall.[48]

Governor Plumer felt thoroughly satisfied with the New
Hampshire court's decision. Anxious for the uncertainty of
litigation to end, for a while he optimistically thought the College trustees might not appeal to the Supreme Court.

It is said Brown & Co intend carrying the suit, by writ of Error to the
supreme court of the U.S. [the Governor wrote.] I should not think they
would adopt such a course, had I not seen too many instances of men suffering of passion, wounded pride & resentments to usurp the place of sound
discretion & mature judgment. I think they can have no rational grounds to
hope for success in the national Court, & that the friends of the University
have nothing to fear from the result, but the expence [sic] & the evils
which proceed from a state of suspense.[49]

Plumer predicted victory in this battle to which he had whole-
heartedly committed himself.[50]

The University trustees, meeting on December 31, voted
to retain John Holmes as counsel.[51] A Massachusetts Congressman for the district of Maine, Holmes had abandoned the Federalist party in 1811 to become a Republican. Not an outstanding lawyer, he was a shrewd, resourceful politician who had
attracted attention owing to his support of the War of 1812.
Governor Plumer endorsed the selection of Holmes;[52] and so
did Woodward, who observed, "What appears at first so forbidding and indeed so likely to impress some with a kind of disgust wears away on further acquaintance—I have thought him
extremely ready—of sound mind and a good lawyer inferiour
to D.W. only in point of oratory—."[53] After agreeing to serve,
Holmes asked the state's attorneys to send him the relevant
papers, especially their briefs.[54] But he did not prepare energetically even though he realized the difficulty of winning.[55]

[48] Burton A. Konkle, *Joseph Hopkinson, 1770-1842* (Philadelphia, 1931);
Warren, "Historical Note on the Dartmouth College Case," *Am. Law Rev.,* XLVI
(Sept.–Oct., 1912), 666.
[49] Plumer Papers (Lib. Cong.).
[50] A typical letter is Plumer to Salma Hale, Jan. 15, 1818, Plumer Papers
(N. H. State Lib.).
[51] William Allen to Salma Hale, Jan. 1, 1818, Dart. Coll. Archives.
[52] Plumer to Hale, Jan. 15, 1818, Plumer Papers (N. H. State Lib.).
[53] Woodward to Hale, Jan. 18, 1818, Dart. Coll. Archives.
[54] Holmes to Allen, Jan. 8, 1818, *ibid.*
[55] Hale to Allen, Feb. 27. 1818, *ibid.*

Management of the defendant's cause actually fell to Salma Hale, Congressman and University trustee. Unlike Allen, Woodward, and Plumer, Hale disapproved the choice of Holmes and unhesitatingly said so in letters to New Hampshire.

Mr. H. came here [he declared] with a very high reputation. The members from the South and west were eager to know and eager to tell who he was. But from the high station in many minds which the good he did in perilous times deservedly placed him, he has now fallen much below that to which I think his talents entitle him. He may not rise to the proper level.[56]

Other friends of the University, such as Secretary of the Navy Benjamin W. Crowninshield and Eleazar W. Ripley, approved Hale's demand for additional counsel.[57] President Allen, Governor Plumer, and the board of trustees did not object, the only obstacle being the difficulty of paying the lawyers' fees.[58] Largely upon his own initiative, Hale employed Attorney General William Wirt.[59] Only recently had this facile, witty Virginian assumed the official duties he would perform for the next dozen years with exceptional skill. He had long experience before state and lower Federal tribunals, though very little in the Supreme Court. But at the moment, Wirt was so overwhelmed with work that he could not give the case the best of his great talents.[60]

The inadequate preparation of both Holmes and Wirt may have been partially due to procrastination by the New Hampshire counsel, Sullivan and Bartlett, in forwarding their briefs to Washington. Hale exhorted Plumer and Allen to hurry the papers on, but it was late February before they arrived.[61]

[56] Hale to Plumer, Jan. 20, 1818, ibid.

[57] Cyrus Perkins to Hale, Jan. 24, 1818, ibid. Crowninshield was Secretary of the Navy, 1814–18, and an overseer of the University. General Eleazar Wheelock Ripley, a nephew of John Wheelock, was one of the lobbyists who drafted the New Hampshire laws.

[58] Woodward to Hale, Jan. 25, 1818, and Woodward to John Harris, Jan. 25, 1818, ibid.; Plumer to Hale, Feb. 5, 1818, Plumer Papers (N. H. State Lib.).

[59] Hale to Allen, Feb. 15, 1818, Dart. Coll. Archives. See also Woodward to Hale, Feb. 18, 1818, and Allen to Hale, Feb. 18, 1818, ibid. Governor Plumer commended Hale's action in a letter of February 16, Plumer Papers (Lib. Cong.), but he declined to make a personal financial contribution for Wirt's fees because "it would cause our political enemies to blaspheme." Plumer to Clement Storer, Feb. 23, 1818, ibid.

[60] Warren, "Historical Note on the Dartmouth College Case," Am. Law Rev., XLVI (Sept.–Oct., 1912), 669–72.

[61] Hale to Plumer, Feb. 7, 1818, Plumer Papers (Lib. Cong.); Woodward to Hale, Feb. 18, 1818, Dart. Coll. Archives; Allen to Hale, Feb. 18, 1818, ibid.;

The University lawyers did not have even a list of the authorities cited in the state court until just before argument. Had Sullivan or Bartlett come to Washington, they would have handled the case more effectively; but the expense of their doing this seemed needless.

At eleven o'clock on March 10, 1818, Webster opened for the plaintiffs. The Court, still occupying a temporary chamber due to wartime damages to the Capitol, was closing a busy term. The only spectators were a few interested lawyers and a small band of New Englanders.[62] Beginning in a conversational tone, Webster summarized the facts with special attention to provisions of the College charter and to alterations worked by the New Hampshire statutes. He continued for more than four hours with one of the most eloquent performances in the Court's history.[63]

The salient characteristic of Webster's argument was an ample exposition of corporate rights under the common law. His purpose was to prove that the state acts violated the New Hampshire constitution, though he realized that this consideration did not fall within the Court's jurisdiction. Inasmuch as the case came from a state tribunal on writ of error, only allegations of conflict between the state statutes and the Federal Constitution were appropriate under the United States Judiciary Act of 1789. This Webster conceded. "Yet it may assist," he declared, "in forming an opinion of their [the laws'] true nature and character to compare them with those fundamental principles introduced into the State governments for the purpose of limiting the exercise of the legislative power, and which the Constitution of New Hampshire expresses with great fulness and accuracy."[64]

There must have been other reasons why he went beyond jurisdictional boundaries. One was undoubtedly the fact that he

---

Plumer to Clement Storer, Feb. 23, 1818, Plumer Papers (Lib. Cong.) ; Hale to Plumer, Feb. 24, 1818, *ibid.;* Hale to Allen, Feb. 27, 1818, Dart. Coll. Archives.

[62] Beveridge, *Marshall,* IV, 236–37.

[63] Webster's argument is printed in *WS,* X, 195–233. In the Dartmouth College Archives there are two manuscript drafts of the argument. The first, ten pages in length, is composed of notes on Mason's and Smith's briefs in addition to Webster's own outline. The second, fifty-five pages in length, is a smoother draft, which was probably used in preparing the printed report of the case.

[64] *WS,* X, 200.

followed Mason's brief so closely; and of course Mason had rightly stressed state constitutional provisions in the New Hampshire Court. Furthermore, Webster was attempting to refute the strong opinion of Chief Justice Richardson, particularly the holding that Dartmouth College was a public corporation. And fundamentally the lawyer lacked confidence in the Federal contract clause to protect corporate charters, which was understandable since the scope of that clause was still unclear.

All relevant judicial decisions and authoritative legal commentaries, Webster contended, classified colleges as eleemosynary institutions, that is to say private charities rather than public or civil corporations. Colleges were unlike civil corporations, organized either for political purposes (cities and counties) or for trading purposes (banks and insurance companies). In the words of Blackstone, they were "constituted for the perpetual distributions of the free alms or bounty of the founder of them, to such persons as he has directed."[65] The will of donors who established colleges was paramount. Thus the founder could act as visitor to govern the corporation. The visitorial right was the founder's private property possessed by him alone or assigned to others, oftentimes trustees or overseers.[66] Among the numerous English cases cited to maintain this doctrine, the one put forward most emphatically was *Phillips* v. *Bury,* in which Chief Justice Lord Holt of King's Bench held Exeter College in Oxford to be an eleemosynary corporation subject to the founder's visitorial power.[67]

These principles, Webster insisted, applied to the present instance. As founder of Dartmouth College, President Eleazar Wheelock had secured a charter establishing an eleemosynary corporation. Later Wheelock assigned the power of visitation to trustees, who then enjoyed certain privileges and immunities. Each trustee held a franchise, no different than any other right to hold private property. The fact that the exercise of that right by the trustees affected the public in the benevolent cause of

[65] 1 Blackstone 471. Webster's position concerning the common law status of corporations was well supported by William Blackstone's *Commentaries on the Laws of England,* I, 467–85, which at this time was a convincing authority in America as well as England.

[66] *WS,* X, 203–10.

[67] 1 Lord Raymond 5, printed in 91 English Reports 900.

education did not make the corporation public or the interest in the College property public.[68]

Webster asserted that the "law of the land" clause in Article Fifteen of the state constitution protected the trustees' rights. He followed Mason's interpretation of the article as limiting legislative power and guaranteeing judicial trial. Challenging Richardson's opinion that a legislative statute was the "law of the land," he expounded the idea later to be known as substantive due process of law. Even an omnipotent Parliament, let alone a less powerful state legislature, would not act in such an oppressive manner. Otherwise law would lack the essential quality of uniformity and would be nothing more than the authority of a capricious majority to confiscate property and transfer it to other persons.[69]

Turning to the contract clause of the national Constitution, Webster said it also prohibited the New Hampshire legislation. Article I, section 10, provides that "No State shall pass any . . . law impairing the obligation of contracts." The lawyer referred to Number Forty-four of the *Federalist,* in which Madison interpreted the clause as a safeguard against fluctuating policies that would permit speculation to triumph over honest industry.[70] In a broad sense, it was a necessary check upon state power in order to maintain the stability of vested rights, a doctrine affirmed on several occasions by this Court. *Fletcher* v. *Peck* (1810) had decided that a state land grant was an executed contract, obligating the state not to rescind its conveyance. *New Jersey* v. *Wilson* (1812), Webster continued, had held "that a grant by a State before the Revolution is as much to be protected as a grant since." *Terrett* v. *Taylor* (1815) was "of all others most pertinent to the present argument. Indeed, the judgment of the court in that case seems to leave little to be argued or decided in this." Justice Story's opinion had protected vested rights in lands of the Episcopalian church in Virginia.

68 *WS*, X, 209–10.
69 *Ibid.,* 211–24. Other articles of the state constitution were also cited to support this contention.
   Thomas M. Cooley, *A Treatise on Constitutional Limitations* (Boston, 1874), 353–54, says that no definition of due process of law has been more often quoted than Webster's in this argument.
70 *Ibid.,* 225.

The decision, resting upon principles of natural justice, had not invoked the contract clause, but it had defined the legal nature of corporations in a way relevant to the Dartmouth College question. The franchises or property rights of *private* corporations, Story had declared, could be transferred only by judicial proceedings, and not by legislative action. Only *public* corporations, said Webster, were subject to legislative supervision "under proper limitations."[71]

Precedents had established the unquestionable rule, Webster argued, that the charter of a private corporation is a contract, unalterable by grantor unless grantees consent. Corporators can accept or reject all changes in the terms of the grant, because it is a contract. In short, such a charter always presumes agreement of both parties.[72] This point, buttressed by English authorities, was obviously essential to plaintiffs' claim of protection under the contract clause and would have far reaching effects upon American constitutional law.

Webster concluded with some reference to practical aspects of the controversy. He found no merit in the apology for what the legislature had done on the ground of necessity. No abuses demanding reform existed; and if they did exist, the consequences of political intervention in the College's affairs would be far more perilous than the abuses themselves. The outcome of Dartmouth's ordeal would affect "every college, and all the literary institutions of the country."

Benefactors will have no certainty of effecting the object of their bounty; and learned men will be deterred from devoting themselves to the service of such institutions, from the precarious title of their offices. Colleges and halls will be deserted by all better spirits, and become a theatre for the contentions of politics. Party and faction will be cherished in the places consecrated to piety and learning.[73]

The attorney added a flourish of Latin, pleading for maintenance of his clients' rights now dependent upon the wisdom of the Court.

After a pause Webster delivered his peroration. Unfortunately for students of history and oratory, there is no

<hr />

[71] *Ibid.*, 226–27. See 9 Cranch 43–55.
[72] *WS*, X, 227–29.
[73] *Ibid.*, 232.

extant record of this peroration in Webster's own words. According to surviving accounts, the lawyer made a very dramatic, emotional appeal to the justices' sympathies for the cause of higher education and, in particular, for the fate of this little school. One version of these remarks, though the exact language is unreliable, has been incorporated in Websterian literature as reflecting the substance and spirit of what he said. Supposedly Webster declared, "It is, sir, as I have said, a small college. And yet *there are those who love it*." Here he expressed his personal attachment to Dartmouth with such tender feeling that he deeply moved his listeners. Then, recovering himself, he reportedly concluded with his customary vibrancy: "Sir, I know not how others may feel, but, for myself, when I see my Alma Mater surrounded, like Caesar in the senate-house, by those who are reiterating stab upon stab, I would not, for this right hand, have her turn to me, and say, *Et tu quoque mi filii! And thou too, my son!*"[74]

A spectator in the Court, Professor Chauncey A. Goodrich of Yale, wrote these words from memory thirty-five years afterward. In 1852, after Webster's death, Goodrich supplied Rufus Choate with his recollection of the famous peroration. Choate made some revisions in the Professor's letter and incorporated it in his eulogy of Webster at Dartmouth College on July 27, 1853.[75] Although the Goodrich-Choate text is not literally accurate, it probably represents the tenor of what the lawyer said.[76] Another observer, Salma Hale, in his correspondence at that time reported that Webster finished with a comparison of Caesar in the Senate House and his alma mater. Then Wirt replied, Hale said, with an analogy between the expiring Roman and President Wheelock's ghost bewailing his former

[74] *Ibid.*, XV, 11–13.

[75] The manuscript from which Choate spoke is now deposited in the Boston Public Library. Pasted onto Choate's draft are sections of Goodrich's letter to him. For information concerning Choate's eulogy, see Samuel G. Brown (ed.), *The Works of Rufus Choate with a Memoir of His Life* (2 vols., Boston, 1862), I, 187–88, and Claude M. Fuess, *Rufus Choate: The Wizard of the Law* (New York, 1928), 208–09, 227–32.

[76] Such are the conclusions of John W. Black, "Webster's Peroration in the Dartmouth College Case," *Quarterly Journal of Speech*, XXIII (Dec., 1937), 636–42; of Carroll A. Wilson, "Familiar Small College Quotations," *Colophon*, III (New Series, Winter, 1938), 7–23; and of Richardson, *Dart. Coll.*, I, 337.

student's [Webster's] ingratitude.[77] Some years later, Justice Story also recalled Webster's conclusion:

And when he came to his peroration, there was in his whole air & manner, in the fiery flashings of his eye, the darkness of his contracted brow, the sudden & flying flushes of his cheeks, the quivering & scarcely manageable movements of his lips, in the deep guttural tones of his voice, in the struggle to suppress his own emotions, in the almost convulsive clenchings of his hands without a seeming consciousness of the act, there was in these things what gave to his oratory an almost superhuman influence. . . . The whole audience had been wrought up to the highest excitement; many were dissolved in tears; many betrayed the most agitating mental struggles; many were sinking under exhausting efforts to conceal their own emotions.[78]

However persuasive it may have been, Webster's argument was vulnerable. As a result of drawing so heavily upon the briefs of Mason and Smith, he discussed some questions outside the Court's jurisdiction. Neither the state constitution nor the common law was sufficient authority to invalidate the New Hampshire acts, yet Webster gave much more attention to them than to the contract clause. Technically, he should have recast his argument to avoid irrelevancy. He did have solid footing in the common law. Blackstone, the most respected authority of the day, clearly affirms the rights of a college founder as Webster expounded them. But the justices did not have to apply the rule.[79] The New Hampshire legislature did not necessarily face the same limits as the King of England; nor, for that matter, did the legislature have the same omnipotence as Parliament. Actually, the decisive question transcended the common law precedents. Had Dartmouth really operated through the years as a private institution? Webster's insistent yes, though quite

[77] Hale to William Allen, Mar. 12, 1818, Dart. Coll. Archives; Hale to William Plumer, Jr., Mar. 24, 1818, Plumer Papers (N. H. State Lib.).

[78] Story's description, probably written in 1830, is in the Webster Papers (Lib. Cong.), XII, 1809–15. It was undoubtedly used by George Ticknor in writing a review, "Speeches and Forensic Arguments of Daniel Webster," for the *American Quarterly Review,* IX (June, 1831), 420–57, as a comparison of Story's and Ticknor's accounts shows.

[79] English law made the distinction of civil and eleemosynary, but not public and private. There were a few American precedents, cited by Webster and particularly applicable to this case. One was *Trustees of the University of North Carolina* v. *Foy,* 5 North Car. Reports 58 (1805), restricting legislative power over an educational corporation. See Edwin M. Dodd, *American Business Corporations until 1860* (Cambridge, 1954), 13–27; Roscoe Pound, *The Spirit of the Common Law* (Boston, 1921), 148–49.

tenable, could be challenged. University counsel had to refute him on this ground to win their case.

John Holmes opened argument for Woodward on March 11 and, by all accounts, made a sorry showing. Education is a public concern, subject to legislative authority, Holmes contended. Dartmouth's charter was not a contract as contemplated by the Constitution; and even if it were, the New Hampshire acts did not impair its obligation. They neither inflicted an injury nor deprived any property, because they merely improved the College government, said the Maine Congressman.[80] Holmes seems to have been the only person satisfied with his performance,[81] for the University partisans painfully felt the contrast between his argument and Webster's. "Mr. Holmes," Salma Hale wrote, "was below our moderate expectations."[82] "Upon the whole," Webster observed, "he gave us three hours of the merest stuff that was ever uttered in a county court."[83] To his friend Smith, Webster remarked, "I had a malicious joy in seeing Bell [one of the New Hampshire judges] sit by to hear him, while everybody was grinning at the folly he uttered. Bell could not stand it. He seized his hat and went off."[84]

Although he had entered the case poorly prepared and had relied upon Salma Hale's prompting at the last moment,[85] Wirt recovered some of the ground lost by his colleague Holmes.[86] Oddly, he first discussed the constitutional clause prohibiting states from passing bills of attainder. Until now no one had mentioned this provision, which Wirt insisted New Hampshire had not violated. But the Attorney General directed his main batteries at the contention that the contract clause protected the Dartmouth trustees. These officers, he answered, did not have private rights so shielded; for the corporation was civil, one in which the people at large had an interest. "Charters to public corporations for purposes of public policy are necessarily subject to the legislative discretion, which may revoke or

80 4 Wheaton 600–06.
81 See Holmes to William Allen, Mar. 12, 1818, Dart. Coll. Archives.
82 Hale to William Plumer, Mar. 12, 1818, Plumer Papers (Lib. Cong.).
83 Webster to Mason, Mar. 13, 1818, WS, XVII, 275.
84 Webster to Smith, Mar. 14, 1818, ibid., 277.
85 Hale to William Plumer, Mar. 12, 1818, Plumer Papers (Lib. Cong.).
86 Wirt's argument is summarized in 4 Wheaton 606–15.

modify them as the continually fluctuating exigencies of the society may require."[87] Despite the merit of this point, Wirt lacked specific information about the early history of the College to support it. Indeed both parties to the suit were prone to speak in generalities—that *all* colleges were public corporations or that *all* colleges were private corporations—instead of emphasizing this *particular* college in New Hampshire.

A rumor later circulated that Wirt did not believe that the University's case was as strong as the College's and that he had said so to Webster, who then reported the conversation to his friends at Hanover. President Allen and Salma Hale were disturbed upon hearing the rumor and called upon Wirt for an explanation.[88] The lawyer quickly denied that he had ever said what was attributed to him. He gave permission for the publication of a letter declaring, "I was never engaged in a disputed cause in which I was more strongly convinced that my client ought to succeed, than in this."[89]

Webster felt compelled to repudiate an alleged remark on his part that Wirt's argument was so inferior it helped the College more than the University. Assuring Wirt that he had capably represented the defendant, Webster said, "In victory or in defeat, none but a fool could *boast* that he was warring, not with giants, but with pigmies."[90] No doubt he was sincere when, on several occasions, he praised Wirt's professional talents,[91] but he was less than honest in complimenting the Virginian on his handling of this case. Privately, Webster wrote to Mason:

He [Wirt] is a good deal of a lawyer, and has very quick perceptions, and handsome power of argument; but he seemed to treat this case as if his side could furnish nothing but declamation. He undertook to make out one legal point on which he rested his argument, namely, that Dr. Wheelock was not

[87] *Ibid.,* 609.

[88] Allen to Hale, Apr. 2, 1818, and Hale to Wirt, Apr. 10, 1818, Dart. Coll. Archives.

[89] Wirt to Hale, Apr. 11, 1818, copy in *ibid.* Wirt also said: "He [Webster] opened the case with great ability, and I remember to have said that I wished him all the success which his cause deserved, but not all that his argument merited, by which I meant to convey my impression that his argument was, in my opinion, much better than his cause."

[90] Webster to Wirt, Apr. 5, 1818, quoted in Everett P. Wheeler, *Daniel Webster: The Expounder of the Constitution* (New York, 1905), 33.

[91] See, for example, Webster to Brown, Mar. 13, 1818, *WS,* XVII, 274, and Webster to Smith, Mar. 14, 1818, *ibid.,* 277.

the founder. In this he was, I thought, completely unsuccessful. He abandoned his first point, recited some foolish opinions of Virginians on the third, but made his great effort to support the second, namely, that there was no contract. On this he had nothing new to say. The old story of the public nature of the use—a charter for the ultimate benefit of the people—in the nature of a public institution—like towns &c. He made an apology for himself, that he had not had time to study the case, and had hardly thought of it, till it was called on.[92]

Salma Hale was much more pleased with Wirt's argument than with Holmes's, yet he was keenly aware of the damaging blows delivered by Webster. "I have been occupied day and night during this week," he wearily observed, "in searching for facts and documents and am almost exhausted. Mr. Wirt could not find time to reflect on the case till Monday evening, and considering his want of preparation spoke with great ability."[93]

Webster's associate, Joseph Hopkinson, closed the *Dartmouth College* case by recapitulating the positions of the appellant and by replying to those of Holmes and Wirt. The reflective, graceful Philadelphian restated the common law rule on private rights of eleemosynary corporations. And because rights conferred by the charter were private, he asserted, there was an obligation of contract binding New Hampshire. The legislature had impaired its obligation when it deprived the College trustees of their visitorial rights, while the trustees had fulfilled their obligation in promoting the education of New England youths.[94]

The end of the term was near when Hopkinson concluded on March 12. Since some of the justices were undecided and the others divided upon this important constitutional question, the Court carried the case over to the following year. Both the College and the University were disappointed, but each hoped that in the coming months it could win over a majority of the bench. They would make determined efforts to do so.

92 Webster to Mason, Mar. 13, 1818, *ibid.*, 274–76. In the Dartmouth College Archives among the "Briefs of the Dartmouth College Case," are Webster's notes summarizing the arguments of opposing counsel. These indicate the casual attention he gave to Holmes and to Wirt on the first day the Attorney General spoke. When Wirt continued the next day after additional preparation, Webster doodled and scratched less and took fuller notes.

93 Hale to William Plumer, Mar. 12, 1818, Plumer Papers (Lib. Cong.).

94 4 Wheaton 615–24. See also MS. brief in Dart. Coll. Archives. Webster was very pleased with Hopkinson's performance. Webster to Brown, Mar. 13, 1818, *WS*, XVII, 274.

As news from the national capital arrived at Hanover, President William Allen and other officers of Dartmouth University were plainly displeased with the performances of Holmes and Wirt. Since the Court had continued the cause to the following term, perhaps the University might be able to reargue it then. So on August 26, 1818, Allen received permission from his trustees to employ new counsel for reargument. Soon he retained William Pinkney to serve with Wirt and to replace the ineffectual Holmes.[95]

Allen now dispatched letters informing Pinkney of the nature of the case. He included copies of the New Hampshire laws of 1816, of Chief Justice Richardson's opinion upholding them, and of Webster's argument at Washington. Besides these, Allen also supplied materials to disprove Webster's contentions that President Eleazar Wheelock and the English donors had founded Dartmouth as a private charity. If Pinkney could show that public beneficence in New Hampshire had established the College, reasoned Allen, then it was undoubtedly a public institution susceptible of public control. He had industriously searched the old papers of Eleazar Wheelock with this object in mind. Reporting these investigations to Pinkney, he concluded that the provincial governor, John Wentworth, had stipulated the terms of the charter, that the crown had contributed lands for the College site, and that Wheelock had given nothing to the corporation.

The keystone of Allen's position was a distinction between Dartmouth College and Moor's Charity School. Wheelock had conducted Moor's School, it will be recalled, for the instruction of Indians at Lebanon, Connecticut, prior to moving to New Hampshire in 1769. Its affairs were supposedly separate from those of the College where white youths were matriculated. Unlike Moor's School, which Wheelock had personally directed as the founder, Dartmouth College had been founded by the crown and was now subject to the state's power, Allen insisted. These were "new facts" which the University's counsel would present in reargument, if the Court were willing.[96]

[95] Vote of the Trustees of Dartmouth University, Aug. 26, 1818, Dart. Coll. Archives.

[96] Allen to Pinkney, Sept. 10, 1818, copy in *ibid.*, and Allen to Salma Hale, Oct. 15, 1818, *ibid.;* Allen to William Plumer, Oct. 15, 1818, Plumer Papers (Lib.

As usual, Pinkney was confident. Joseph Hopkinson talked with Pinkney during a passage through Baltimore in November, 1818. "I suppose he expects to do something very extraordinary in it," Hopkinson wrote, "as he says Mr. Wirt 'was not strong enough for it, has not back enough.' "[97] By early December the papers for Pinkney's use were on the way.[98] For further information, Pinkney conferred with Cyrus Perkins, secretary of the University after Woodward's recent death. Although Perkins was impatient with the Maryland attorney's delay, he said, "Mr. P[inkney] will come out in the majesty of his strength and professes to feel strong in the cause—hopes that Mr. W[ebster] will appear on the floor again, from which it is to be inferred that he feels ready & able to meet him on the question."[99]

The College party knew about these preparations by the University. As early as September 26 President Francis Brown understood Allen's purpose in examining the Wheelock papers. On that date Brown wrote a letter to Webster in which he summarized rather accurately the points he expected in reargument. He believed that Pinkney would also attempt to show that Dartmouth was similar to the universities in England, regarded as public institutions, and unlike the English colleges founded as private charities.[100] In his reply to Brown, Webster was unconcerned. It did not matter what the old correspondence contained, he remarked, because "the charter declares Dr. Wheelock to be the *founder* & I do not see how it can be denied that was such." He conceded that English universities and colleges were different kinds of corporations, the former being civil and the latter, eleemosynary. But the only resemblance between Dartmouth and an English university, in his opinion, was that both conferred degrees, a power some colleges possessed. Brushing off the University's "new facts" as not "formidable," he would rely upon the terms of the charter to explain the nature of the corporation. Thus, at common law, a college charter naming a

---

Cong.). The University side was shifting its emphasis from the *object* or *use* of the institution to the nature of its *founding* in order to meet Webster's argument.

[97] Hopkinson to Webster, Nov. 17, 1818, *WS,* XVII, 289.

[98] Salma Hale to William Allen, Dec. 4, 1818, Dart. Coll. Archives.

[99] Quoted in Richardson, *Dart. Coll.,* I, 341.

[100] Brown to Webster, Sept. 26, 1818, "Briefs in the Dartmouth College Case," Dart. Coll. Archives. See also Timothy Farrar to Webster, Jan. 2, 1819, *ibid.*

founder created an eleemosynary corporation, a private charity to be governed by the founder alone.[101]

Webster was reluctant to reopen the case. As a result, the College officers grew uneasy about the prospect of employing another attorney if the Court permitted Pinkney to speak. To pacify Webster, Brown said he would be satisfied if the lawyer merely replied to Pinkney without making another formal argument.[102] Though Webster opposed going over the whole ground, he agreed to answer the Marylander; however, he preferred a decision without additional argument.[103]

Notwithstanding his opposition to this movement for reargument, Webster himself disliked the shape the legal questions had taken. He had argued that the statutes violated the state constitution and the common law; but he realized that, according to the Federal judiciary act of 1789, these were not issues that could be appealed to the Supreme Court from the state tribunal. Strictly, the only question was whether New Hampshire had violated the national Constitution.

Even before argument at the capital, he and his associates adopted a plan to surmount this handicap. In letters to Mason, Smith, President Brown, and Trustee Charles Marsh, in December, 1817, Webster recommended new actions against the University in the Federal Circuit Court of New Hampshire. This would permit inquiry into all aspects of the controversy, he said. The Circuit Court could take jurisdiction because of diversity of state citizenship of the parties, arranged by sale or lease of College lands to citizens of Vermont. In this court the College could claim violations of the state constitution, the common law, and principles of natural justice.[104] Conveniently, this

---

[101] Webster to Brown, Sept. 28, 1818, *ibid.;* Webster to Brown, Nov. 9, 1818, *WS,* XVII, 288. Webster believed that Pinkney would argue that even though, by the common law, the King could not alter a corporate charter, Parliament in its omnipotence could do so. Thus the New Hampshire legislature succeeded to the powers of Parliament. Webster to Jeremiah Mason, Dec. 12, 1818, Webster Papers (New Hampshire Historical Society). This point had been advanced, but not emphasized, by the University counsel in the state court and in the Supreme Court.

[102] Brown to Webster, Sept. 26, 1818, "Briefs in the Dart. Coll. Case"; Charles Marsh to Brown, Nov. 4, 1818, Dart. Coll. Archives; Brown to Webster, Nov. 4, 1818, *ibid.*

[103] Hopkinson to Webster, Nov. 17, 1818, *WS,* XVII, 289.

[104] Webster to Brown, Dec. 8, 1817, Dart. Coll. Archives. This includes Webster's copy of a letter by him to Charles Marsh of the same date on the same subject.

was the circuit of Justice Joseph Story, who had encouraged such steps, reported Webster, by "sundry sayings."[105] These cases would probably go on up to the Supreme Court and, he thought, would involve broader grounds than the *Woodward* case.

By early January, 1818, Webster had convinced Brown that the strategy was desirable and should be set in motion without delay. Brown then directed the College secretary to inquire into a convenient method of initiating new suits.[106] Actually Mason devised the form of the cases through conveyances of land to Vermont citizens who then sued University officials, citizens of New Hampshire, for ejectment.[107] In March, when the Court continued the *Woodward* case to the next term, Webster was all the more anxious "to have an action in which all the questions arise."[108] A secondary reason was the precarious state of Woodward's health, for if he died before the 1819 term the College might have to abandon its original case.[109] So Marsh, one of the plaintiffs in the new "cognate cases," busily prepared for the May term of the Circuit Court. Webster passed on assurances that Story would expedite the cases so that the Supreme Court could hear them at the 1819 term.[110] "I have no doubt," the lawyer wrote, "he will incline to send up the new cause in the most convenient manner, without giving any opinion, and probably without an argument. If the district judge will agree to divide [in the judgment] without argument, *pro forma*, I think Judge Story will incline so to dispose of the cause."[111]

The cases[112] came before the Circuit Court of Ports-

See also Webster to Mason, Dec. 8, 1817, *WS*, XVI, 39. It will be recalled that Webster had actually advanced extensive arguments based upon the state constitution and upon the common law. Technically, however, these were not questions within the Supreme Court's jurisdiction in the *Woodward* case.

[105] Webster to Smith, Dec. 8, 1817, *ibid.*, XVII, 268.

[106] Brown to Mills Olcott, Jan. 10, 1818, Dart. Coll. Archives.

[107] Timothy Farrar to Brown, Feb. 7, 1818, *ibid.;* Webster to Brown, Feb. 14, 1818, *ibid.;* Charles Marsh to Brown, Feb. 27, 1818, *ibid.*

[108] Webster to Brown, Mar. 11, 1818, *WS*, XVI, 40; Webster to Mason, Mar. 22, 1818, *ibid.*, XVII, 278.

[109] Charles Marsh told President Allen that this was a reason, but he could not be expected to give a reliable explanation to his opponent in the litigation. Allen to William Plumer, Mar. 26, 1818, Plumer Papers (Lib. Cong.).

[110] Webster to Brown, Mar. 30 and Apr. 12, 1818, *WS*, XVII, 279, 280.

[111] Webster to Mason, Apr. 23, 1818, *ibid.*, 281.

[112] *Hatch* v. *Lang, Pierce ex dem. Lyman* v. *Gilbert*, and *Marsh* v. *Allen.* They are not reported in the *Federal Cases.* But see Shirley, *Dart. Coll. Causes*, 3

mouth in May, 1818, with the College pressing hard for their prompt disposition and with the University wishing delay or preferably abatement. The suits were said to arise from fictitious transactions, which Mason privately admitted, but the Court gave little weight to that objection.[113] Story granted continuance to the fall term, but, as Marsh observed,

the court made the most positive injunction on the defendants to plead in season and be prepared for trial early the next term, and it was suggested that an adjourned term would be holden for their trial if necessary in order that some one or more of them might be entered in the Supreme Court at next term. The Judge intimated that this was of great importance as the action now there [the *Woodward* case] did not perhaps present all the questions that would naturally arise out of the controversy and as it was time the controversy should be finished, the judge assured the parties that nothing should be wanting on the part of the court to place the actions in such train as would insure their final decision.[114]

Marsh was pleased with Story's sympathetic attitude, while the friends of the University naturally had other feelings.[115]

In October both sides consented to enter in the records of the cases special verdicts, drawn up as findings of the jury that the King had granted the charter of 1769 and that the state had passed the laws of 1816. In addition to copies of these items, the parties could agree to insert other papers in the records when they went up to the Supreme Court. Story and the district judge signed a *pro forma* certificate of division of opinion. The attorneys for the University proposed to add numerous documents, including copies of Eleazar Wheelock's will and New Hampshire statutes relating to the College. In December College counsel consented to this.[116]

When the College initiated the cognate cases in the Circuit Court, the University party was uncertain what course to adopt.[117] At the May term it asked for continuance, after it had

---

and *passim;* Lord, *Dart. Coll.,* 145–56; and William Allen to William Pinkney, Sept. 10, 1818, Dart. Coll. Archives.

[113] Richard Ela to William Plumer, Jr., May 5, 1818, Plumer Papers (N.H. State Lib.) ; Mason to Marsh, Sept. 11, 1818, Dart. Coll. Archives.

[114] Marsh to Brown, May 2, 1818, quoted in Lord, *Dart. Coll.,* 154.

[115] Marsh to Brown, May 18, 1818, Dart. Coll. Archives. See also Webster to Hopkinson, July 3, 1818, copy in "Personal Papers, Miscellaneous," Lib. Cong.

[116] Lord, *Dart. Coll.,* 159.

[117] Allen to Salma Hale, Apr. 2, 1818, Dart. Coll. Archives; Eastman to Allen, Apr. 7, 1818, *ibid.*

failed to abate the suits. At the October term, however, it decidedly changed its view of the cases. Now it saw in them an
opportunity to introduce the "new facts," which would prove
that Dartmouth, in contrast to Moor's Indian School, had always
been a public institution under governmental control. President
Allen sent his counsel such information as he had uncovered in
the Wheelock papers for incorporation into the records. He also
sent similar materials to Pinkney for use at Washington.[118]
Discontented with the earlier defense of the *Woodward* case,
the University attempted to get these "new facts" before the
Supreme Court either by way of reargument or through the
cognate cases. For its own ends the University now seized what
had originally been a College maneuver to broaden the cause.

Both sides felt confident about the *Woodward* case.

I have no accurate knowledge of the manner in which the judges are
divided [Webster observed]. The chief [Marshall] and Washington, I
have no doubt are with us. Duval and Todd perhaps against us; and the
other three holding up. I cannot much doubt but that Story will be with us
in the end, and I think we shall finally succeed.[119]

Salma Hale was no less hopeful that the University would prevail and, in fact, predicted success with only one or two justices
dissenting.[120] Governor Plumer had no doubts concerning victory,
but he and President Allen disliked delay because it hurt the
University financially.[121]

Notwithstanding their optimism, the opposing groups
conducted extensive campaigns to gain support of public opinion
and to convert the undecided judges. The University's strategy
was to circulate widely the opinion of Chief Justice Richardson
in the state court upholding the New Hampshire statutes. A
month before delivery of the opinion, Woodward suggested
such a course, which, in a sense, was simply a continuation of the
preceding political struggle involving Dartmouth.[122] By January, 1818, with Plumer's enthusiastic approval, the Richardson

118 Allen to William Plumer, Oct. 15, 1818, Plumer Papers (Lib. Cong.).
119 Webster to Smith, Mar. 14, 1818, *WS*, XVII, 276. See also Webster to
Brown, Mar. 13, 1818, *ibid.,* 274–75; Hopkinson to Brown, Mar. 13, 1818, Dart.
Coll. Archives; E. Porter to Brown, Apr. 14, 1818, *ibid.*
120 Hale to Allen, Apr. 2 and 8, 1818, *ibid.*
121 Plumer to Hale, Mar. 26, 1818, Plumer Papers (N.H. State Lib.); Allen
to Plumer, Mar. 26, 1818, Plumer Papers (Lib. Cong.).
122 Woodward to Plumer, Oct. 2, 1817, Plumer Papers (N.H. State Lib.).

opinion was published "to silence the clamors of the plaintiffs," who, it was said, misrepresented the true meaning of the decision.[123] Soon the principal goal was to place pamphlet copies in the hands of the Supreme Court justices and prominent lawyers at Washington before argument there in March.[124] Hale did this and found that the bar "applauded" the opinion.[125] What the justices thought he did not say.

The College understood the value of publicity as early as the University did, but it acted less promptly. For several months, while the state and Federal courts were considering the case, President Brown anxiously urged printing and distributing the arguments of the College lawyers. By doing so, declared Brown, the College might win its battle with the University to recruit students.[126] Webster was wary, because he wished to avoid the appearance of improper conduct while the case pended. On that ground, in December, 1817, he brusquely refused Isaac Hill's request to publish his argument in the Republican Concord *Patriot*.[127] Gradually the desirability of proselyting weakened Webster's avowal of decorum. By April, 1818, he had printed a few copies of his Supreme Court argument and showed them to persons in Boston. The lawyer insisted, however, that he was not "publishing the creature" and that "these copies are and will remain, except when loaned for a single day, under my own lock and key."[128] In time, numerous people read it—Chief Justice Isaac Parker of Massachusetts, Justice Story, President Brown, Benjamin Gilbert at Hanover, Jacob McGaw of Bangor, and many of the College students.[129] By autumn enough

[123] Plumer to Woodward, Oct. 11, 1817, Plumer Papers (Lib. Cong.) ; Woodward to Plumer, Nov. 20, 1817, *ibid.;* Plumer to William Plumer, Jr., Jan. 13, 1818, Plumer Papers (N.H. State Lib.) ; Plumer to Hale, Jan. 15, 1818, *ibid.*

[124] Plumer to Hale, Feb. 5, 1818, *ibid.* The Governor wrote, "Would it not be proper that the Council [Holmes and Wirt] should furnish each Judge a copy?"

[125] Hale to [Allen], Feb. 15, 1818, Dart. Coll. Archives; Hale to Plumer, Feb. 17, 1818, Plumer Papers (Lib. Cong.).

[126] See, for example, Brown to Timothy Farrar, Sept. 23, 1817, Farrar Papers (New Hampshire Historical Society). It will be noted that this letter was written more than a month prior to the state court's decision. Other correspondence in the Farrar Papers shows the same opinion expressed by College partisans.

[127] Hill to Webster, Dec. 16, 1817, Webster Papers (N.H. Hist. Soc.) ; Webster to Hill, Dec. 27, 1817, *ibid.*

[128] Webster to Mason, Apr. 23, 1818, *WS,* XVII, 280–81.

[129] Isaac Parker to Webster, Apr., 1818, quoted in Ephraim A. Otis, "The Dartmouth College Case," *American Law Review,* XXVII (July–Aug., 1893), 535;

copies were in circulation to make it meaningless to stop short of full publication, a step now taken in all righteousness.[130]

Obviously the target of the propaganda spread by both sides was the Court. Webster had correctly estimated the division of the judges: Marshall, Washington, and Story for the College; Todd and Duval for the University; and Johnson and Livingston undecided. The plaintiffs needed the vote of either Johnson or Livingston, whereas the defendant had to have the votes of both. Whatever would be done had to be delicately contrived. Indirect but promising was the method of acting through an intermediary, the eminent New York jurist, Chancellor James Kent. In the summer of 1818 the rivals ardently courted Kent in the hope that he would exert his influence upon Johnson and Livingston in their behalf.

Early in August the learned Chancellor and his wife took a vacation tour up the Connecticut Valley to enjoy the beautiful New England scenery and to refresh their spirits. Stopping at Windsor, Vermont, they were entertained by Josiah Dunham, a dedicated University partisan, who presented his point of view with some zeal. Then the Kents went on to Hanover where they strolled around the green and viewed the College buildings. In the evening President Allen and his professors called upon the Chancellor at his hotel, though, according to Kent's later account, they said nothing about the pending dispute.[131] Nonetheless, with some dexterity the University people placed in Kent's hands a copy of Chief Justice Richardson's opinion, which, strange as it may seem, he said he was "enabled to purchase after some search." After reading it the next day upon his return to Windsor, Kent recalled, "It appeared to me on a hasty perusal of it that the Legislature was competent to pass the laws in question, for I was led by the Opinion to assume the

Webster to Hopkinson, July 3, 1818, copy in "Personal Papers, Miscellaneous," Lib. Cong.; Webster to Brown, July 16, 1818, WS, XVII, 284–85; Webster to Jacob McGaw, July 27, 1818, Dart. Coll. Archives.

130 Brown to Webster, Sept. 19 and 26, 1818, "Briefs in Dart. Coll. Case," Dart. Coll. Archives; Webster to Brown, Sept. 28, 1818, ibid.; Webster to Brown, Nov. 9, 1818, WS, XVII, 288.

131 Kent's Journal, I, and Kent to William Johnson [of New York], Aug. 22, 1818, Kent Papers (Lib. Cong.); Shirley, Dart. Coll. Causes, 253; Lord, Dart. Coll., 152–53; Richardson, Dart. Coll., I, 339.

fact that Dartmouth College was a public establishment for purposes of a general Nature."[132]

The College officers were worried. When the Chancellor had visited Hanover, they had not had the opportunity to talk with him. They feared the weight of his influence if directed against them, and they fully appreciated its value if exercised for them. Consequently Trustee Charles Marsh sent Kent a letter, stating the College's positions in the case and enclosing copies of Webster's argument and of the 1769 charter. This had the intended effect, for Kent replied that

the fuller statement of facts in Mr W. argument, in respects to the origin & reasons & Substance of the charter of D C° & the Sources of the Gifts, *gives a new Complexion to the case,* & it is very probable that If I was now to set [*sic*] down & seriously study the case with *the facts at large before me,* that I should be led to a different conclusion from the one I had at first formed.[133]

To insure Kent's conversion, President Brown visited him at Albany in September and discussed the case at great length. Confidently, Brown told Webster that

There is no doubt, that by the Argument & the Charter he is brought completely over to our side; & he has a full impression of the importance of the question. I believe he will take every proper & prudent measure to impart correct views to others. While I remained in Albany, another copy of your Argument fell into his hands, which, he said, agreeably to the strong wish of Judge Johnson, he should transmit to him.[134]

Brown's confidence was well-founded. The wavering justices, Johnson and Livingston, would vote for the College, making certain a victory for the old trustees.[135] During this

---

[132] Kent to Charles Marsh, Aug. 26, 1818, Dart. Coll. Archives.

[133] *Ibid.*

[134] Brown to Webster, Sept. 15, 1818, Farrar Papers. As a member of the New York Council of Revision in 1804, Kent had objected on constitutional grounds to alterations in the charter of New York City. Brown was aware of this precedent. *Ibid.* See Charles Warren, *The Supreme Court in United States History* (3 vols., Boston, 1923), I, 476 n. 1 and Brown to Webster, Sept. 8, 1818, Farrar Papers. Shirley, *Dart. Coll. Causes,* believes that the New York precedent influenced Kent's views on the College question.

[135] Brown wrote to Webster, Sept. 19, 1818: "N[ew] E[ngland] & N.Y. are *gained.* Will not this be sufficient for our *present* purposes? . . . the current from this part of the country is setting so strongly toward the south, that we may

period, Johnson met with Kent at Albany, and they may have talked about the Dartmouth controversy. Johnson's hesitancy may have been merely a reluctance to apply the contract clause to the case rather than any uncertainty about the invalidity of the New Hampshire laws. In *Fletcher* v. *Peck* (1810) Johnson had preferred to invoke the principles of natural justice rather than the contract clause, and later he believed the *ex post facto* clause was a more appropriate vehicle for prohibiting retroactive legislation. At any rate, he now seemed willing to concur with the Chief Justice on the ground that the College was a private institution.[136] By what process of thought Livingston arrived at his conclusions is unknown. But it is possible that Kent, assisted by De Witt Clinton, influenced him also to concur.[137]

Several accounts say that Justice Story favored the University side prior to the Supreme Court argument of March, 1818, and that he was undecided for a time afterward. In support of such assertions, it is said that Story himself drafted the state statutes and that Governor Plumer appointed him a University overseer. No evidence that the Justice wrote the legislation exists. And though Plumer did indeed tender the appointment, Story declined it.[138] On the other hand, there are strong indications of Story's pro-College sentiments from beginning to end, the strongest being his handling of the cognate cases. Webster's correspondence in the months before his argument at Washington did not reflect any fear of Story's position, in fact just the opposite. Later, when the lawyer circulated copies of his brief, he gave Story five of them to send "to each of such of the judges as you think proper."[139] Story may have assisted in winning over the two hesitant justices.[140]

---

safely trust to its force alone to accomplish whatever is necessary." It is reasonable to believe that Brown was referring to Story of Massachusetts, Livingston of New York, and Johnson of South Carolina. "Briefs in Dart. Coll. Case," Dart. Coll. Archives.

[136] Donald G. Morgan, *Justice William Johnson: The First Dissenter. The Career and Constitutional Philosophy of a Jeffersonian Judge* (Columbia, So. Car., 1954), 214–15. See Johnson's opinions in *Fletcher* v. *Peck*, 6 Cranch 143–48, and in *Ogden* v. *Saunders*, 12 Wheaton 271–92.

[137] A copy of Webster's argument was placed in the hands of Clinton. Brown to Webster, Sept. 15, 1818, Farrar Papers.

[138] See Lord, *Dart. Coll.*, 143.

[139] Webster to Story, Sept. 9, 1818, *WS*, XVII, 287.

[140] Chief Justice Marshall's role must, of course, not be overlooked. His nationalism and economic conservatism drew him naturally to the College side.

When the Court opened its term on February 1, 1819, Pinkney was present, prepared to reargue *Dartmouth College* v. *Woodward* or to defend one of the cognate cases. "I suppose," Webster predicted, "[Pinkney] will move for a new argument in the case of Woodward. It is most probable perhaps, that he will succeed, in that object; altho I do not think it by any means certain."[141] Marshall was doubtless aware of Pinkney's intentions. But the next day, as the lawyer stood to make a petition, the Chief Justice immediately began reading his opinion and thereby avoided the discomfort of ruling on the motion.[142]

After reciting the facts of the record, Marshall took notice of both the magnitude and the delicacy of the question before him.[143] "However irksome the task may be," he declared, the Court had a "duty from which we dare not shrink."[144] His analysis of the provisions of the College charter led him to remark with some abruptness, "It can require no argument to prove, that the circumstances of this case constitute a contract."[145] Dogmatic as this statement may seem, Marshall amplified the point later in his opinion. There he conceded that the framers of the Constitution did not have in view such rights as the Dartmouth trustees claimed, but "it is necessary to go farther, and to say that, had this particular case been suggested, the language would have been varied, as to exclude it."[146] In the absence of such an exception, broad construction of the contract clause was justified.

Like Webster, the Chief Justice was more interested in the nature of this corporation, whether it was public or private, than in the hitherto unsettled question whether corporate grants generally were contracts within the meaning of the Constitution.

Beveridge, *Marshall,* IV, 221, 223. The personal leadership that Marshall gave to the Court was an element in the College's favor.

In December, 1817, a friend of the College, Benjamin J. Gilbert of Hanover, during a visit at Richmond, Virginia, had attempted unsuccessfully to talk with Marshall. He had, however, managed to get a copy of the College charter and other papers into the Chief Justice's hands. Lord, *Dart. Coll.,* I, 153.

[141] Webster to Timothy Farrar, Feb. 1, 1819, Webster Papers (N.H. Hist. Soc.).

[142] Beveridge, *Marshall,* IV, 260–61; Webster to Jeremiah Mason, Feb. 4, 1819, *WS,* XVI, 43.

[143] The entire opinion is in 4 Wheaton 624–54.

[144] *Ibid.,* 625.

[145] *Ibid.,* 627.

[146] *Ibid.,* 644.

On the basis of the charter, Marshall concluded that Eleazar Wheelock had founded the College and that private donors had financed it. "It is then an eleemosynary, and, as far as respects its funds, a private corporation," he ruled.[147] He gave great weight to the rights and privileges of the donors and of the trustees acting for them. In conferring these rights the crown had assumed an obligation which its successor, the state, could not subsequently impair. Admittedly, under the common law Parliament, as distinguished from the King, could exercise its omnipotence by annulling such property interests, shocking though that might be; but in the United States after 1789 the contract clause of the Constitution prohibited states from impairing the obligation of contracts.[148]

Of course Marshall could correctly say that a state legislature did not possess powers equal to Parliament's, yet he declined to take the next logical step of wholly rejecting the common law rule on corporations. He closely followed precedents safeguarding donors' interests and founders' privileges instead of the rights of those benefiting from educational trusts. Although in New Hampshire the public was the beneficiary, it was not entitled to regulate the college. Marshall and Webster looked at the *origins* of charitable corporations in evaluating their objects. The principal object, then, was to protect the property of the trust, which would in turn assure the performance of the trustees' functions.

From this point the Chief Justice had a straight path to his decision. Did the New Hampshire acts impair the obligation of a contract and thereby violate the Constitution? They did, he concluded. The state had plainly misused its powers by entirely changing the character of the College charter, contrary to the will of the original donors and of their successors, the trustees. He reversed the state court's judgment.[149]

Washington and Story filed concurring opinions, considering the same questions that Marshall had posed: (1) was the College charter a contract within the meaning of the Con-

147 *Ibid.,* 633–34.
148 *Ibid.,* 643, 651–52.
149 *Ibid.,* 650–64.

stitution; and (2) if so, did the state statutes impair the obligation of that contract? In a short opinion, Washington cited precedents to prove that colleges were private corporations, were governable only by their private patrons, and were protected by the contract clause.[150] The erudite Story probed deeply into the common law in "an inquiry into the nature, rights, and duties of aggregate corporations." Referring to numerous authorities, particularly Blackstone's *Commentaries* and Lord Holt in *Phillips v. Bury,* he concluded that there were two classes of corporations, public and private. A college was invariably a private, charitable entity because private persons founded the corporation, though it did have public purposes. Dartmouth College, then, was such an institution, whose donors and trustees had property rights immune from the state's interference. Such rights, said Story, established a contractual obligation that a state must not impair. Taken as a whole, Story's opinion canvassed the broad legal questions that interested Webster and could have applied to the cognate cases initiated by the old trustees.[151]

On the day of the Court's decision, Webster dispatched several letters to his friends in New Hampshire, announcing the College's victory and pointing out that only one justice, Duval, dissented and another, Todd, was absent. Marshall's opinion, he wrote to his brother Ezekiel, "was very able and very elaborate; it goes the whole length, and leaves not an inch of ground for the University to stand on." In a note to President Brown, he said he felt "a load removed from [his] shoulders much heavier than they have been accustomed to bear."[152] But he urged the College people to celebrate their glorious triumph with a "sense of moderation, liberality, & magnanimity," so as not to alienate

150 *Ibid.*, 654–66.

151 *Ibid.*, 666–713. Story cited with approval a Massachusetts case holding that a state could not alter a corporate charter "unless *a power for that purpose be reserved to the legislature in the act of incorporation.*" *Ibid.*, 708. After the Dartmouth College decision many states inserted such reserve clauses in new charters. Usually the power to revoke was asserted only where cause could be shown. Dodd, *Am. Bus. Corporations,* 141–42.

152 Webster to Ezekiel Webster and Webster to Brown, Feb. 2, 1819, *WS,* XVII, 300.

the popular good will that the school then enjoyed.[153] This was sound advice for the financially debilitated College if it was to recover from the damage the controversy had inflicted.

Disappointment and anger pervaded the University ranks.[154] That side believed that the decision was not only bad constitutional law but was politically dangerous to the rights of the states. Governor Plumer repeated the familiar warning that the Supreme Court was consolidating national power at the expense of the states.[155] Expressed in this fashion, criticism of the judges might have elicited widespread support in various quarters. Even the nationalistic John Quincy Adams reportedly disapproved Marshall's disposition of the case. But at the moment other matters occupied the attention of the defenders of states' rights.[156]

A more substantial ground for complaint was the haste with which the Court had proceeded in the 1819 term despite its knowledge that Pinkney wished to make a second argument. Cyrus Perkins, Salma Hale, and Plumer were annoyed that the Court had not considered the "new facts" relative to the crown's role in founding the College through extensive donations.[157] The counsel and officers of the University now explored means to reopen the cause. "I am, notwithstanding what has occurred at Washington, still of the opinion that the laws of N.H. of 1816 are strictly and literally constitutional [wrote the Governor]; & I am inclined to think a Court will ultimately be obliged so to decide."[158]

If Pinkney was to succeed in getting a re-examination of the legal questions, he had to do it now by way of the cognate cases. In late February, however, Marshall remanded these

[153] Webster to Timothy Farrar, Feb. 9, 1819, Webster Papers (N.H. Hist. Soc.).

[154] Clement Storer to William Plumer, Feb. 2, 1819, Plumer Papers (Lib. Cong.); Cyrus Perkins to William Allen, Feb. 2, 1819, Dart. Coll. Archives; Lord, *Dart. Coll.*, 161.

[155] Plumer to Salma Hale, Feb. 13 and April 8, 1819, Plumer Papers (Lib. Cong.).

[156] Hale to Plumer, Feb. 26, 1819, *ibid.* The Congressional debates concerning the admission of the state of Missouri were underway. A sharp controversy over the status of the national bank was also in progress.

[157] Plumer to Clement Storer, Feb. 15, 1819, Plumer Papers (Lib. Cong.); Hale to Plumer, Mar. 29, 1819, *ibid.*; Perkins to William Allen, Feb. 2, 1819, Dart. Coll. Archives.

[158] Plumer to Allen, Mar. 17, 1819, Plumer Papers (Lib. Cong.).

cases to Story's Circuit Court, owing to Webster's refusal to admit the additional facts to the records.[159] The liberality that the College attorneys had formerly shown on this point in New Hampshire now vanished at the capital. Webster's letter of this period often referred to the cognate cases and bubbled with optimism.[160] He doubted that Pinkney was serious in his professed wish to go further. "Pinkney sent back this cause to get rid of it," Webster said. "He talked, however, and blustered, because among other reasons the party was in a fever and he must do something for his fees. As he could not talk in court, he therefore talked *out* of court. I believe his course is understood."[161]

The College continued to oppose the introduction of new facts in the Circuit Court and to insist upon swiftly concluding the cases. In any event, it felt assured that Story would remain favorable. Webster wrote to Mason, who would again represent the College:

As to the College Cause, you may depend on it that there will be difficulty in getting delay in that case, without reason. I flatter myself that the judge will tell the defendants that the new facts which they talk of, were presented to the minds of the judges at Washington, and that, if all proved, they would not have the least effect on the opinion of any judge; that unless it can be proved that the king did not grant such a charter as the special verdict recites, or that the New Hampshire General Court did not pass acts as are therein contained, no material alteration of the case can be made.[162]

At Portsmouth, May 1, 1819, Story delivered the opinion of the Circuit Court, disposing of the cases in conformity with the *Woodward* decision. The University lawyers did not then have the "new facts" ready for submission, since the papers had not arrived from Washington. The judge granted them more time and withheld judgment in the opinion he had read.[163] On

---

[159] Webster to Jeremiah Mason, Feb. 24, 1819, *WS*, XVI, 44; Webster to Jeremiah Smith, Feb. 28, 1819, *ibid.*, 44–45.

[160] Webster to Brown, Feb. 23, 1819, *ibid.*, XVII, 301–02; Webster to Mason, Feb. 24, 1819, *ibid.*, XVI, 44; Webster to Brown, Feb. 25 and Apr. 14, 1819, *ibid.*, XVII, 303, 304.

[161] Webster to Mason, Apr. 13, 1819, *ibid.*, XVI, 49.

[162] *Ibid.*

[163] Lord, *Dart. Coll.*, 166; Webster to Hopkinson, May 9, 1819, copy in "Personal Papers, Miscellaneous," Lib. Cong.

May 27 the papers were before Story, who thereupon ruled that they did not contradict provisions of the corporate charter (thus that the institution was founded as a private charity) and ordered execution of judgment for the College.[164]

The University had already ceased operations. When news of the Supreme Court decision in the *Woodward* case reached Hanover in February, joyous College partisans seized possession of the school buildings, from which they had been evicted two years earlier. President Allen reluctantly turned over the keys and halted instruction of the handful of University students. In its brief lifetime Dartmouth University had been a skeleton organization created by state law but supported neither by local public opinion nor by legislative appropriations. Heavily indebted and deserted by many of its former friends, it expired with few mourners at its side. Governor Plumer, who almost alone had envisioned it as a truly liberal, non-sectarian institution of learning, was disillusioned by the adverse turn of events. John Wheelock and William H. Woodward were dead, and the University itself was an unhappy memory among the defeated party.[165]

Even before the *Woodward* decision, the College side planned publication of a book reporting the case in the state and Federal courts. General direction of the enterprise fell to Webster, though the book appeared under the editorship of Timothy Farrar, Jr., his former law partner of Portsmouth.[166] Securing copies of the justices' opinions and arranging to pay the official reporter for the right to publish them, Webster ap-

---

[164] Webster to Mason, May 27, 1819, *WS*, XVI, 53; Webster to Brown, May 30, 1819, *ibid.*, XVII, 306–07; Webster to Phillip Carrigan, May 30, 1819, Webster Papers (N.H. Hist. Soc.); Shirley, *Dart. Coll. Causes*, 204–05.

[165] For descriptions of the operations and the closing of the University see Richardson, *Dart. Coll.*, I, 352–71, and Lord, *Dart. Coll.*, 120–27, 131–37, 164, 167–74, 682–86. Much valuable material can be found in the Dartmouth College Archives and in the Plumer Papers at the Library of Congress and the New Hampshire State Library.

Plumer was already disappointed with the shape of the University. "She appears to be following the old tradition," he wrote, "and seems more anxious to please the priesthood than to pursue a manly and expedient course to fit men for the business and duties of this world." Plumer to Salma Hale, Dec. 28, 1818, Plumer Papers (Lib. Cong.).

[166] See Farrar to Webster, Jan. 18, 1819, Farrar Papers.

plied himself to the project with lively interest during the spring of 1819.[167] Not only did he write out a version of his own argument, but he also drafted Hopkinson's from notes sent to him.[168] There was difficulty in obtaining a brief from Wirt, since the Attorney General was reluctant to revive his hastily prepared argument in print. Furthermore, until the termination of the cognate cases in May, Wirt refused to cooperate with Webster's venture because it might prejudice the University's chances for victory.[169] The volume also included the arguments and opinion at the state court and appendices containing pro-College documents.[170] In collecting all these materials, Webster assumed primary responsibility, while Farrar managed relations with the printer.

Farrar encountered trouble in getting printed copy as soon as promised, and by June Webster was quite dissatisfied with the slow rate of progress. The lawyer scolded Farrar for the delay and regretted that he had ever undertaken the venture. Henry Wheaton awaited copy to use in his official reports, a situation that embarrassed Webster.[171] Worst of all was the dubious accuracy of the sheets as they came from the press. To prevent serious errors, he sent proofs of the Supreme Court opinions to Story, who had agreed to examine them.[172]

167 Webster to Farrar, Feb. 4, Mar. 12, Mar. 22 and Apr. 3, 1819, Webster Papers (N.H. Hist. Soc.). During this period of the Court's history the Reporter did not have a verbatim record of counsel's arguments.

168 Webster to Hopkinson, Mar. 22, 1819, *WS*, XVI, 47; Hopkinson to Webster, Apr. 19, 1819, *ibid.*, XVII, 305; Webster to Hopkinson, May 9, 1819, copy in "Personal Papers, Miscellaneous," Lib. Cong.; Hopkinson to Webster, May 21, 1819, "Briefs in Dart. Coll. Case," Dart. Coll. Archives. In the College Archives are manuscript notes, briefs, and opinions used in the preparation of the book.

169 Wirt to Webster, Apr. 28, 1819, Webster Papers (Lib. Cong.).

170 Webster referred to the printed versions of Mason's and Smith's arguments "bunglingly put together by me." Webster to Smith, May 12, 1819, *WS*, XVII, 306.

"As to Ichabod's [Bartlett's] argument," he declared, "I am decidedly of the opinion, that I would *not* publish any abuse of the Trustees, or of the Counsel. If he has not decency enough to leave such slang out, I would not publish his argument. . . . 50 or 60 pages!—Good Heavens!—and all slang!—do get it abridged." Webster to Farrar, May 18, 1819, Webster Papers (N.H. Hist. Soc.).

171 Webster to Farrar, June 19, 1819, *ibid.;* Webster to Mason, June 28, 1819, *WS*, XVII, 307.

172 Webster to Farrar, June 23, 1819, Webster Papers (N. H. Hist. Soc.); Webster to Story, Mar., 1819, *WS*, XVI, 46; Story to Farrar, July 3, 1819, Farrar Papers.

Finally, in August, "the creature," as the exasperated Webster called it, was published.[173] Up to the present day it has been the standard report of the *Dartmouth College* case. Both the Federal and the state court reporters reprinted the relevant portions of Farrar's edition so that they, as well as later students of history and law, benefited from the work of Webster and Farrar. Of course, the object in bringing out the book was not wholly altruistic, for Brown, Webster, and their friends recognized the urgency of inspiring as much favorable sentiment as possible. For the College to heal the deep wounds inflicted by the lengthy controversy, this was indispensable; and Farrar's *Report of the Case of the Trustees of Dartmouth College against William H. Woodward* was intended to accomplish such a propagandizing purpose.

The *Dartmouth College* case became a landmark in constitutional history, establishing the principle of vested rights of corporations. Not only educational but all types of corporations could now claim the protection of the contract clause against state legislation. In an era of economic expansion such as the early nineteenth century, a legal doctrine of this kind was useful and generally acceptable in spite of criticism then and later.[174] The Court may have extended the scope of this constitutional provision beyond its originally intended meaning; yet some other device, the *ex post facto* clause or perhaps natural justice, might well have served to arrive at the same end. Furthermore, where state action seemed desirable, means were found to justify it, the College precedent notwithstanding.[175] The most tenable

---

[173] Webster to Mason, no date, *WS*, XVII, 311. The bibliographical citation is Timothy Farrar, *Report of the Case of the Trustees of Dartmouth College against William H. Woodward. Argued and Determined in the Superior Court of Judicature of the State of New Hampshire, November 1817. And on Error in the Supreme Court of the United States, February 1819.* Portsmouth, N. H.: J. W. Foster, 1819. 406 pp. A highly favorable review, unsigned but probably written by Warren Dutton, appeared in the *North American Review*, X (1820), 83–115. Chancellor Kent refused to review the book because he expected "the doctrine involved in that case will shortly be brought before our Court of Errors. . . ." Kent to Story, Aug. 3, 1819, *Proceedings of the Massachusetts Historical Society*, Second Series, XIV (1901), 413.

[174] Benjamin F. Wright, Jr., *The Contract Clause of the Constitution* (Cambridge, Mass., 1938), 243–59; James Willard Hurst, *Law and the Conditions of Freedom in the Nineteenth-Century United States* (Madison, Wisc., 1956), 11–18, 22–29, and *passim*.

[175] The state's police power and reserve clauses inserted in subsequent charters were two such means. See Association of American Law Schools (ed.),

grounds of criticizing Marshall's decision are not usually assumed. These are his refusal to hear further arguments by counsel concerning the early history of *this* corporation and his sweeping application of a common law rule to an incomplete statement of facts. Had Pinkney been permitted to make another argument, however, the College lawyers could still have convincingly shown that Dartmouth had operated through the years as a private college.[176]

Webster's role has frequently been the subject of commentary, but too often it has been a matter of worshiping or abusing him. An accurate evaluation must avoid both. In his favor, obviously, one can mention his eloquent delivery of the argument, even though he drew the substance from the research of others. Whatever the desirability of incorporating the common law rule on charitable corporations, Webster did make a sound statement of it. On the whole, he was correct from the standpoint of strict law in emphasizing the origins of the institution in order to prove its private nature. In the realm of constitutional law, of course, he was on new, uncertain ground. *Fletcher* v. *Peck* (1810), holding that a state could be a party to a contract within the meaning of the Constitution, was a compelling precedent for the College decision. But since a corporate charter by a state had not previously been construed as a contractual obligation, the lawyer wished to broaden the questions before the Supreme Court as much as possible. To do this, he transcended the jurisdictional limits of that tribunal when he relied upon the state constitution and natural justice. And in pressing the cognate cases prior to the *Woodward* decision, he and Justice Story entered a relationship most unusual for a judge and an attorney.

"Power of the State to Alter Corporate Charters," *Selected Essays on Constitutional Law,* II, 352–59; Robert L. Hale, "The Supreme Court and the Contract Clause," *Harvard Law Review,* LVII (1944), 638–63; Dodd, *Am. Bus. Corporations,* 29–31, 141–42.

Throughout this period lawyers and judges attached much importance to natural law as a limitation upon legislative power. Dodd, 149–50.

176 The Court would nevertheless have had before it other facts in addition to the provisions of the charter of 1769 and the statutes of 1816. By taking greater notice of the factual background, Marshall might have devised a judicial standard which would have been a more satisfactory guide in handling future contract cases. Maurice G. Baxter, "Should the Dartmouth College Case Have Been Reargued?" *New England Quarterly,* XXXIII (March, 1960), 19–36.

How did the case affect Dartmouth College? Manifestly it saved this institution from being extensively remodeled by the legislature. Instead of becoming a state university, Dartmouth remained a small private New England college with a proud tradition and a distinctive flavor. Indeed later generations of loyal Dartmouth men have felt their alma mater miraculously escaped destruction.[177] But the immediate result of the controversy was a disastrous deterioration of the College's financial condition. While the litigation progressed, tenants on the College lands stopped paying rent, thereby cutting off a principal source of income at the very period when expenses were abnormally heavy. President Brown desperately solicited gifts and begged loans in order to resuscitate the school's treasury.[178] The case did not, however, fix upon the College an entirely inflexible form of government, because in practice the trustees themselves voluntarily altered the charter to adjust to changing circumstances. For example, in 1891, the alumni gained the privilege of electing five trustees, thus making the board a different kind of body than the self-perpetuating one of an earlier day. At numerous times College authorities willingly cooperated with the state of New Hampshire, as in fact they had before 1816.[179] Finally, the case established Dartmouth as a symbol of academic freedom from capricious political meddling, a symbol that would mean much to many other educational institutions in the future.[180]

The effects upon Webster were also considerable. For his professional standing the case had great significance. He became one of the leaders of the bar and launched a long, successful career unsurpassed to this day. The lawyer also received a thou-

[177] See Richardson, *Dart. Coll.,* I, 345–46.

[178] *Ibid.,* 347–49, 360–63, 367–70; Brown to Webster, Sept. 19, 1818, "Briefs in Dart. Coll. Case," Dart. Coll. Archives. Stricken by tuberculosis, oppressed by the burdens of his office, Brown died the year after the Supreme Court decision.

[179] Richardson, *Dart. Coll.,* II, 578–82, 650–60; William J. Tucker, *My Generation: An Autobiographical Interpretation* (Boston, 1919), 249–413.

[180] Richard Hofstadter and Walter P. Metzger, *The Development of Academic Freedom in the United States* (New York, 1955), 219–20. A contrary view has been taken by many authors with some justification. But often these critics have been principally dissatisfied with the subsequent broad application of the doctrine of the case to all classes of corporate charters.

It is interesting to notice that William Allen, following the demise of Dartmouth University, served as president of Bowdoin College. Here he was deprived of his position by legislative action and then regained it by a suit on the grounds of the Dartmouth College decision. Richardson, *Dart. Coll.,* I, 345.

sand-dollar fee for his legal services—far more than any other attorney on either side. Though he was eager to aid the College in its hour of peril, he was likewise interested in the compensation he would receive.[181] After the decision the trustees voted a resolution of thanks to the College counsel, Mason, Smith, Hopkinson, and Webster. At the commencement in August, 1819, the Phi Beta Kappa dinner honored Webster. And the trustees further expressed their gratitude by commissioning portraits of the four, completed some years later.[182] Writing to President Brown about the outcome of the battle, Hopkinson said, "I would have an inscription over the door of your building, 'Founded by Eleazar Wheelock, Refounded by Daniel Webster.' "[183] The College later followed this suggestion by placing such an inscription on a bronze tablet at the entrance to Webster Hall. The veneration with which Dartmouth has remembered Webster's contributions appeared in President William J. Tucker's remarks at the Webster Centennial in 1901: "The relation of Mr. Webster to his College, his living and his posthumous relation, is unique. It is doubtful if the name of any educational institution in the land is so inseparably blended with the name of a graduate, or even of a founder, as is the name of Dartmouth with that of Daniel Webster."[184]

---

181 *Ibid.*, 363–64. Hopkinson received five hundred dollars; Smith, $180; Mason, one hundred dollars; Sullivan and Bartlett, one hundred dollars each; Wirt, three hundred dollars; Pinkney, $350. Webster also received fifty dollars for his argument in the state court.

Webster and Brown exchanged candid letters on the subject of legal fees. See, for example, Webster to Brown, Nov. 9, 1818, *WS*, XVII, 287–88.

182 Claude M. Fuess, *Daniel Webster* (2 vols., Boston, 1930), I, 243–44; Richardson, *Dart. Coll.*, 367.

183 Hopkinson to Brown, Feb. 2, 1819, *WS*, XVII, 301. On the centennial of Webster's death, in October, 1952, the trustees of Dartmouth College placed a plaque at his grave in the Winslow Burying Ground (near the site of the lawyer's home at Marshfield). The marker commemorates his service in safeguarding the constitutional liberties of the College and other institutions like it.

184 Tucker, *My Generation*, 290. The occasion was the hundredth anniversary of Webster's graduation from Dartmouth.

V

THE CONTRACT CLAUSE

The decision in *Dartmouth College* v. *Woodward* suggested broad possibilities of protection by the contract clause for American corporations and for all who could claim vested rights. In the next thirty years the Court probed many of these possibilities as it worked its way from case to case. In a large sense, the recurrent problem was to identify the boundaries of a forbidden area laid out by the contract clause into which states could not trespass. Webster played a leading role in this important chapter of constitutional history.

One class of contract cases during the latter half of the Marshall era involved state power to pass bankruptcy legislation. Of the two leading cases, *Sturges* v. *Crowninshield* (1819) and *Ogden* v. *Saunders* (1827), Webster participated in the second but not the first. Specifically, the questions were whether and to what extent states could relieve insolvent debtors in the absence of a national statute. But generally the question was whether the contract clause limited state economic regulations with either retrospective or prospective effects, or both. It is apparent that the point was quite controversial when one notices that on this subject the Chief Justice, for the only time in his judicial career, was in the minority concerning a constitutional issue.

In *Sturges* v. *Crowninshield* the plaintiff challenged a New York insolvency act on the grounds that Congressional power to pass uniform bankruptcy laws was exclusive and that the state statute impaired the obligation of contracts.[1] In an opinion for the unanimous Court, Marshall made a surprising concession to states' rights by holding that the Congressional bankruptcy power was not exclusive and that therefore the states could act where Congress had not. After examining the *nature* of the power, he concluded that "it is not the mere existence of the power, but its exercise, which is incompatible with the exercise of the same power by the States."[2] At that moment, and indeed throughout most of the nineteenth century, there was no national bankruptcy statute.[3] So the New York measure survived this test. Marshall probably recognized that unfortunate debtors needed some protection against oppressive penalties, such as imprisonment for debt. Congress seemed unwilling or unable to afford that protection, but there was a vast body of state legislation.[4] Yet when he considered the applicability of the contract clause, he quickly reclaimed much that he had just conceded. The obligation of a contract was the debtor's liability to perform his agreement, he said; and any state law which discharged all future liability, as this one did, impaired the obligation, thus violating the contract clause. States could legislate concerning the remedy available to the creditor against a debtor, but they could not remove the debtor's obligation altogether.

Aside from the dubious justification for extending the

[1] 4 Wheaton 122–208. In the following discussion the words "bankruptcy" and "insolvency" will be used interchangeably. At this time there was much confusion about the legal definitions of the words. It was often said that bankruptcy statutes applied only to traders and merchants and discharged them from all future liability, while insolvency statutes applied to everyone but only discharged the person of the debtor from imprisonment. Many state laws, however, had characteristics both of bankruptcy and insolvency. The Constitution, Article I, section 8, paragraph 4, empowers Congress to establish uniform laws on the subject of bankruptcies but says nothing about insolvency. Chief Justice Marshall saw that the line of distinction between the two was becoming increasingly blurred and therefore refused to decide whether they were the one or the other.

[2] *Ibid.*, 196.

[3] There had been a national bankruptcy law passed in 1800 but repealed in 1803.

[4] See citations in Kurt H. Nadelman, "On the Origin of the Bankruptcy Clause," *The American Journal of Legal History*, I (July, 1957), 215–28.

contract clause to the field of bankruptcy,[5] the clarity of the *Sturges* opinion is open to criticism. In this case New York had passed the law after the contract had been made; consequently, as a precedent, the decision only forbade retrospective statutes. But throughout his opinion the Chief Justice made no distinction between retrospective and prospective acts, and it seemed wholly possible that he did not wish to distinguish between them. Despite his statement that "this opinion is confined to the case actually under consideration,"[6] Marshall left the matter in doubt. Perhaps acts applying to future contracts might also be unconstitutional.

This possibility seemed all the more likely when at the same term (1819) the Court decided *McMillan* v. *McNeill*.[7] A short, misleading opinion held that a Louisiana bankruptcy law did not protect a debtor who had made a contract in South Carolina. Later comment on the case shows that the Court simply refused to approve the extraterritorial effect of the statute; however, confusion resulted since the state had passed the law *before* the date of the contract. A credible interpretation of the decision was that the statute could not affect *future* contracts even in the state of Louisiana. The Court invited such an interpretation by the statement that "the circumstances of the State law, under which the debt was attemped to be discharged, having been passed before the debt was contracted, made no difference in the application of the principle" of *Sturges* v. *Crowninshield*.[8] If the principle of *Sturges* was that only retrospective legislation was unconstitutional, then the Court could not have been invoking it in *McMillan* v. *McNeill*, though it said it was doing so.

The uncertainty created by these cases lasted until the decision in *Ogden* v. *Saunders* (1827).[9] The parties made a contract after the passage of a state insolvency law. George Ogden, the original defendant, relied upon a New York act of 1801 in refusing to pay bills of exchange drawn in 1806. Now

---

[5] Benjamin F. Wright, Jr., *The Contract Clause of the Constitution* (Cambridge, 1938), 48, disapproves the application of the contract clause to state bankruptcy laws.

[6] Wheaton 207.

[7] *Ibid.*, 209.

[8] *Ibid.*, 212–13.

[9] 12 Wheaton 213.

as plaintiff in error, he was represented by an impressive array of legal talent in his appeal to the Supreme Court at two terms, 1824 and 1827. Seven lawyers altogether, at one term or the other, argued for the validity of the statute: David B. Ogden (the only attorney appearing for that side at both terms), Attorney General William Wirt, Henry Clay, Charles G. Haines, Edward Livingston, Walter Jones, and William Sampson. Attacking the law for the defendant in error, Saunders, were Henry Wheaton and Webster. Here was the explicit question of state power to enact bankruptcy legislation affecting future contracts.

Counsel for Ogden contended that the bankruptcy power was not exclusively national but shared by the states and Congress. On this point they could comfortably depend upon the *Sturges* precedent and merely repeat a few arguments which that opinion had accepted. The more difficult aspect of the case related to the contract clause, and on this they concentrated their attention. The obligation of a contract, they said, derives from "the law of the place," that is to say positive legislation of the states. Any agreement is binding only insofar as such laws enforce it. Thus persons entering a contract are aware of this fact and give their implied assent to the operation of bankruptcy acts. Indeed these acts become part of the contract from the beginning and cannot possibly impair its obligation. Admitting with some reluctance that the contract clause prohibited retrospective laws, Webster's opponents insisted that laws, like this one, governing future contracts were clearly valid. Besides, the very placement of the contract clause in the tenth section of Article I of the Constitution proved that the framers were thinking of retrospective, not prospective legislation. It was part of a series of prohibitions upon the states, including the passage of bills of attainder and *ex post facto* laws, both by their nature retrospective.[10]

Webster and Wheaton presented their case with vigor and, as the future would reveal, with unwarranted confidence.[11] They contended that the national bankruptcy power was exclusive, thereby asking the Court to reconsider its concurrent-power

[10] *Ibid.*, 226–37.
[11] Story's description of Webster's argument in the Webster Papers (Library of Congress), XII, 18015; Wheaton to Webster, Nov. 30, 1823, *ibid.*, I.

holding in *Sturges* v. *Crowninshield*. Aware of Justice Washington's preference for exclusive national authority, they might have been addressing this argument to him primarily.[12] Like their opponents, however, the two lawyers chiefly concerned themselves with the contract clause. The heart of their disagreement with advocates of state power was their definition of the obligation of contracts. To the question what creates an obligation, they answered that it is universal, natural, or moral law and not positive or statutory law. A party to a contract, said Webster, would still be obligated to perform an agreement if he moved to a desert isle over which "no law of society extends."[13] Positive legislation can only provide remedies available to the creditor and protective to the debtor, but it must never impair the obligation by discharging all liability to pay a debt.[14] Furthermore, a statute has nothing to do with a contract until it is broken. Since the making of a contract perforce precedes the application of the statute to that contract, all such statutes operate retrospectively. They cannot go further than to alter the remedy for the non-fulfillment of an obligation previously assumed. The contract clause consequently protects rights originating from natural law. Indeed, if any law is read into a contract, Webster insisted, it is this constitutional clause, of which both parties are aware.

What Webster sought was the broadest possible coverage by the contract clause. Although he looked upon all bankruptcy legislation, by its nature, as operating retrospectively, he declared that the contract clause would still control prospective legislation as well. The tenth section of Article I in the Constitution, he said, did not confine other prohibitions upon state power to retrospective statutes—for example, coinage of money, emitting bills of credit, and making anything but gold and silver coin

[12] On circuit in 1814, Justice Washington had ruled that the national bankruptcy power was exclusive. *Golden* v. *Prince,* 10 *Federal Cases* 542. As it will be shown below, Washington proved to be the pivotal member of the Court.

Wheaton's argument is in 12 Wheaton 214–26 and Webster's in *WS*, XI, 25–40.

[13] Logically, natural law would also be superior to positive legislation by Congress. Webster did not consider this possibility.

[14] Statutes on usury and frauds could discharge the debtor's liability because contracts affected by them were not regarded as legal agreements.

a tender in payment of debts. He repelled plaintiff's assertion that the contract clause prohibited only retrospective legislation because the framers located it in a series with the clauses on bills of attainder and *ex post facto* laws (admittedly retrospective only).[15] Most of the attorneys and justices undertook this kind of word analysis throughout the hearing and decision of *Ogden* v. *Saunders*. But another argument by Webster, calculated to have an even more persuasive effect upon conservatives on the bench, referred to circumstances at the time of the Constitutional Convention. Thus the great consideration of policy in the minds of the framers was to place the credit of the nation upon a sound footing, to guard against "great public mischiefs" threatening not merely the rights of private property but, more significantly, the financial health of the country.[16]

Webster lost the case by the narrowest margin. Four of the seven justices, Washington, Johnson, Thompson, and Trimble, upheld the New York statute, with Story and Duval joining Marshall in dissent. Each of the majority filed separate opinions, but they agreed on fundamentals.[17] All four acknowledged the difficulty of the questions, yet they thought that in doubtful cases involving state power the Court ought to presume the states were acting constitutionally. Though they readily conceded that natural law could and did attach the obligation to a contract, all four believed that positive law enacted by the states did also. Where the two conflicted, positive law was superior to natural law. By an analysis of the language of Article I, section 10 of the Constitution, all four concluded that the contract clause prohibited retrospective (but not prospective) legislation since it

15 To prove exclusive national power, Webster would collate sections 8 and 10 of Article I in the Constitution. Thus Congress shall have power to establish uniform laws of bankruptcy, but no state shall pass any law impairing the obligation of contracts.

16 *WS*, XI, 34–35.

17 This Webster did not believe. He wrote to Nicholas Biddle on February 20, 1827: "You see what a fire the judges have made on the question of State Bankrupt laws. No two of those who are *for* the validity of such laws agree in their *reasons*. Those who are *against* their validity, concur entirely. Is there not a saying—if there be not let it go for a new one—that truth is one; but error various." *Ibid.*, XVI, 141.

Washington's opinion is in 12 Wheaton 254–70; Johnson's, *ibid.*, 271–92; Thompson's, *ibid.*, 292–313; Trimble's, *ibid.*, 313–31.

was placed in the same series with the *ex post facto* clause. States could therefore pass bankruptcy laws affecting *future* contracts and could do so notwithstanding any principle of natural law.

The opinions of Johnson and Washington are especially interesting because they show the compromise that lay behind the *Sturges* decision some years earlier. Washington said he then thought, and still did, that the Congressional bankruptcy power was exclusive, as against state power, but that he would abide by the *Sturges* ruling that the states possessed concurrent power if they did not impair the obligation of past contracts. Johnson observed that he had favored full concurrent state power but had yielded to prohibition on retrospective legislation in order to preserve state power over future contracts.[18] Washington's willingness to stand by the compromise lost the case for Webster.

It was no small consolation to Webster to hear the Chief Justice deliver a dissenting opinion[19] which unreservedly accepted his view of the contract clause.[20] The obligation of a contract, said Marshall, derives from the universal principles of natural law, not from municipal legislation. An individual's rights "to acquire property, to dispose of that property according to his own judgment, and to pledge himself for a future act," he declared, are "not given by society, but are brought into it."[21] Consequently, as Webster had contended, a state bankruptcy law does not affect a contract until an insolvency occurs. In all instances this point of time would follow both the making of a contract and the passage of the law, so that the distinction between retrospective and prospective legislation was meaningless. In short, Marshall's position was that the contract clause forbade legislation, retrospective or prospective, whenever it discharged the debtor's liability to pay his debt, or, in other words, impaired the obligation. If the clause did not have this meaning, warned the Chief Justice, "one of the most important features

[18] Johnson said, "The minority thought it better to yield something than risk the whole." *Ibid.*, 272.

[19] *Ibid.*, 332–57.

[20] See Story's comment, Webster Papers (Lib. Cong.), XII, 18015. Webster's argument, said Story, "coincides in reasoning & conclusion" with Marshall's opinion.

[21] 12 Wheaton 346. Marshall's natural-law theory of contracts is analyzed in Nathan Isaacs, "John Marshall on Contracts: A Study in Early American Juristic Theory," *Virginia Law Review*, VII (Mar., 1921), 413–28.

in the constitution of the United States, one which the state of the times most urgently required, one on which the good and the wise reposed confidently for securing the prosperity and harmony of our citizens, would lie prostrate, and be construed into an inanimate, inoperative, unmeaning clause."[22]

A part of *Ogden* v. *Saunders* often given insufficient attention was a second decision two weeks following the first. The parties to the contract were Saunders, a citizen of Kentucky, and Ogden, a citizen of New York. The judges now heard argument by counsel on the question whether a state bankruptcy law applied to a creditor who was a citizen of another state, such as Saunders. According to Justice Johnson, the Court reserved this point in the earlier hearing. He said that the record sent up by the lower Federal court did not show the grounds of its judgment against the constitutionality of the statute. There were at least two possible grounds: (1) the contract clause; or (2) the inapplicability of the statute to a citizen outside the state's jurisdiction. In order to obtain an opinion on point one, which was more controversial, counsel at Washington had reserved argument, with the assent of the Supreme Court, on point two.[23] The second decision held that New York's law could not operate upon a Kentucky citizen. This time Justice Johnson was with Marshall, Story, and Duval, the former dissenters.[24] Citing several American precedents, Johnson rejected the British practice of reciprocity in giving effect to foreign bankruptcy laws.[25] For Johnson, it was a matter of jurisdiction of the courts. A state could not control the judicial processes concerning bankruptcy either of other states or, as in the present instance, of the United States.[26]

Like other great constitutional cases in American history, *Ogden* v. *Saunders* seems to have been contrived to elicit from the Court a definition of state and national powers over a subject

[22] 12 Wheaton 339.

[23] *Ibid.*, 271–72, 357–58.

[24] Johnson's second opinion is in *ibid.*, 358–69.

[25] He cited *Harrison* v. *Sterry*, 5 Cranch 298 (1807), and decisions of courts in Massachusetts, South Carolina, and Pennsylvania. More important than these in Johnson's reasoning may have been principles of international law and natural justice. Conrad Reno, "Ogden v. Saunders Reviewed," *American Law Register* (New Series, 1888), 611–26.

[26] This case came up from the Federal Circuit Court of Louisiana.

of current political and economic interest.[27] The fact that the parties made the contract twenty years previously, the fact that ten years had elapsed before they appealed the case to the Supreme Court, and the fact that both lawyers and judges were so willing to rest the first decision on an unclear record of the original judicial proceedings, all forcibly suggest that the controversy was not so much a law suit involving two private parties as it was a question of broad public policy. If the Court had been as hesitant to pronounce upon the limits of state power as all five opinions professed, it could have insisted upon a clarification of the record before the first decision. Should it have done this, it would then have simply restated the ruling in *McMillan v. McNeill* (1819) that a state bankruptcy statute did not have extraterritorial effect. Though doubtless an appropriate case would soon have presented the question of the limits imposed by the contract clause, this was not such a case.

The eagerness of both sides to have a judicial definition of the bankruptcy power can be understood if one considers the movement then underway to enact a national law. During the preceding decade Wheaton, Webster, Story, and Johnson had each drafted bankruptcy bills which they hoped Congress would pass to replace a short-lived law of 1801–1803.[28] Nearly every session of Congress in the 1820's had before it such proposals; and Webster, drawing upon Story's advice and suggestions, had been in the midst of the campaign.[29] Only days before the Court decided the *Ogden* case, the Senate rejected a bankruptcy bill after long debate. It was an issue dividing commercial and agrarian interests. And the latter, favoring continued reliance upon state statutes, defeated the measure.[30]

[27] Some of the many cases that come to mind are *Fletcher* v. *Peck* (1810), *Martin* v. *Hunter's Lessee* (1816), and *Pollock* v. *Farmers' Loan and Trust Co.* (1895).

[28] Joseph Story to Henry Wheaton, Dec. 13, 1815, *Life and Letters of Joseph Story* (2 vols., Boston, 1851), I, 396; Donald G. Morgan, *Justice William Johnson* (Columbia, So. Car., 1954), 118.

[29] Charles Warren, *Bankruptcy in United States History* (Cambridge, 1935), 27–51; Morris Weisman, "Story and Webster—And the Bankruptcy Act of 1841," *Commercial Law Journal*, XLVI (Jan., 1941), 6–8; Webster to Story, Nov. 19, 1825, *Proceedings of the Massachusetts Historical Society* (Boston, 1901), Second Series, Vol. XIV (1900–01), 405.

[30] *Register of Debates in Congress*, 19 Cong., 2 sess., 2–3, 22–28, 66–68, 76–210, 223–27, 276–88, 577. The speeches in the Senate made frequent reference to the pending case in the Supreme Court.

An immediate result of the *Ogden* decision was to demolish whatever lingering chances there were for a national law. The compromise of the *Sturges* case, recognizing state concurrent authority, survived; and Webster's efforts failed temporarily. But the real significance of the second decision in *Ogden* becomes obvious when placed against the economic background. With the advent of a severe depression in 1837, clamor for a national, uniform law again arose. State acts were inadequate, argued Webster and others in Congress, for they could not operate outside their particular jurisdictions. As the nation's economy grew to interstate proportions, the necessity for a national bankruptcy policy intensified. In 1841 Webster and Clay succeeded in passing a log-rolled law, but it lasted only briefly.[31] Except for adopting another short-term measure of the Reconstruction period, Congress did not see fit to act until 1898. Thus for most of the nineteenth century the country lacked a national bankruptcy law, though persistent agitation, heightening during hard times, demonstrated a felt need for one.[32]

Through the years the contract clause proved to be somewhat effective in striking down retrospective, repressive state legislation. But late in the century the due process clause of the Fourteenth Amendment provided the sort of protection Webster had hoped to get from the contract clause. The Court invoked due process to invalidate prospective as well as retrospective statutes found unreasonable or confiscatory. Had Webster won the first decision in *Ogden* v. *Saunders,* this would have been possible several decades earlier in constitutional history.

Another pivotal contract case was *Charles River Bridge* v. *Warren Bridge,* decided in 1837, the year Taney became the Chief Justice. This, in Webster's opinion, was a much greater setback to his expansive doctrine of vested rights than the bankruptcy case had been. Again the Court reduced the possible boundaries of the contract clause. Though the decision did not reject the *Dartmouth College* precedent, it restricted the privileges corporations could claim under their charters and the Constitution.

---

[31] Warren, *Bankruptcy in U.S. Hist.,* 52–87; Glyndon G. Van Deusen, *The Jacksonian Era, 1828–1848,* in Henry S. Commager and Richard B. Morris (eds.), *The New American Nation Series* (New York, 1959), 161–62.

[32] Warren, *Bankruptcy in U.S. Hist.,* 105, 127, 144–45.

In 1785 the Massachusetts legislature incorporated a company to construct and operate a bridge across the Charles River from Boston to Charlestown. Ready for traffic the following year, the bridge company had authority to collect tolls for forty years. The state later extended this period to seventy years when it chartered another bridge to connect West Boston and Cambridge some distance away but presumably offering competition to the first bridge. At the site of the Charles River Bridge a ferry, whose receipts went to Harvard College, had operated since the mid-seventeenth century. The charter obligated the bridge company to pay an annual sum to the college in compensation for its loss of income from the discontinued ferry.[33]

In time the bridge became a very profitable enterprise. From an initial capitalization of $51,000 its stock rose to the value of $280,000 in the 1820's. But for that very reason there were complaints that the proprietors did not provide facilities of transportation equivalent to the tolls. Animosity toward the bridge corporation soon led to political agitation. Beginning in 1823, the Massachusetts legislature received a stream of petitions urging construction of another bridge, this one toll-free. Generally, foes of Charles River Bridge were Jacksonians, aligned against the conservative elements of old Federalists and National Republicans, though differences of countryside and city also underlay the controversy.[34] The proprietors once consulted Webster concerning their constitutional rights, but the lawyer answered noncommittally.[35] At last the legislature passed an act in March, 1828, incorporating the Warren Bridge company to erect a structure closely parallel to the existing bridge and to collect tolls for no more than six years, after which it would be state-owned and free to all pedestrians and vehicles. On Christmas Day that same year, the new Warren Bridge, located only 260 feet away from the Charles River Bridge on the Charlestown end, was opened to traffic. In the alloted time it would stop charging tolls, with ruinous effects upon its unwilling competitor.[36]

[33] 11 Peters 423–28.

[34] Charles Warren, *History of the Harvard Law School* (3 vols., New York, 1908), I, 512–19.

[35] Draft of Webster's letter to "Gentlemen," Mar. 20, 1826, Claude H. Van Tyne (ed.), *The Letters of Daniel Webster* (New York, 1902), 117–18.

[36] Warren, *Hist. Harvard Law School*, I, 519–20.

The old bridge company immediately attempted to protect its rights. Retaining Webster and Lemuel Shaw (later the state's eminent chief justice) as counsel, it filed a bill in the Massachusetts Supreme Court for an injunction to forbid construction of Warren Bridge. This was in June 1828. Then followed a sequence of answers by the defendants and amended bills by the plaintiffs so that it was October, 1829, when Webster and Shaw argued the case on its merits. Meanwhile the completion of the Warren Bridge defeated the initial object of these proceedings, and now all that the Charles River Bridge proprietors could expect was some kind of indemnification.[37]

The central point in the arguments of Webster and Shaw[38] was that Charles River Bridge had an exclusive right to the line of travel between the two termini, Boston and Charlestown.[39] This right, they contended, derived from two sources: (1) the ferry franchise held for many years by Harvard College and transferred to the plaintiffs by implicit terms of the bridge's charter of 1785; and (2) the charter itself which necessarily prohibited such destructive competition as that set up by the act of 1828 incorporating Warren Bridge. They gave great weight to the ferry right. Webster devoted over half his argument to show that the long accepted rule of the common law concerning ferries upheld his clients' complaint. Obviously the weakest link in this chain of reasoning was the absence of a provision in the charter specifically conveying the College's rights to the bridge company. But Webster insisted an inference to that effect could be drawn from the requirement that Charles River Bridge compensate the College for its loss of the ferry right.

Constitutionally, the lawyer maintained that the statutes of 1785 and 1792 were contracts obligating Massachusetts not to diminish the value of the bridge's tolls. Since the act of 1828 impaired this obligation, it violated the contract clause of the

[37] 6 Pickering 376–408 (Mass., 1828); 7 Pickering 347–71 (1828–29). Webster and Shaw failed to obtain a preliminary injunction while the bridge was going up, but they did succeed in obtaining a ruling that the court had equity jurisdiction in such a controversy.

[38] Shaw's argument is in 7 Pickering 391–402; Webster's, *ibid.*, 427–43, reprinted in *WS*, XV, 347–63.

[39] Then, and in later arguments, the contention was that the old bridge's exclusive right was to the "line of travel" from Boston to Charlestown, but not across *all* parts of the river.

Constitution. Again Webster had to put forward a loose construction of the 1785 charter inasmuch as the document did not directly confer an exclusive franchise. Opposing counsel urged strict construction, which would not permit Charles River Bridge to assume the ferry rights or to enjoy freedom from competition.[40]

Though the manner of construing the act of incorporation was the principal constitutional issue, this case raised other questions. Webster and Shaw declared that the state had taken the bridge's property (a right to tolls fundamental to the franchise) for public use without adequate compensation. The eminent domain clause of the state constitution, they said, forbade this.[41] At bottom were differing views about the fairness of the 1828 legislation. The old bridge company saw its property arbitrarily confiscated, contrary to principles of constitutions and natural justice.[42] The new bridge company answered that the state had merely promoted necessary public works as a stroke against exploitative monopoly.

Finally, on January 12, 1830, each of the four judges of the Massachusetts Supreme Court delivered an opinion. They were divided, with two upholding the statute of 1828 and two concluding it was invalid. As a result, the Court did not grant the relief for which Charles River Bridge had petitioned.[43] The politically-minded Jacksonian, Marcus Morton, rejected Webster's arguments in every particular. As compelling as constitutional-legal considerations, in his thinking, were social-economic ones. Expressing his fears of an exclusive franchise by the old bridge, he asserted that monopolies must not thwart economic improvements.[44] On the other hand, Chief Justice Isaac Parker, Webster's good friend,[45] thought that Charles River Bridge had

40 Warren Bridge counsel's argument, 7 Pickering 403–27.

41 The attorneys for Warren Bridge denied that eminent domain had been used. Contrast this position with that of other counsel for the same side at the Supreme Court as described below.

42 Webster insisted that the taking of property must be by judicial procedure, not by legislative action. *WS*, XV, 358–60.

43 7 Pickering 443–533 (1830).

44 *Ibid.*, 443–66. Justice Samuel S. Wilde concurred with Morton, but showed sympathy for the Charles River Bridge proprietors, who, he believed, had been treated unjustly though having no legal recourse.

45 There are numerous letters from Parker to Webster in the Webster Papers at the Library of Congress, showing the close friendship of the two. See, for example, Volume II, number 15686, dated Feb. 10, 1827.

an exclusive right, well within the protection of the contract clause. Like most other jurists of his day, Parker firmly believed natural law governed human affairs. And his opinion in this case rested quite as much upon tenets of natural justice as upon the contract clause. The state legislature, said Parker, had flagrantly trod upon those tenets.[46]

That very day, Shaw began preparing an appeal to the Federal Supreme Court.[47] And a year later, at the 1831 term, Webster and Warren Dutton presented their case in opposition to Attorney General William Wirt and Walter Jones. There is nothing noteworthy to say about this hearing, since the only argument whose contents are now known is Wirt's, and it closely followed the briefs sent up from the lower court.[48] In any event, neither side could convince the necessary four justices, though Webster and Dutton came very close. Marshall, Story, and Thompson favored the claim of the old bridge, Baldwin would have dissented, McLean and Johnson were undecided, and Duval was absent.[49]

So the case lay on the docket term after term as illnesses and vacancies on the bench prevented a decision. Meanwhile Warren Bridge had become a free highway, and the old corporation had lost nearly all its revenue. It also had poorer prospects of winning its cause. Taney, whose disapproval of exclusive transportation franchises was well-known,[50] now headed the Court

[46] 7 Pickering 506–33. Only one of the four justices thought that the College ferry rights were conveyed to the bridge. And only one justice thought that the state had exercised eminent domain in an unconstitutional manner. The principal constitutional difference between the justices concerned the contract clause.

[47] Shaw to Webster, Jan. 12, 1830, Webster Papers (Lib. Cong.). See also an undated memorandum on the right and procedure of appeal in the Webster Papers (New Hampshire Historical Society), VI, 178.

[48] MS. notes by Simon Greenleaf, "Arguments of Counsel in the case Charles River Bridge vs. Warren Bridge delivered in S. C. U. States Jan. term 1837" (Harvard University Law Library). This is a valuable collection of notes by Geenleaf, who argued the case for the defendants in 1837, and contains detailed information on all the arguments at the second hearing in 1837 but on only Wirt's argument at the first hearing in 1831. See also Warren, *Hist. Harvard Law School*, I, 525–27.

[49] Charles Warren, *The Supreme Court in United States History* (3 vols., Boston, 1923), II, 233.

[50] In 1833, Taney had written a legal opinion saying that a state legislature could not confer a monopoly upon a New Jersey railroad company because this would unconstitutionally alienate the sovereignty of future legislatures and would obstruct economic progress. The opinion is printed in *Niles' Register*, XLV (Nov. 2, 1833), 151–52.

and sat with other recently appointed Jacksonians unfriendly toward corporate privileges.[51]

For a week in January, 1837, the judges heard the second arguments. Again Webster and Dutton represented the plaintiff; but the defendant had employed new attorneys, Simon Greenleaf and John Davis. Greenleaf, a brilliant young law professor at Harvard and Justice Story's colleague there, was arguing against the College's financial interest in the old bridge.[52] Davis was a veteran Massachusetts politician. Very much impressed by the performances of all four lawyers, Story wrote an interesting commentary on what he heard.

Every argument [said Story] was very good and beyond expectation, and that is truly no slight praise, considering all circumstances. Our friend Greenleaf's argument was excellent,—full of ability, point, learning, condensed thought, and strong illustration,—delivered with great presence of mind, modestly, calmly, and resolutely. It was every way worthy of him and the cause. It has given him a high character with the Bench and with the Bar, and placed him in public opinion exactly where you and I could wish him to be, among the most honored of the profession. He has given Dane College new *éclat,* sounding and resounding fame; I speak this unhesitatingly. But at the same time I do not say that he will win the cause. That is uncertain yet, and will not be decided under weeks to come. I say so more resolutely because on some points he did not convince me; but I felt the force of his argument, exhibiting a great deal of acuteness and power of thinking. Dutton's argument was strong, clear, pointed, and replete with learning. Webster's closing reply was in his best manner, but with a little too much of *fierté* here and there. He had manifestly studied it with great care and sobriety of spirit. On the whole, it was a glorious exhibition for old Massachusetts; four of her leading men brought out in the same cause, and none of them inferior to those who are accustomed to the lead here. The audience was very large, especially as the cause advanced;—a large circle of ladies, of the highest fashion, and taste, and intelligence, numerous lawyers, and gentlemen of both houses of Congress, and towards the close, the foreign ministers, or at least two or three of them. . . .[53]

51 James M. Wayne and Philip P. Barbour.

52 The College not only received annual sums from Charles River Bridge in accordance with the provisions of the Charter of 1785 on the ferry rights but it also owned a good deal of stock in the bridge company. Warren, *Hist. Harvard Law School,* I, 542.

53 Story to Charles Sumner, Jan. 25, 1837, Sumner Papers (Harvard University Library). The letter is printed in William W. Story (ed.), *Life and Letters of Joseph Story* (2 vols., Boston, 1851), II, 265–66. See also Story to W. W.

Beginning argument for Charles River Bridge, Warren Dutton, Webster's associate, capably went over the ground covered at previous hearings. The bridge corporation succeeded to the College's ferry rights, the charter of 1785 implicitly granted an exclusive franchise, and the 1828 statute authorizing Warren Bridge unconstitutionally impaired the contractual obligation of Massachusetts, he contended. To meet the highly important question whether a grant could imply an exclusive right, Dutton painstakingly explored the common law. Even royal grants in England, he declared, were often construed liberally for the grantee unless they proceeded from the king's "bounty" or "grace."[54] And in this country under republican government the rule of construction was justly all the more liberal toward the grantee. Whenever government made a grant upon a valuable consideration (such as Charles River Bridge offering new transportation as a public utility), it construed the grant liberally for the recipient.[55]

In their turn the Warren Bridge counsel, Greenleaf and Davis, insisted upon strict construction of the grants of 1785 and 1792.[56] They denied that the College ferry had ever had an exclusive franchise for transportation across the Charles River. But if so, they continued, then the legislature extinguished the right when it chartered Charles River Bridge and thus did not convey any such right to that corporation. Nor could an exclusive franchise for the bridge be presumed in the absence of specific terms in the charter, for the sound rule of construction was that "nothing passes by implication."[57] Otherwise monopolies would frustrate essential improvements in public works; and so it was a matter of public right against a private right. To convince the Court on this subject, Davis referred to the enormous profits of the old bridge company. Despite Greenleaf's later remark that

Story, Jan. 28, 1837, printed in Warren, *Hist. Harvard Law School,* I, 534; Warren, *Sup. Ct. in U.S. Hist.,* II, 295–97.

[54] Dutton's view seems well supported in Blackstone's *Commentaries,* II, 347.

[55] 11 Peters 428–61; Greenleaf, "Arguments in Charles River Bridge Case."

[56] Greenleaf's argument is in 11 Peters 461–73 and Davis' in *ibid.,* 474–514. See also the full notes in Greenleaf, "Arguments in Charles River Bridge Case."

[57] Counsel for Warren Bridge emphasized a Massachusetts legislative report of 1792, which extended the period of the old bridge's franchise but declared that the franchise was not exclusive.

his side avoided everything "peoplish," he seems to have mined that vein.[58]

Greenleaf skillfully discussed other, substantially new points.[59] The Court, said the Professor, did not have jurisdiction because the state now owned Warren Bridge and it would be impossible for the bridge's original proprietors (against whom the petition was directed) to obey a judicial decree. Consequently this was really a suit against Massachusetts, prohibited in the Federal courts by the Eleventh Amendment. Furthermore, this was not a proper suit in equity, Greenleaf contended, since adequate remedy, such as financial compensation, was available in a court at law. The state court had therefore erred in assuming equity jurisdiction.

But the most striking aspect of Greenleaf's argument was the heavy emphasis he gave to the state's power of eminent domain. In the first place, Massachusetts could not have granted Charles River Bridge an exclusive franchise because it could not bargain away an essential attribute of sovereignty which future legislatures had the power to exercise, the power of eminent domain.[60] In the second place, old charters and contracts were subject to this power of the state. The state may have taken the old company's toll rights for public use, but the adequacy of compensation for the taking was a question for only the state to decide.[61] Greenleaf's colleague, John Davis, would have categorically denied the proprietors any compensation, because the damages were consequential, he said, and not direct.

The final argument in the case was Webster's. Extant reports of what he said indicate that he rambled from point to point, often retracing his steps in order to refute defendant's counsel.[62] According to Greenleaf, Webster had threatened to

---

[58] Greenleaf to Charles Sumner, Jan. 24, 1837, Sumner Papers.

[59] See printed page setting down the main points of the Warren Bridge counsel in Greenleaf, "Arguments in Charles River Bridge Case."

[60] Greenleaf was aware of Taney's opinion concerning the New Jersey transportation companies in 1833 and here restated Taney's views. See note 50 above.

[61] Justice McLean adopted this argument as the basis of his opinion.

[62] Richard Peters, the Supreme Court reporter, appended the following note to his report of Webster's argument: "The reporter was disappointed, in what he believed a well founded expectation of receiving a full statement of Mr. Webster's argument, made out by himself; or his notes, from which, with other aids, he could have given the argument more at large." 11 Peters 514. The argu-

" 'tear our arguments to pieces,' and abuse me. The former will puzzle him; the latter I doubt not he will do, as he was observed to be very uneasy and moody during the whole defense."[63] At any rate, it was a spirited performance, as the lawyer fought strenuously for the cause of vested rights. Several times Webster jabbed aggressively at his opponents, particularly Greenleaf, to whom he referred as the professor parading his "super-learning."

One essential for winning the case was to counteract the emotional sentiment generated against the old bridge company on the ground that it was a grasping monopoly. This Webster valiantly attempted to do. Franchises to bridges and other public utilities, said both Webster and Dutton, were not monopolies in the true legal definition. Only an exclusive privilege conferred by the sovereign to trade in some article (sugar, coffee, cotton, and so forth) in derogation of the common right was a monopoly. Building a bridge was not a common right possessed by one and all. Then the attorney sought to separate the rights of the plaintiffs from the economic position they may have earlier enjoyed. "If there was a contract, the question [before the Court] is not what was the amount of profit to be derived from it, but what was its provisions."[64] The movement for chartering Warren Bridge had unfairly victimized his clients, Webster asserted. "It began in a clamor about monopoly—that all bridges were held by the people—and that what the State wanted it might take. That was bad enough in taverns and bar rooms and garrets in Essex County and was very little better when dressed with more decorum of appearance, and advanced in this Court."[65] And to the argument that an exclusive bridge franchise hindered internal improvements he replied that failure to uphold these vested rights would discourage such improvements far more. All those who might venture new enterprises would be frightened away if their investments were vulnerable to shifting currents of inflamed public opinion.

---

ment is printed in *WS*, XV, 322–47. See the fuller summary in Greenleaf, "Arguments in the Charles River Bridge Case," on which much of the following discussion is based.

[63] Greenleaf to Charles Sumner, Jan. 24, 1837, Sumner Papers.
[64] *WS*, XV, 323.
[65] Greenleaf, "Arguments in Charles River Bridge Case."

At various junctures the lawyer upheld the Court's power to decide the case. To defendant's contention that this was now a suit against the state because it had assumed control of Warren Bridge Webster responded that the new bridge proprietors were the party named on the record and that, strictly speaking, this was not an action prohibited by the Eleventh Amendment. Here he cited *Osborn* v. *Bank of U. S.* (1824).[66] He also attacked the assertion that the original petition was not a proper one in a court of equity, for, he said, the Massachusetts judiciary act of 1827 was ample authority.[67] His most vigorous argument on the subject of jurisdiction, however, was to support the Supreme Court as the final arbiter of the Constitution, the best protector of property rights against oppressive state legislative assault. The Massachusetts legislature, he observed, was itself uncertain about the validity of the 1828 statute and had passed it by a very small margin with the knowledge that the courts would strike it down if it were unconstitutional. Much less convincingly, Webster added that the state supreme court had divided *pro forma* in order to place the questions of the case before the Federal court.[68] The justices therefore should not unnecessarily defer to legislative discretion but should consult their own "enlightened conscience."[69]

Of course the main body of Webster's argument repeated familiar points: transfer of the College's ferry rights to Charles River Bridge, an exclusive franchise conferred upon that corporation by loose construction of the 1785 state charter, and rigorous application of the contract clause in behalf of vested rights. One after the other he developed these points to their farthest limits.[70]

The phase of the case which Webster now thought was most ominous related to the state's power of eminent domain. He seemed both alarmed and angered that Greenleaf and Davis

[66] 9 Wheaton 738. See the discussion of this case in a later chapter.

[67] See Chief Justice Parker's opinion upholding jurisdiction in 6 Pickering 376.

[68] No evidence to support this statement has been discovered.

[69] *WS*, XV, 347. Webster is supposed to have said that he had the "deepest reverence for the principles which enables this Court to correct improvident, inconsiderate, intemperate and hasty and sometimes ignorant legislation." Greenleaf, "Arguments in Charles River Bridge Case."

[70] Much less was said about the rule of construing corporate charters in Webster's argument than in Taney's opinion.

introduced it at this late moment. As Webster said, defendant's counsel in the state court and at the first argument in Washington had not relied upon eminent domain. Nor had three of the four state judges thought this power applicable to the controversy. If the Court confined its attention to the record, he concluded, it would hold that eminent domain had "no bearing" on the case whatever. Nevertheless, the plaintiffs themselves had repeatedly raised the question by denying that the state had exercised the power correctly or had even intended to exercise it. And regardless of what had been said before, it was quite logical to bring in eminent domain to counterbalance the contract clause, even though the latter might be the only *constitutional* issue.[71] In other words, the defense attorneys were not, as Webster charged, injecting an altogether novel or irrelevant issue. Whether their argument was sound was another matter.

There were two distinct and separate positions that Webster assumed with regard to eminent domain. First, he challenged the statement that the state could not bargain away this sovereign power by entering into such a contract as the charter of 1785. Once a state granted an exclusive franchise, he contended, it could not rescind the franchise perhaps under any circumstances and certainly not by issuing another, competing franchise.[72] Where the national contract clause and the state's power of eminent domain conflicted, the contract clause would be superior. Second, Webster argued that the state had not exercised eminent domain in a proper, constitutional manner. In this position, he implied that the state could have taken the franchise of the bridge for public use if it had made adequate compensation for the taking. The contract clause would be no bar to eminent

[71] The question of eminent domain by itself was related only to the *state* constitution, for the eminent domain clause of the Fifth Amendment in the United States Constitution did not apply to state legislatures, only to Congress. *Barron* v. *Baltimore,* 7 Peters 243 (1833). The Judiciary Act of 1789 required that a question involving the *national* Constitution be at issue in a case appealed from the state tribunals to the Federal Supreme Court. Thus, though the contract clause was the only such constitutional question, the proper exercise of eminent domain might be an exception to the prohibition to impair the obligation of contracts.

[72] Here he was referring to the appropriate procedure for eminent domain. Merely issuing another franchise was not appropriate, he thought, because judicial process was necessary.

Citing *New Jersey* v. *Wilson,* 7 Cranch 164 (1812), wherein the Court upheld an exemption from taxation because it was a contract with a state, Webster argued that a sovereign power could be alienated by a state charter.

domain, then, if procedure were correct. This incidentally was also Dutton's contention.[73] These two positions of Webster's offered different possibilities for a judicial rule either to prohibit or to limit eminent domain vis-á-vis the contract clause. At that stage of constitutional development the Court had not yet settled upon a doctrine.

Webster realized beforehand that the Court's decision would be against his clients.[74] Perhaps his friend Story, much dissatisfied with the new Democratic complexion of the bench, may have told him what to expect. But for reasons obvious enough to all, the attorney himself could have readily predicted defeat. The recent Jacksonian appointees, Taney, Barbour, and Wayne, could be expected to join Baldwin, who had been the only justice ready to approve the state legislation at the first argument. And they did. Taney delivered the Court's opinion in which the other three concurred. McLean thought the Court did not have jurisdiction, which meant, in effect, he also upheld the state statute. Story, followed by Thompson, delivered his long-prepared opinion in dissent.

Next to the *Dred Scott* case, the Chief Justice's opinion in *Charles River Bridge* v. *Warren Bridge* is the one for which he is best known.[75] Unquestionably it is an impressive, but often misunderstood, document. One can characterize it as typical of Taney's judicial craftsmanship. Where possible he avoided answering non-essential questions, and throughout he displayed a keen awareness of the practical consequences of the decision. Although he did not repudiate the precedents of the Marshall period, specifically the *Dartmouth College* rule that corporate charters were contracts in a constitutional sense, he made it perfectly clear that a new era had arrived.

Taney began with a brief consideration of the relationship of Harvard's ferry rights and the old bridge's franchise. He found no ground to presume the transfer of the ferry rights to the bridge proprietors. There were, he held, no conveyance or assignment, no indication of such a transaction in the charter

73 11 Peters 453–59.
74 Fletcher Webster to Daniel Webster, Feb. 24, 1837, Van Tyne (ed.), *Letters of Webster,* 209, and Mar. 6, 1837, Webster Papers (New Hamp. Hist. Soc.), VII, 85 [letter erroneously mounted with those of 1839].
75 11 Peters 536–53.

of 1785, and no equitable claim that could be maintained. Nor would he consult the old law on ferries in search of a rule to determine the bridge's rights, for this would unduly recognize anachronistic "feudal grants." Not only did Taney de-emphasize this aspect of the case, but he gave no notice whatsoever to the subject of eminent domain. Thus the Court deferred a definition of this power to a future occasion. Moreover, he completely ignored the questions of jurisdiction.

Taney directed nearly all his attention to laying down a rule for interpreting the corporate charter. Not at all surprisingly, he evoked strict construction. Learned lawyer that he was, he discovered numerous English and American precedents to support the rule.[76] The one case upon which he leaned most heavily was a recent English decision, *Stourbridge Canal* v. *Wheely* (1831). The English court had narrowly interpreted a parliamentary charter conferring the right to take tolls and had denied the grantees anything "not clearly given them."[77] The sound rule, well established by American courts too, said Taney, was "that in grants by the public, nothing passes by implication."[78] Yet it is obvious that Taney was not quite so dogmatic as this statement might suggest. Elsewhere in his opinion, and on other occasions, Taney acknowledged that *some* charter rights were implied.[79] In the present instance Taney concluded that the Massachusetts legislature had not intended to grant an exclusive franchise. As proof for this conclusion, he referred to a report of a state legislative committee in 1792 declaring that the Charles River Bridge proprietors did not have the sole right of transportation across the river. If Taney was really rejecting all implications, he need not have taken the trouble to explore legislative *intention* and could have stopped with a reading of the statutes only.

Legalisms notwithstanding, Taney's main concern was

[76] He cited *Jackson* v. *Lamphire*, 3 Peters 289; *Beatty* v. *Lessee of Knowles*, 4 Peters 168; *Providence Bank* v. *Billings*, 4 Peters 514; and *U.S.* v. *Arredondo*, 8 Peters 738.

[77] 2 Barn. and Adol. 793, in 109 English Reports 792–97.

[78] 11 Peters 546.

[79] In his legal opinion concerning the New Jersey railroad monopoly of 1833, as described in note 50 above, Taney wrote: "This pledge on behalf of the state, is not given in express and direct terms, but it may be finally *implied* from the words of the law." [Italics added.] *Niles' Register*, XLV (Nov. 2, 1833), 151.

with the economic effects of the decision. He disliked special corporate privileges, particularly monopolies, though he was not unfriendly to all corporations in this age of industrialization. Accepting the complainant's argument for implied privileges, he believed, would lead to insuperable difficulties.

The millions of property which have been invested in rail roads and canals, upon lines of travel which have been before occupied by turnpike corporations, will be put in jeopardy. We shall be thrown back to the improvements of the last century, and obliged to stand still, until the claims of the old turnpike corporations shall be satisfied.[80]

The Chief Justice was convinced that

in a country like ours, free, active, and enterprising, continually advancing in numbers and wealth; new channels of communication are daily found necessary, both for travel and trade; and are essential to the comfort, convenience, and prosperity of the people. . . . While the rights of private property are sacredly guarded, we must not forget that the community also have rights, and that the happiness and well being of every citizen depends on their faithful preservation.[81]

McLean's opinion was one of several puzzling ones he delivered during his judicial career.[82] It did not affect the outcome of the case, inasmuch as Taney's opinion reflected the unified position of the Court's majority; however, it touched upon some questions that would recur in succeeding years. The Ohioan thought that the old bridge company correctly claimed implied rights under the charter, and that there was a contract.[83] Nevertheless the state had not impaired the obligation of this contract, he believed, because it had exercised the power of eminent domain. That power, if it exists in the state, must be above the contract, he asserted. Of course the state must adequately compensate the owners when it takes property for public use, but determining the adequacy of compensation, he continued, was entirely a question for the state courts. The

[80] 11 Peters 553.
[81] *Ibid.,* 547–48.
[82] 11 Peters 554–83. McLean often yielded to the temptation to comment at length upon aspects of cases unrelated to the specific grounds of his opinions. See, for example, his opinion in *Groves* v. *Slaughter,* 15 Peters 503–08 (1841).
[83] McLean reluctantly followed Marshall's holding in *Fletcher* v. *Peck* (1810) that *executed* contracts (grants, etc.) were covered by the contract clause of the Constitution. He would have preferred to apply the clause only to *executory* contracts. 11 Peters 572–74.

Federal courts therefore did not have jurisdiction.[84] The best way to classify McLean's opinion is to say that he concurred with the majority but on jurisdictional grounds. Among the many weaknesses of the opinion was his unnecessary discussion of the bridge company's rights under the charter if these rights could never be protected against eminent domain. And he made no effort to discover whether the facts of the case showed that the state had actually exercised eminent domain.[85]

Not long after the first argument of the *Charles River Bridge* case in 1831, Justice Story had written an elaborate opinion upholding the rights of the old company.[86] Now, six years later, he delivered the opinion in dissent substantially as he had first drafted it.[87] It was a lengthy and thorough canvass of the law concerning grants. On every point Story approved the arguments of Webster and Dutton, while exhaustively countering the views of the majority. He did so with much animation, for the seemingly gross injustice to the plaintiffs profoundly disturbed him.[88]

Relentlessly Story demolished the aphorism that in a grant nothing passes by implication. *Royal* grants were sometimes construed strictly against the grantee under the common law he said, but often they were liberally construed.[89] The present question before the Court, however, was a different one, because it arose from a *legislative* grant. And in the circumstances, it was always necessary to identify legislative intentions

[84] *Ibid.*, 580.

[85] It will be noticed that McLean accepted Greenleaf's argument concerning eminent domain. Cf. *West River Bridge* v. *Dix* (1848) discussed below. McLean also indicated that he was greatly influenced by the desirability of carrying forward internal improvements. 11 Peters 583.

Justice Baldwin's opinion concurring in the decision was published separately in his *A General View of the Origin and Government of the United States* (Philadelphia, 1837), 134-69.

[86] In late 1831 Story wrote to Jeremiah Mason, asking Mason to read and criticize the opinion which he had drafted. Mason agreed and may have done so. Story to Mason, Nov. 19, 1831, George S. Hilliard (ed.), *Memoir and Correspondence of Jeremiah Mason* (Cambridge, 1873), 335; Mason to Story, Nov. 24, 1831, *ibid.*, 336; Story to Mason, Dec. 23, 1831, *ibid.*, 336-37.

[87] 11 Peters 583-650.

[88] Story to Mrs. Story, Feb. 14, 1837, quoted in Warren, *Hist. Harvard Law School,* I, 535-36.

[89] Blackstone, *Commentaries,* II, 347, says it was "usual," in order to allow a liberal construction of a royal grant, for the crown to provide that the grant was not made at the suit of the grantee but "by the special grace, certain knowledge, and mere motion of the king."

to allow the reasonable implications of a grant. Story read the recent English decision in *Stourbridge Canal* v. *Wheely* differently than Taney did. Despite the judge's statement that nothing could be claimed from a grant that was "not clearly given," Story pointed to the further passage in the opinion holding that it was "therefore incumbent upon [the grantees] to shew that they have a right clearly given by *inference* from some of the other clauses [of the act]."[90] By and large, Story was right about his common law.

The more one studies the *Charles River Bridge* case, the plainer it is that the differences between the lawyers and judges on each side came down to the point of economic policy. Story and Webster feared that a decision against the plaintiffs would deter internal improvements. The outlay of new capital would be uncertain, property would be unsafe, stockholders would be alarmed. The old bridge, they thought, was not an odious monopoly (as the Jacksonians labelled it). It was a sign of enterprise and progress, which the state arbitrarily undermined. In this case the constitutional positions of Taney on the one hand and Story and Webster on the other were closer than first apparent.[91] Their economic theories were farther apart.

Conservative sentiment on the decision was understandably hostile. Webster himself, while complimenting Story upon "the ablest, and best written opinion, I ever heard you deliver," declared that Taney had "completely overturned" the contract clause of the Constitution.[92] The passage of time did not cause him to change his mind about the Chief Justice's "ingenious, elaborate, and sometimes half shame-faced apology for what is wrong."[93] James Kent shared this feeling. The famous New York jurist, champion of property that he was, remarked that after reading Taney's opinion he "dropped the pamphlet in

90 Italics added. 109 English Reports 796.

91 Edwin M. Dodd, *American Business Corporations until 1860* (Cambridge, 1954), 126. Like Webster, Story thought that a state could alienate its power of eminent domain by granting an exclusive franchise. His position here was, of course, different than Taney's. 11 Peters 641–45.

92 Webster to Story [no date but probably soon after the decision of Feb. 12, 1837], Story (ed.), *Story*, II, 269.

93 Webster's speech before a committee of the Massachusetts legislature, Jan. 20, 1845, *WS*, XV, 399.

disgust and read no more." "If the Legislature can quibble away, or whittle away its contracts with impunity," Kent prophesied, "the people will be sure to follow."[94] In subsequent times, others have looked upon the case as a massive blow against corporate privileges, as working a substantial change in the constitutional doctrine of the old days of John Marshall.[95]

Today the *Charles River Bridge* case does not seem nearly so revolutionary. There were, after all, precedents in the Reports, cited by Taney, for the majority decision. And the distance between the legal theories of the majority and minority was not great. In the context of other contract clause cases during Taney's time, the truth is that this decision did little damage to vested rights generally.[96] Equally true, nonetheless, is the fact that the Charles River Bridge stockholders suffered an enormous financial loss. Ironically, the public at Boston, in whose interests the Court supposedly delivered a bold stroke, later had to pay tolls to the state to pass over both the Warren and the Charles River Bridges![97]

A few years after the *Charles River Bridge* decision another case posed the question whether to construe corporate charters loosely or strictly. *Planters' Bank of Mississippi v. Sharp* (1848) tested the constitutionality of a Mississippi statute prohibiting banks from transferring by endorsement promissory notes payable to them. The state's object had been to strengthen its earlier requirement that banks which made loans in its own paper had to receive the same, oftentimes depreciated paper in repayment of the loans. It was thought that banks had been transferring promissory notes of their debtors in order to evade that requirement. Did the Mississippi law impair the obligation

94 Kent to Story, Apr. 18 and June 23, 1837, quoted in Warren, *Hist. of Harvard Law School*, I, 539.

95 See for example, Roscoe Pound, "The Charles River Bridge Case (7 Pick., 344, 1829)," *Massachusetts Law Quarterly*, XXVII (Oct., 1942), 17–21.

96 Wright, *Contract Clause*, 63–65; Charles G. Haines and Foster Sherwood, *The Role of the Supreme Court in American Government and Politics, 1835–1864* (Berkeley, 1957), 43. As shown in *Planters' Bank of Mississippi v. Sharp* (1848), discussed below, even the Taney Court did not always apply the rule.

97 Warren, *Hist. Harvard Law School*, I, 530, 541–42. In 1841, during the administration of none other than the one-time counsel for Warren Bridge, Governor John Davis, the Massachusetts legislature provided for the payment of $25,000 for the surrender of the title and charter of Charles River Bridge.

of contract in the bank charters which authorized discounting bills and notes and other such transactions?[98]

In this controversy Webster represented the debtor Sharp, relying upon the state statute in opposition to the creditor bank. As a lawyer, he was therefore arguing the side of the case where his personal convictions did not lie. The bank's charter did not expressly confer the right to endorse promissory notes, he contended, and consequently by a strict construction of the charter this power could not be implied. Interestingly, he did not cite the *Charles River Bridge* case. Nor was the transfer of these notes necessary to the exercise of a granted power, he said. In discussing the latter point he made some tenuous observations about banking operations, which he would never have uttered outside the courtroom.[99]

Justice Woodbury, speaking for a majority, held the Mississippi law violated the contract clause. He thought that the bank's charter expressly authorized it to transfer notes. But if this were not true, he believed the charter implied such a right as necessary and proper to do those things that were expressly authorized. In other words, he did not follow the rule of strict construction that nothing passes by implication.[100] Daniel and Taney dissented, with the former filing an opinion which declared that no such right as claimed could be implied.[101] Though the majority seemed to reject the principle of the *Charles River Bridge* decision, neither Woodbury nor Daniel so much as cited, let alone discussed, that case.

At this 1848 term, the same Court which protected a corporation's rights through liberal construction of its charter refused to extend protection under the contract clause against a state's power of eminent domain. In *West River Bridge* v. *Dix*, for the first time in its history, the Supreme Court defined

[98] 6 Howard 301–07. A companion case of *Baldwin* v. *Payne*, involving the same questions, was argued and decided with the *Sharp* case.

[99] *Ibid.*, 310–16. Webster is reported to have said: "Is the power to transfer notes essential to the proper business of banking? On the contrary, it is entirely subversive of it. It is endorsing other people's paper,—mere brokerage. When the paper is assigned, interest upon it ceases to the bank. No well-conducted bank is ever reduced to such an emergency as to be obliged to sell paper." *Ibid.*, 316.

[100] *Ibid.*, 318–333.

[101] *Ibid.*, 336–43. McLean concurred with the majority on the separate ground that the state law unconstitutionally deprived the creditor's right to sue in the courts. *Ibid.*, 335–36.

that important function of sovereignty known as eminent domain. By doing so, it picked up a question lengthily discussed in the *Charles River Bridge* case but left unanswered.

Vermont incorporated a bridge company in 1795 and permitted it to take tolls from traffic across West River. In time people of the vicinity felt that the toll bridge was a "sore grievance"; and so they petitioned the county court to take the bridge and make it part of a new free highway. This was done in due course under a state law of 1839 empowering county courts to take real estate and franchises for the public use with adequate compensation. The Vermont Supreme Court affirmed these proceedings. It rejected the corporation's complaint that the statute of 1839 authorizing resumption of the franchise violated the contract clause of the Constitution. Thereupon the bridge company appealed to the Federal Supreme Court.[102]

Webster and Jacob Collamer represented West River Bridge in this path-marking case. The principal points in their brief resembled Webster's argument in the *Charles River Bridge* case concerning the relationship between the contract clause and eminent domain.[103] In the event of conflict between the two, as in the present instance, the attorneys contended the contract clause was always superior. Whenever a corporation could find cover for its franchise under the contract clause, it was immune from the state's power of eminent domain. Webster conceded that a government could take real estate for public use but could not take a franchise. Consequently corporations would usually enjoy much fuller protection than individuals. Indeed the Constitution, he insisted, absolutely forbade a state from rescinding or impairing a charter under color of eminent domain. Finally the lawyer expressed alarm at the extremes to which the doctrine of eminent domain might stray. "It is easy to see," he warned, "that, by a very slight improvement on the proceedings in this case, and in pursuance of the avowed principle, . . . the most levelling ultraisms of Anti-rentism or agrarianism or Abolitionism may be successfully advanced."[104]

---

102 *Ibid.*, 507–12.
103 *Ibid*, 513–21.
104 *Ibid.*, 521. Except for reference to Kent's *Commentaries,* Webster included no citations in his brief, not even to Story's dissenting opinion in the *Charles River Bridge* case.

Fortunately for the future development of American transportation, the Court decided against Webster's clients. That steady friend of state sovereignty, Justice Daniel, delivered the majority opinion fully accepting the argument of the defendant in error.[105] Daniel was ecstatic in his exposition of the state's capacity to act in the interest of the public. "This power, denominated the *eminent domain* of the State," declared Daniel, "is, as its name imports, paramount to all private rights vested under the government, and these last are, by necessary implication, held in subordination to this power, and must yield in every instance to its proper exercise."[106] All contracts, including charters of incorporation, were therefore made with the knowledge that eminent domain was paramount. As an implicit part of every contract, the exercise of this power could not impair the obligation of a contract. Daniel saw nothing sacred in a franchise as compared with other classes of property. "A franchise is property and nothing more," he held.[107] The Justice concluded by saying that it was unnecessary, and beyond the Court's jurisdiction, to inquire into the adequacy of compensation awarded to the bridge company or to review the form of proceedings in the state tribunals. These were matters solely for the state to determine, according to its own discretion.

It was on the last point that Justice Woodbury disagreed with Daniel.[108] Though he concurred with the holding that eminent domain did not violate the contract clause, Woodbury would have preferred to lay down a standard to judge a given case. He was unwilling to place so much confidence in the state itself. The bridge franchise should not have been taken unless "the further exercise of the franchise as a corporation is inconsistent or incompatible with the highway to be laid out."[109] Mere convenience would be an insufficient reason to resume the charter, for there must be a showing of genuine necessity. But in the present circumstances as demonstrated in the record, the purpose of taking the franchise was "eminently for the public

[105] *Ibid.*, 529–36. Counsel for the defendant was Samuel S. Phelps of Vermont. His able argument is in *ibid.*, 521–29.
[106] *Ibid.*, 532.
[107] *Ibid.*, 534.
[108] Woodbury's well written opinion is in *ibid.*, 539–49.
[109] *Ibid.*, 544.

use."[110] Woodbury's standard of reviewing such cases might have been a just and useful one. The Court did not then adopt it; nor, by and large, did it later venture very far in any direction. Federal judicial review seldom restrained the states' broad power of eminent domain.[111]

Both theoretical and practical grounds justified state power. The origins of eminent domain go back in history many centuries, as early as the ancient Roman period. During the seventeenth and eighteenth centuries natural-law writers, such as Grotius and Vattel, developed the concept systematically. English and American common law accepted the principle of enforced sale with adequate compensation.[112] By the early nineteenth century, at the time of the *West River Bridge* case, numerous precedents in the state judicial reports provided the Supreme Court with a well-formulated doctrine.[113] And practically, there was the desirability of fostering internal improvements and public utilities. Just as it had in the *Charles River Bridge* case, the Court now recognized that turnpike charters must not hinder railroad building, that old franchises must not discourage new bridges and highways, and that previous legislative generosities must not defeat any one of many future economic policies.

The constitutional effect of the *West River Bridge* decision, then, was to establish a substantial limitation upon corporate privilege. Instead of accepting Webster's version of the contract clause as an insurmountable barrier against fundamental state power, the judges held that eminent domain was

110 *Ibid.,* 547.

111 Dodd, *Am. Bus. Corporations,* 127–30; Edward S. Corwin (ed.), *Constitution . . . Analysis and Interpretation* (Washington, 1953), 1062–70. Lawrence, *Wayne,* 106.

112 Philip Nichols, *The Law of Eminent Domain: A Treatise on the Principles Which Affect the Taking of Property for Public Use* (2 vols., Albany, 1917, 2nd ed.), I, 1–23; Arthur Lenhoff, "Development of the Concept of Eminent Domain," *Columbia Law Review,* XLII (Apr. 1942), 598–638; J. A. C. Grant, "The 'Higher Law' Background of the Law of Eminent Domain," *Wisconsin Law Review,* VI (Feb. 1931), 67–85.

113 Chief Justice Lemuel Shaw of Massachusetts pioneered in developing the doctrine of eminent domain. One of his notable decisions was in *Boston Water Power Co.* v. *Boston,* 23 Pickering 360 (Mass., 1839), holding that a corporate franchise was subject to eminent domain and that the national contract clause was not violated. Daniel cited the precedent in his *West River Bridge* opinion. Leonard W. Levy, *The Law of the Commonwealth and Chief Justice Shaw* (Cambridge, 1956), 118–35.

inalienable. A state could not contract it away in a charter. The Court furthermore retreated from the large, perhaps overly burdensome responsibility suggested by Woodbury to rule upon many particulars of a case. The weakness of Daniel's opinion was that it might well permit the states through pretense or fiction to claim they were exercising eminent domain while actually obviating the contract clause or some other constitutional provision. To prevent these maneuvers the state constitutions or the good sense of the people themselves would have to be depended upon. Webster, and to some extent Woodbury, was not disposed to entrust the fate of vested rights in such hands. The majority thought otherwise.

Reviewing Webster's record in contract-clause cases after the *Dartmouth College* decision, one finds that he participated in four altogether. In three of these he represented parties claiming vested rights, and in all three he lost. A qualification must be made, however, concerning the bankruptcy case, for he did win the second decision, a rather considerable victory. The fourth case, in which he unsuccessfully defended state power, was by far the least important one; and his argument was entirely perfunctory.[114]

Clearly the set of judicial currents was against Webster's version of the contract clause in the last years of the Marshall Court and the early years of the Taney Court. In *Ogden* v. *Saunders* Webster failed to make the contract clause a prohibition on prospective as well as retrospective legislation. In the *Charles River Bridge* case the Court rejected his loose-constructionist rule of interpreting corporate charters. And in the *West River Bridge* case he did not succeed in setting up the contract clause as an absolute barrier to state power of eminent domain. It was also during this era that the police power was

---

[114] Webster's other vested rights cases in which constitutional questions were involved, but not the contract clause, were: *Pawlet* v. *Clark,* 9 Cranch 292 (1815); *Society for Propagation of Gospel* v. *New Haven,* 8 Wheaton 464 (1823); *Wilkinson* v. *Leland,* 2 Peters 627 (1829).

In another case, *Mason* v. *Haile,* 12 Wheaton 370 (1827), Webster argued that Rhode Island had violated the contract clause by special legislation discharging a debtor from his bond. But the Court through Justice Thompson held that the state had not affected the *obligation* of a contract, only the remedy available to the creditor—in this instance, imprisonment of the debtor.

These cases are discussed in Chapter VI.

developing into an additional basis for state action and an important counterweight to vested rights.[115]

Just as significant, if not more so, was the ground which proponents of vested rights, like Webster, did not lose. The second decision in *Ogden* v. *Saunders* really made it impossible for Congress to leave the subject of bankruptcy to the states, because in a nationalizing economy state legislation within each separate state jurisdiction would not serve the needs of the country. The *Charles River Bridge* opinion of Taney, though establishing the rule of strict construction of charters, was not so severe as might first appear. As shown in this very opinion, in *Bank of Mississippi* v. *Sharp,* and in many other cases, the Court would allow implications in corporate charters. The power of eminent domain, affirmed in the *West River Bridge* case, did not prove to be the radical instrument that Webster and the conservatives feared it might be. By the mid nineteenth century it was plain that the Court was pursuing a route somewhere between the differing position of Taney and Webster.[116] The contract clause would still amply protect vested rights.

[115] See *Brown* v. *Maryland,* 12 Wheaton 419 (1827) ; *N.Y.* v. *Miln,* 11 Peters 102 (1837) ; *Stone* v. *Mississippi,* 101 U. S. 814 (1880).

[116] Taney's differences with the majority of the Court are illustrated not only in the Mississippi bank case but also in *Piqua Branch of Bank of Ohio* v. *Knoup,* 16 Howard 369 (1854), wherein it was held that a state could contract away its taxing power. See Carl B. Swisher, *Roger B. Taney* (New York, 1936), 390–92, and Wright, *Contract Clause,* 63–65.

VI

THE RIGHTS AND USES
OF PROPERTY

Besides his contract-clause cases, Webster handled many others concerning the relationship of governmental power and property rights. Occasionally the question related to national policy, but usually it involved state power. And though in the course of his practice he naturally represented some clients who relied upon state authority to restrict the rights of property, much more often he opposed that authority. Altogether, his cases tested a wide variety of rights: land claims, debtor-creditor relations, copyrights, patents, wills, and many others. Out of such cases, a pattern of his legal thought emerges. Whenever possible, he believed, government must recognize claims of title to ownership with all its benefits and must assure a large measure of freedom in the uses of property. If legislative bodies, state or Federal, did not act as liberally as they ought, then the judiciary should accept responsibility for protecting property. First principles of justice drawn from natural law and abundant precedents from the common law were both available for the task. An advantage of resorting to either was its essential generosity toward private rights. Furthermore, the bench might perhaps apply them to circumstances covered unsatisfactorily by constitutional and statutory provisions.

Even an attorney of Webster's ability, however, had difficulty convincing the Court that it ought to ignore longstanding, explicitly declared public policies. In *Johnson* v. *McIntosh* (1823), a hopeless case from the beginning, he put forward a tenuous claim by the plaintiff to a large tract in Illinois based upon an alleged sale of lands by the Indians to speculators on the eve of the Revolution. The defendant, on the other hand, had later purchased the lands from the national government. Did the Indians have such a title to their lands that they could sell to private individuals? And if so, was the sale legal in the face of the British Proclamation of 1763 and of subsequent \Virginia legislation prohibiting these transactions? Webster elaborately maintained the affirmative to both questions. But the whole history of Indian relations was against him, and a decision in his favor would have caused a more chaotic situation than one could imagine. Without qualification, Marshall rejected plaintiff's position. After a thorough review of policies and practices of various nations, Marshall concluded that the Indians held their lands by rights of occupancy, subordinate to the titles established through discovery by the European nations. Consequently individuals could purchase the lands only from these nations or their successors, in this instance the United States.[1]

A few years later the Court heard a series of cases concerning very extensive land claims in Florida, dating back to the pre-1819 Spanish period. These suits raised complicated questions of evidence, for the original documents allegedly proving grants of thousands of acres were usually lost or unavailable. Offered instead were copies or copies of copies, the authenticity of which was dubious. Or if they were authentic, it was said, favor seekers had obtained the grants by corrupting or deceiving Spanish colonial officials. A number of cases, furthermore, involved the construction of treaties relating to Florida and a review of diplomatic history underlying the treaties. Many original grantees had sold their interests to American entrepreneurs, who would now profit enormously by favorable judicial decisions. In these cases Webster and his fellow lawyers received quite sizeable fees for their services.[2]

[1] 8 Wheaton 543–605 (1823).
[2] Gustavus Myers, *History of the Supreme Court of the United States* (Chicago, 1918), 321–53, is a detailed, but highly subjective, treatment of the cases.

At first, the Court found ways and means to disapprove some of the Spanish grants. In *Foster and Elam* v. *Neilson* (1829) Marshall turned away claimants to a West Florida area by holding that other branches of the Federal government had not recognized it as Spanish soil.[3] But *U.S.* v. *Arredondo* (1832) lowered the barriers. Fernando Arredondo alleged title to about three hundred thousand acres in northeastern Florida, granted in late 1817 on condition that he begin to settle the area within three years. He had lost his case before the Board of Land Commissioners, established by Congress to examine such claims; but the courts treated him more generously.[4] Counsel for the United States were Richard K. Call (an attorney from Florida chiefly responsible for preparing the government's briefs in these suits), Wirt, and Attorney General Taney; for Arredondo were Joseph White, John Berrien, and Webster. This array of talent on each side indicated the financial importance of the case. Only the principal points of the five-day-long arguments are reported, but it is safe to guess that they left little unsaid.

Justice Baldwin in one of his longest and most tortuous opinions, and he was never noted for laconism, affirmed Arredondo's claims. First, he held the Spanish intendant had authority to make the grant. The burden of proof that the grant was illegal, said Baldwin, fell upon the United States, not the grantee. Unless convinced otherwise, the Court would presume that the process had been orderly. Second, he held that the Board could not deny the grant because Arredondo had failed to settle the area. Hostility of the Indians and disarrangements caused by the cession of Florida to another sovereignty required liberal

One is persuaded, however, to agree with Myers' condemnation of the questionable claims.

During the early 1820's Webster had obtained large fees in representing claimants before a special Federal commission on claims for Spanish commercial depredations. See Chapter I.

[3] See Chapter III.

[4] 6 Peters 691–705 (1832); Charles Warren, *The Supreme Court in United States History* (3 vols., Boston, 1923), II, 241–45; Myers, *History of the Sup. Ct.*, 326–36. By the terms of the Florida Treaty (1819), all Spanish land grants made prior to 1818 were to be confirmed. But a disagreement between the United States and Spain concerning many last-minute grants had delayed American ratification of the treaty until 1821.

principles of equity.[5] On this point, Baldwin may have felt some misgivings as he heard Justice Thompson's aroused dissent, which appears to have had a sounder foundation in strict law.[6]

Even larger victories were now possible. In *Mitchel* v. *U.S.* (1835) Webster presented the claim of a group of speculators to over a million acres of land in the Gulf area of Tallahassee and St. Mark's. They traced their title to Indian cessions in payment of debts and damages to certain trading companies. One wonders how justice could have demanded such an indemnity. At any rate, Webster argued that the Spanish governor had confirmed this vast acquisition and that the United States was bound by the Florida Treaty to respect it. Justice Baldwin agreed. Taking the trail he had blazed in *Arredondo,* he presumed the authority of Spanish officials to validate the cession and unhesitatingly accepted the authenticity of evidence despite an absence of many original documents.[7] Not satisfied with all this, Mitchel later attempted to secure title even to the site of St. Mark's fort, but this time the Court rejected Webster's appeal.[8]

Far more of Webster's cases on vested rights concerned state rather than national policy. One that reveals his legal ideas rather well is *Mason* v. *Haile* (1827). Here the lawyer represented a creditor, the plaintiff, who challenged the validity of state acts discharging a debtor, one Nathan Haile, from bonds he had given to assure payment of his debts. The bonds had obligated Haile to remain in jail until his debts were "lawfully discharged." But this debtor, like others of the day, sought and received special relief from the Rhode Island legislature which freed him from jail and discharged his debts. Webster argued that the bonds were contracts within the meaning of the

[5] 6 Peters 706–49. The Treaty of 1819 had two official forms, one in English and the other in Spanish. Baldwin followed the Spanish version, which was made liberal to grantees. After the *Arredondo* decision, Webster moved for a reargument of the case in order to prove that the grants were good even if the English version were used; but the Court denied the motion. Webster to Story, undated letter, Story Papers, XXXI, 91 (Massachusetts Historical Society).

[6] 6 Peters 749–59. Thompson thought the English version of the Treaty ought to be followed.

[7] 9 Peters 711–63 (1835).

[8] 15 Peters 52–92 (1841). The question concerning the land occupied by the fort had been referred to the lower court in Baldwin's opinion of 1935.

See also Webster's legal opinions supporting the validity of other Spanish grants. *WS*, XV, 310–21.

Constitution and that the state had impaired their obligations. Almost casually, he also suggested that the legislative acts "might even be considered void on general principles, independent of the positive prohibition in the constitution, as being retrospective laws interfering with vested rights." Cursory though this remark was, the meaning was plain. Extraconstitutional and extrastatutory standards, philosophically oriented and judicially discovered, might determine the issue. Justice Thompson's opinion for the Court evaded these difficult questions by holding that the state had merely acted upon the remedy, not the obligation, of a contract and that this was part of a long established legal system in Rhode Island.[9]

Again in *Wilkinson* v. *Leland* (1829) Webster invited bold judicial initiative.[10] The Rhode Island legislature had authorized sale of certain lands to satisfy claims of creditors after the owner's death. Descendants of the deceased brought action against purchasers of the property on the ground that the state had wrongly devested their rights. John Whipple and William Wirt represented Wilkinson and others, the purchasers who relied upon the state law.[11] Whipple eloquently maintained that a Federal Court could not invalidate a state statute on the basis of natural justice. Such a judgment could only rest upon a clause of the United States Constitution, he declared.[12] Attacking the state statute in behalf of the descendants, Leland and others, Webster put forward the opposite view with equal force. *Legislative* action of this kind was outright confiscation, without a hearing, without notice to the parties, without the *judicial* procedures that a state of this Union must follow, declared Webster. He did not contend that the law violated the contract clause. "Though there may be no prohibition in the Constitu-

---

[9] 12 Wheaton 370–83 (1827). The contract clause prohibits state impairment of the *obligation* of a contract. Changing the judicial remedy available to the creditor, according to Thompson, did not impair the obligation. See Washington's dissent, *ibid.*, 379–83.

[10] 2 Peters 627–63 (1829).

[11] The Circuit Court had declared the legislative act invalid, and Wilkinson now appealed.

[12] Thus the only basis could be Article VI of the Constitution, providing that the Constitution, laws, and treaties of the United States "shall be the supreme law of the land." Wirt contended that the act violated no constitutional clause, such as those on *ex post facto* laws, contracts, or a republican form of government. 2 Peters 631–41, 648–53.

tion," he said, "the legislature is restrained from committing flagrant acts, from acts subverting the great principles of republican liberty, and of the social compact; such as giving the property of A to B."[13]

Webster lost the case, but Justice Story expressed ample sympathy for his proposition.

That government can scarcely be deemed to be free [Story observed], where the rights of property are left solely dependent upon the will of a legislative body, without any restraint. The fundamental maxims of a free government seem to require, that the rights of personal liberty and private property should be held sacred. At least no Court of Justice in this country would be warranted in assuming, that the power to violate and disregard them,—a power so repugnant to the common principles of justice and civil liberty,—lurked under any general grant of legislative authority, or ought to be implied from any general expressions of the will of the people.[14]

To support this strong statement of inherent judicial power to protect vested rights, Story cited his own opinion in *Terret* v. *Taylor* (1815), in which he had in fact invoked the principles of natural justice to disapprove legislative resumption of a land grant.[15] However, the Justice found it unnecessary to go so far in the present case, because on another point he ruled against Webster's side. Estates like the one in question, he held, were devised subject to all liens of debts. Inasmuch as the devisees' rights had these legal infirmities, the state law had not devested them.[16]

Counsel and Court explored another aspect of the rela-

---

[13] *Ibid.,* 647. Webster's whole argument, pages 641–48. He did, however, mildly assert that the Rhode Island legislature was wrongly exercising judicial power and that therefore the state did not have a republican form of government, as required by the Constitution. Contrast this with his defense of the Rhode Island charter in *Luther* v. *Borden* (1849), discussed in Chapter III. The major part of his argument was devoted to various objections to the form of proceedings that had been followed with respect to the sale of the lands.

[14] 2 Peters 657.

[15] 9 Cranch 43 (1815). Story would have liked to have decided the *Dartmouth College* case on grounds of natural justice. See Chapter IV.

[16] Whole opinion, 2 Peters 653–63.

In *Leland* v. *Wilkinson,* 6 Peters 317 (1832) and 10 Peters 294 (1836), the Court upheld the land sales in the face of further challenges by Webster in behalf of Leland.

As previously indicated, Webster did argue some cases in behalf of state power over vested rights, but none is sufficiently noteworthy to justify discussion here. *Pawlet* v. *Clark,* 9 Cranch 292 (1815); *S. P. G. F. P.* v. *New Haven,* 8 Wheaton 464 (1823); *Carver* v. *Jackson,* 4 Peters 1 (1830).

tionship between legislative statutes and judge-made law in *Wheaton* v. *Peters* (1834). Especially significant because it was the Court's first copyright case, this controversy presented the novel issue whether the common law protected literary property when Congress had legislated on the matter. A Federal common law rule might conceivably secure an author's rights, or more probably a state's common law remedy might be available, wherever he could not rely upon the statute. If either of these possibilities existed, there were broad implications for the whole body of American law.

Webster's friend, Henry Wheaton, was the central figure of the case. Graduate of Brown in his native Rhode Island, Wheaton was a New York lawyer-politician, journalist, respected expert on international law, and in his late years American minister to Denmark and Prussia.[17] From 1816 to 1827 he was Reporter of the Supreme Court, whose decisions (together with notes, arguments by counsel, and judges' opinions) he skillfully reported each year. In those days the Court Reporter published his work privately and derived most of his salary from sales. Wheaton's successor, Richard Peters, soon after assuming office, decided to bring out a six-volume abridgement of all reports from 1790 to 1827 known as *Peters' Condensed Reports* and sold at a lower price than the original editions.[18] Against this threat to his future income from the *Reports* the incensed Wheaton sought protection in the courts. At Federal Circuit Court in Philadelphia Judge Joseph Hopkinson dismissed his petition for a perpetual injunction to stop Peters' project. From this decision he appealed to the Supreme Court at the 1834 term. The issue was whether Wheaton possessed a copyright, either at common law or under national statutes.[19]

Major responsibility for preparing and arguing Wheaton's case fell to Elijah Paine, but Webster had also been engaged far in advance and was quite familiar with the facts of this

---

[17] Elizabeth F. Baker, *Henry Wheaton, 1785–1848* (Philadelphia, 1937).

[18] *Ibid.*, 123–26.

[19] *Ibid.*, 127; 8 Peters 591–95. Judge Hopkinson's opinion is reprinted in the Appendix to 8 Peters. He decided the case at a time when Justice Baldwin was not sitting with him, a circumstance angering Wheaton. Baldwin subsequently dissented in the Supreme Court—that is, believed Wheaton's rights had been violated.

strange controversy.[20] Paine and Webster depended primarily upon the common law to maintain Wheaton's copyright.[21] English courts had recognized the right to literary property, they said, as early as the sixteenth century. Even though in 1710 Parliament had passed a statute securing copyrights to authors and publishers for limited terms, the lawyers contended that a perpetual common law right remained. Judicial precedents to support this argument, however, were not so well settled as Paine and Webster pretended. Two English cases on the eve of the Revolution were all they could turn to: (1) *Millar* v. *Taylor*,[22] decided by King's Bench in 1769, had upheld a common law copyright concurrent with a statutory right; but (2) *Donaldson* v. *Beckett*,[23] decided by the House of Lords in 1774, had ruled that the statute had taken away the whole common law right. The former case was better law than the latter, Paine and Webster asserted, because the twelve judges in *Donaldson* v. *Beckett* were evenly divided, and it was only because Lord Mansfield refrained from giving an opinion in the House of Lords that the question was determined six to five against the common law right.[24] In any event, the Parliamentary statute did not apply to America, but the common law rule did. Pennsylvania had adopted the common law, continued the attorneys, and thus Wheaton was entitled to a copyright under it.[25]

They pursued this line of reasoning because Wheaton was quite uncertain about his rights under the Congressional copyright laws of 1790 and 1802. Despite an unproved and probably unprovable statement that he had complied with statutory provisions in registering and giving public notice of his publications, his counsel argued that these procedures were not indispensable

20 Wheaton to Webster, Nov. 25, 1828, and July 22, 1831, Webster Papers (Lib. Cong.) ; Paine to Webster, Dec. 6, 1831, Webster Papers (New Hampshire Historical Society).

21 Paine's argument is in 8 Peters 595–617; Webster's, 651–54. The Reporter drew from Charles Sumner's notes of Webster's argument. Sumner to Simon Greenleaf, undated letter of 1834, Edward L. Pierce, *Memoir and Letters of Charles Sumner* (4 vols., Boston, 1877–93), I, 135–36, 136 n. 1.

22 98 English Reports 201–66.

23 1 English Reports 837–49.

24 98 English Reports 262.

25 Their argument was also that the English common law must apply because there had not been a Pennsylvania decision on the subject.

to a copyright.[26] Here Paine and Webster encountered a previous Circuit Court decision to the contrary and no doubt recognized the difficulty of securing statutory protection.[27] So their chief hope lay in the argument that Congress lacked constitutional power, and had not intended in its copyright legislation, to supersede the common law right. Instead of a national exclusive power, they insisted there was a concurrent state power to afford a common law remedy to authors and publishers.

Justice McLean delivered the majority opinion, completely rejecting the arguments of Paine and Webster. On every point he agreed with Peters' counsel, Charles J. Ingersoll and John Sergeant, that Wheaton could not hold a common law copyright and had not satisfactorily proved compliance with Federal statutes.[28] *Donaldson* v. *Beckett* (1774) in the House of Lords laid down the "well settled" rule that the common law remedy had been entirely taken away by the Parliamentary statute, McLean declared. Besides, there was no common law of the United States, he said. "The federal government is composed of twenty-four sovereign and independent states; each of which may have its local usages, customs and common law. There is no principle which pervades the union and has the authority of law, that is not embodied in the constitution or laws of the union. The common law could be made a part of our federal system," he concluded, "only by legislative adoption."[29] Thus if there were a common law copyright, it would have to be maintained under the common law of Pennsylvania; but McLean found no decision on the subject in that state. Furthermore, he held, the

---

[26] Applicants for copyrights were required to deposit copies of books at the office of the Secretary of State, to record the title in the office of the clerk of the appropriate district court, and to print the record in the newspapers. *U.S. Statutes at Large*, I, 124–26, and II, 171–72. The *Annals of Congress* for 1790 do not reveal whether these were meant to be requirements *indispensable* to copyright protection. In addition, the Supreme Court Reporter was required by other legislation to deposit eighty copies of each volume of his reports with the Secretary of State. Wheaton had apparently complied with this more expensive requirement, though not with some of the others.

[27] Justice Washington's opinion in the Federal Circuit Court of Pennsylvania. *Ewer* v. *Coxe*, 8 *Federal Cases* 917–20 (1824). Washington relied upon analysis of the statutes' language instead of upon English or American precedents.

[28] Ingersoll's and Sergeant's argument, 8 Peters 618–51 (1834). McLean's opinion, *ibid.*, 654–68.

[29] *Ibid.*, 658. Webster and Paine had not claimed a right under the common law of the United States, but only under that of Pennsylvania. Ingersoll, for the other side, had denied that there was a national common law.

national Constitution and copyright statutes occupied the whole
field and left no room for concurrent state power. Consequently
Wheaton must prove he had followed statutory requirements
(which were mandatory, not merely directory) for registering
his claim to copyright. The case was remanded to the Circuit
Court for a jury to determine this question. Finally, McLean all
but extinguished Wheaton's prospects with the terse remark that
"the court are unanimously of opinion, that no reporter has or
can have any copyright in the written opinions delivered by this
court; and that the judges thereof cannot confer on any reporter any such right."[30]

From the viewpoints both of legal history and desirable
policy, the Court's decision was perhaps more supportable than
the position of Paine and Webster. Of course the English precedent, *Donaldson* v. *Beckett* (1774), did hold that a statute
had taken away all common law remedy. Yet this solitary case,
in which both the learned judges Mansfield and Blackstone were
with the minority, did not settle the question as conclusively as
McLean asserted. Blackstone himself, and others, later erroneously interpreted the decision to mean merely that the common
law remedy was limited, but not abolished, by the statute.[31] In
America during the late eighteenth and early nineteenth centuries
whether a common law copyright existed was not a closed question. The copyright clause of the Constitution did not specifically
confer exclusive Congressional power.[32] Nor was there more

[30] 8 Peters 668. Although the judicial *opinions* could not be copyrighted, other
valuable parts of Wheaton's Reports presumably could have been. The notes, reports of arguments by counsel, and appendices were such material. Peters's *Condensed Reports* paraphrased many of Wheaton's notes, omitted arguments by counsel, and deleted concurring and dissenting opinions, the most serious weakness of all.
Today the set is seldom used.

[31] Blackstone, *Commentaries,* II, 405–07.

[32] Article I, sec. 8, par. 8 of the Constitution provides that Congress shall
have power "to promote the progress of science and useful arts, by securing for
limited times to authors and inventors the exclusive right to their respective
writings and discoveries." One early indication of sentiment favoring national exclusive power is *Federalist 43:* "The States cannot separately make effectual provision for [the copyright of authors]." Story in his *Commentaries on the Constitution,* III, secs. 1146–51, said the intent of the framers was not to permit concurrent
state power.

See the excellent summary of the early history of copyright law in England
and America in William W. Crosskey, *Politics and the Constitution in the History
of the United States* (2 vols., Chicago, 1953), II, 477–80, 486. He concludes that the
constitutional clause was intended to remove all common law protection of copyright
and to delegate the entire power to Congress.

than a handful of cases up to 1834 that threw any light at all on the subject. But some judicial pronouncements, as well as political sentiment, had opposed the applicability of the common law by itself (without reference to statutes) to cases in the Federal courts.[33] Moreover, statutory protection would operate more effectively in the interests of authors and the public. It would be vested only after the holder had followed prescribed procedures, would terminate at some future date, and would not remain in possession of the publisher for all time to come. One great abuse, against which advocates of statutory protection had complained on both sides of the Atlantic, had been the common law doctrine of *perpetual* copyright possessed by publishers whose interests were not always the same as those either of authors or of the reading public. The case of *Wheaton* v. *Peters* clarified a point of longstanding doubt and, more significantly, provided a rule still accepted today. Authors can now claim common law rights before they publish their works, but afterward they can rely only upon the copyright statutes.[34]

Strict application of a sound rule of law does not, however, always do moral justice in individual cases. Such may have been true in this instance. Suffering heavy financial losses and embittered by what he felt to be "the unjust and illiberal manner" in which he had been treated, Henry Wheaton firmly believed that not only the unprincipled Richard Peters but false friends on the bench had victimized him. Wheaton charged that Story had corresponded with Judge Hopkinson before the case came up to Washington and had promised he would confirm the Circuit Court's decision against the copyright. And Webster had in his possession, asserted Wheaton, "something in writing under the hand of one of their learned Bench which, if made public, would condemn him [Story] to infamy."[35] Story himself was uncomfortable about the decision; his old friend Wheaton broke with him completely, and his usually steady admirer Chancellor Kent protested the "severity" of the decision. But it was,

---

[33] Justice Chase on circuit in *U.S.* v. *Worral,* 2 Dallas 384 (1798) ; Marshall on circuit in *Livingston* v. *Jefferson,* 15 *Federal Cases* 660 (1811) ; the Supreme Court in *U.S.* v. *Hudson,* 7 Cranch 32 (1812), and *Jackson* v. *Chew,* 12 Wheaton 153 (1827).

[34] Philip Wittenberg, *The Law of Literary Property* (Cleveland, 1957).

[35] Baker, *Wheaton,* 129–31.

wrote the Justice, one of the "many bitter cups we are not at liberty to pass by."[36]

A kind of property similar to a copyright is the patent. Not long before the *Wheaton* case Webster argued *Pennock* v. *Dialogue* (1829),[37] posing one of the first patent questions to the Court. As he would for authors in *Wheaton,* the lawyer asked for very broad protection of inventors, but with no more success. His client had perfected an air and water hose, for which he obtained a patent some years later. Prior to filing for a patent he had assigned the use of the hose to another person for a consideration. Did this constitute "public use" in legal terms? And did it therefore nullify the inventor's statement to the patent office, as required by the law of 1793, that his hose was previously "not known or used"? Webster contended it did not, but this time the English precedents were quite clearly against him.[38] So Story, speaking for the Court, held an inventor must strictly comply with the Congressional statute. If he permitted public use of his invention before filing an application for a patent, he forfeited his rights.

This was an age of invention, a time of scientific and technological progress. As a result American courts heard a constantly increasing number of patent cases. An example is *Goodyear* v. *Day* (1852), the leading case in a series of about three dozen concerning Charles Goodyear's invention of a process for vulcanizing rubber.[39] Known as the "India Rubber Case," it typified the difficulties of the inventor in securing his rights and benefits against the perennial interloper. In addition to its legal and economic significance, interest in the controversy was heightened by the circumstances of the hearing by Federal Circuit Court at Trenton, New Jersey. In March, 1852, Secretary of State Webster came up from Washington to make what would be his last full-scale oral argument. Goodyear had overcome the seventy-year-old cabinet member's reluctance to represent him

[36] Kent to Story, April 11, 1834, *Proceedings of the Massachusetts Historical Society,* Second Series, XIV (Boston, 1901), 417; Story to Kent, May 17, 1834, William W. Story (ed.), *Life and Letters of Joseph Story* (2 vols., Boston, 1851), II, 182.

[37] 2 Peters 1–24.

[38] *Ibid.,* 4–7. He said that, unlike the United States, England had granted patents as exceptions to her statutes against monopolies. Statute of 21 James I, ch. 3.

[39] 10 *Federal Cases* 678–84 (1852). See other cases in this volume.

by offering a fee of ten thousand dollars and five thousand more if the decision was favorable. Here was a windfall that would enable Webster to pacify some of his numerous creditors.[40] Both he and his opponent Rufus Choate showed the spectators they had lost little of the eloquence for which they were famous.[41] The outcome was a victory for Goodyear. But in the course of gaining it, Webster won an important point for patent claimants generally. On the question whether the Court should submit the issues of fact from the massive record to a jury, he convinced the judges that they themselves could determine the issues on equitable grounds and grant an injunction.[42] In Webster's opinion this meant that inventors' rights would be safer in the hands of sober-minded judges than in those of juries who might be swayed by popular cries of monopoly against patent holders.

Efforts to place property under the protection of a national common law, separate from state systems, were persistent. Despite judicial refusals to declare a Federal common law to punish crimes and to protect various private rights (such as copyrights), these efforts bore some fruit. In certain branches of the law there would indeed be a body of rules uniform for the whole country and perhaps more generous toward business enterprise.

A long step in this direction was *Swift* v. *Tyson* (1842).[43] At the 1840 term Webster apparently made an oral argument in the case; and then in 1842 his associate, Thomas Fessenden, submitted their printed brief under Fessenden's name only.[44] Their opponent was the rising young lawyer and author Richard Henry Dana. At issue was a principle of commercial law relating to bills of exchange. Swift, Webster's client, brought an action

[40] Other parties interested in maintaining Goodyear's patent promised Webster another thousand dollars if he won. George Griswold to Webster, Mar. 18, 1852, *WS*, XVI, 665, n. 2. Shortly after the decision and just before his death, Webster reminded Griswold of the promise. Oct. 8, 1852, *ibid.*, 665.

[41] Samuel G. Brown (ed.), *The Works of Rufus Choate with a Memoir of His Life* (2 vols., Boston, 1862), I, 508–09. Webster's argument is in *WS*, XV, 437–72. The eleven-page manuscript brief is in the Webster Papers (Lib. Cong.), VIII.

[42] Justice Grier's opinion, 10 *Federal Cases*, 683–84 (1852).

[43] 16 Peters 1.

[44] Thomas Fessenden to William T. Carroll, Jan. 18 and 23, 1840, Clerk's File, MS. Records of the Supreme Court (National Archives); Warren, *Sup. Ct. in U.S. Hist.*, II, 362–63. Warren refers to Webster's associate as William P. Fessenden.

in the United States Circuit Court of New York for non-payment of a bill of exchange against Tyson, who relied upon decisions of the state courts in his defense. The central question was whether the Federal courts had to apply the rule laid down by the state decisions. Section thirty-four of the Judiciary Act of 1789 provided that "the *laws* of the several States, except where the Constitution, treaties, or statutes of the United States shall otherwise require or provide, shall be regarded as rules of decision, in trials at common law [by the courts of the United States] in cases where they apply."[45] Were state judicial decisions "laws" within the meaning of the Act of 1789? Or did the word "laws" refer only to state statutes and constitutions? Webster and Fessenden answered "no" to the first question and "yes" to the second. Such a matter of importance to the general commerce of the nation as bills of exchange, they also insisted, demanded uniform national rules instead of conflicting state rules. The Court therefore ought to apply a "common mercantile law" for all the states. A final point of the printed brief which Webster may have developed orally at some length, referred to the power of Congress to regulate "commerce between the states." Therefore, to follow differing state decisions on bills of exchange, then serving as an important instrument of business for the nation, would infringe upon this Congressional power.[46]

Dana responded energetically to this mode of reasoning. His brief, as contained in the Reports, barely suggests what must have been a strong argument. The Court's own precedents forbade its declaring, by mere judicial fiat, a common law for the whole nation. If Congress had not done so, or constitutionally could not, neither could the Court. Dana's prediction of what would occur if his opponents' arguments were accepted, was remarkably accurate from the viewpoint of later history. There would be, he warned, just one more system of rules, a national one in addition to those of the several states, all of which would lead to perpetual conflict between the courts of the two levels of government.[47]

[45] *U.S. Statutes at Large*, I, 92. Italics added.
[46] 16 Peters 3-9 (1842).
[47] *Ibid.*, 10-14. Dana did not cite *Wheaton* v. *Peters*, which would have supported his argument.

In a majority opinion that would subsequently be a fertile source of discussion, Story held the Court must lay down its own rule of commercial law because general principles beyond local usages were involved. State judicial decisions were not "laws" within the meaning of the Act of 1789, he said; and though the Supreme Court would give the most "deliberate attention and respect" to the decisions, it did not have to follow them.[48] For nearly a century *Swift* v. *Tyson* provided the basis for an expanding system of court-made law within Federal jurisdiction. Critics attacked the decision, however, as an unfair haven for corporations seeking more lenient treatment by Federal judges than the corporations might receive from state judges. In 1923 Charles Warren, noted historian of the Court, presented evidence to show that Story had not interpreted the Judiciary Act of 1789 as its framers had intended.[49] And in 1938 Justice Brandeis delivered the *coup de grâce* to *Swift* v. *Tyson* by holding that Story's opinion was not only legally erroneous but unconstitutional as well.[50] Since that date the Federal Courts have religiously followed state rules of decision in this area of law. Some scholars believe, however, that Story and Webster were right when they emphasized the snarls that would result from diverse systems of state commercial law.[51]

If property rights were as extensive as Webster believed them to be, what were the boundaries? Though a person or a corporation might enjoy the maximum freedom to use property, there were still some limits to these uses. One property holder could not commit a wrong upon another in the supposed exercise of his rights. Nor could he do certain things that would conflict with public policy or flagrantly violate the community's sense of essential good and right. Such was the question in *Vidal* v. *Girard's Executors* (1844). As counsel in this case, Webster challenged a will devising property for purposes which allegedly undermined the religious values of society. It was true that he represented disappointed heirs putting forward their claims to the property, but more significantly he was now contending for

48 *Ibid.,* 14–22.
49 "New Light on the History of the Federal Judiciary Act of 1789," *Harvard Law Review,* XXXVII (1923), 81–90.
50 *Erie Railroad Co.* v. *Tompkins,* 304 U.S. 64 (1938).
51 Crosskey, *Politics and the Const.,* II, 856–60, 904–05, 912–37.

restrictions upon the testator's discretion in disposing of his estate. In this sense, his role was to oppose a private property right when it might transgress standards of public ethics.

At Philadelphia, on December 26, 1831, the wealthiest man in the United States died. He was Stephen Girard, merchant prince and banker. Girard had personified in his lifetime the American dream of success achieved through natural capacity, intense industry, and favorable circumstances. Born in Bordeaux, France, and receiving little formal education, Girard had gone to sea as a boy. He had come to Philadelphia during the Revolution and soon made a fortune in shipping, other forms of commerce, and banking. His career had been distinguished not only by his amazing Midas-like touch in business affairs but also by his deeply felt civic responsibility. To the dismay of his nieces and nephews, the childless widower had decided upon a most unusual last act of benevolence. Gathered around the casket, Girard's relatives were shocked when they heard his will read. The old man had left each of them disappointingly small bequests and had given the bulk of his estate, worth about seven million dollars, to the city of Philadelphia to establish a school for orphan boys.[52]

With his customary exactitude Girard prescribed the kind of school he wished. The location, the construction of buildings (to be surrounded by a ten-foot wall), the food and clothing of the students, the subjects of instruction—more practical than theoretical—all were carefully specified. The school must accept only poor, white, orphan boys between the ages of six and ten. The boys could remain until they were fourteen, or at the most eighteen, when the institution would bind them out to "suitable occupations." The provision of the will which became most controversial required that

no ecclesiastic, missionary, or minister of any sect whatsoever, shall ever hold or exercise any station or duty whatever in the said college; nor shall any such person ever be admitted for any purpose, or as a visitor, within the premises appropriated to the purposes of the said college.

In making this restriction, I do not mean to cast any reflection upon

[52] Henry E. Wildes, *Lonely Midas: The Story of Stephen Girard* (New York, 1943); Cheesman A. Herrick, *Stephen Girard Founder* (Philadelphia, 1923); John B. McMaster, *The Life and Times of Stephen Girard* (2 vols., Philadelphia, 1918).

any sect or person whatsoever; but, as there is such a multitude of sects, and such a diversity of opinion amongst them, I desire to keep the tender minds of the orphans, who are to derive advantage from this bequest, free from the excitement which clashing doctrines and sectarian controversy are so apt to produce; my desire is, that all the instructors and teachers in the college shall take pains to instil into the minds of the scholars the purest principles of morality, so that, on their entrance into active life, they may, from inclination and habit, evince benevolence towards their fellow-creatures, and a love of truth, sobriety, and industry, adopting at the same time such religious tenets as their matured reason may enable them to prefer.[53]

Girard's relatives decided to challenge the validity of the will in the Federal Circuit Court, which after much delay dismissed their bill in equity in 1841. Their intention from the outset had been to appeal to the Supreme Court, and this they now did.[54] Arguments were heard at Washington in 1843; but owing to absences on the bench, the Court ordered reargument for the following term.

It was early February, 1844, when *Vidal* v. *Girard's Executors* again came on. Into the small courtroom pressed a great throng of spectators, lawyers from far and near interested in the keenly contested legal issues, Congressmen from the chambers above in the Capitol, fashionably dressed women who distracted attention from the judicial proceedings, many persons simply attracted by the color and excitement of the scene. In the aisles and corners, around the attorneys' tables, behind and between the judges' desks were the people fortunate enough to squeeze inside. Hundreds not so fortunate were turned away. Several newspapers assigned reporters to the case. The New York *Herald* carried long daily dispatches describing the setting and commenting upon the arguments.[55]

The Court, Justice Story presiding in the absence of the

---

[53] The sections of the will relating to the school are printed in 2 Howard 129–38 (1844).

[54] In his brief at Washington, Webster said the case was not even argued in the Circuit Court because that court in *Magill* v. *Brown* (1833) had previously decided a similar question in such manner that it was "useless to renew the argument." 2 Howard 172. The *Magill* case will be discussed below.

[55] New York *Herald*, Feb. 7, 8, and 10, 1844; Warren, *Sup. Ct. in U.S. Hist.*, II, 398–403. The following account of the proceedings draws heavily from the *Herald* dispatches.

Chief Justice, showed no inclination to hurry. For ten days counsel probed to the fullest each and every question. When they were done, they had attempted all that learning and oratory could accomplish. Commencing for the plaintiffs and thus attacking the will was the veteran Walter Jones, who spoke for two and a half days. On the other side to defend Girard's bequest was Horace Binney of Philadelphia, drawn out of retirement for this occasion. Binney took more than three days, as he made one of the most brilliant arguments in the Court's history. His associate, John Sergeant, continued for the next two days. Finally came Webster, filling out Jones's points, contending against the profound effect that Binney had made, unremittingly assailing the "anti-Christian" testament of Girard.

In his own calm and competent way Jones performed his task well, though observers eager for display complained about his "soporifics."[56] The city of Philadelphia, Jones maintained, was incapable of taking the trust for establishing and administering Girard's school. He explored the early English doctrine of charitable uses, which, he said, did not support such devises as this one at common law. The purposes and beneficiaries of these trusts were too uncertain for the courts to protect them with the usual rules and remedies. Therefore in Queen Elizabeth's time, Parliament had passed a statute of charitable uses conferring upon the chancellor jurisdiction at equity over these trusts.[57] Pennsylvania, continued Jones, had adopted the common law but not the statute of 43 Elizabeth (1601). Lacking equity jurisdiction, the courts in that state could not care for Girard's charitable bequest, and so it was void. Furthermore, the corporate charter of the city of Philadelphia did not authorize it to take the trust; and since a corporation has only limited powers explicitly granted, the city could not act.[58] The attorney's con-

---

[56] 2 Howard 143–46 (1844); New York *Herald,* Feb. 7, 1844.

[57] The statute of 1601 is said to have been passed to counteract earlier prohibitions of devises to religious societies. The prohibitions had had the purpose of preserving royal revenue that otherwise might have been lost through alienation by mortmain under the rules of feudal tenure. During Henry VIII's time, such a prohibition had been part of the Reformation attack upon the old religious societies whose charities had been called "superstitious uses." William Blackstone, *Commentaries,* II, 272, 376; III, 428.

[58] This was a weak point because Pennsylvania had enacted a law in 1832 authorizing the city to take the trust. Furthermore, any defect in the charter could readily be remedied through amendment by the state. The Court had already de-

cluding point was that the will's provision excluding ministers of the church from the school was anti-Christian, thus repugnant to the state constitution, laws, and public policy. This position he left for Webster to develop in greater depth.

Horace Binney rose to defend the validity of the charity. Though past the prime of life, he was still a handsome figure. His large frame, well-proportioned features, pure white hair, and gold rimmed spectacles gave him a striking physical appearance. His elocution was perfection itself. Distinctly and harmoniously the words flowed forth to his captivated audience. Occasionally he made an excursion into literature or philosophy to illustrate a general principle, but seldom did he wander very far from his solidly built legal argument. "It has been like a huge screw," wrote a reporter, "slowly turning round on its threads, but at last coming down on the object to be squeezed with irresistible power."[59]

The core of Binney's massive brief was his contention that charitable uses were and ever had been encouraged by Anglo-Saxon jurisprudence.[60] His goal was to pulverize the foundation of Webster's and Jones's point that chancery courts could not execute such trusts without statutory authorization. An obstacle to this purpose was a Supreme Court decision by Chief Justice Marshall in *Baptist Association* v. *Hart's Executors* (1819), holding that a devise by a Virginia citizen to a religious society could not be supported in a court of equity without statutory jurisdiction and was too vague and uncertain to be supported in a court of law.[61] Skillfully, Binney elected to sidestep the *Hart* case by showing that Pennsylvania's policy, unlike Virginia's, had always encouraged charitable uses. Nevertheless when he had finished, he had in effect demolished the *Hart* ruling.

---

cided that a city could take a trust. See *Inglis* v. *Sailor's Snug Harbor,* 3 Peters 99 (1830), which Webster lost after an unusually vigorous argument.

[59] New York *Herald,* Feb. 10, 1844; Nathan Sargent, *Public Men and Events* (2 vols., Philadelphia, 1875), II, 212–13; Charles C. Binney, *The Life of Horace Binney* (Philadelphia, 1903), 215–26.

[60] Binney's argument is summarized in 2 Howard 146–64.

[61] 4 Wheaton 1. Marshall relied upon what he thought was the policy of Virginia on the subject. In 1792 Virginia had repealed all the English statutes, including 43 Elizabeth on charitable uses, which had previously been the law of the state. In the *Girard* case Jones had apparently not emphasized the *Hart* precedent, and Webster gave it slight attention.

Binney knew more about the legal history of charitable trusts in 1844 than Marshall had in 1819. In the meantime the English Record Commission had published a calendar of proceedings in chancery, from which Binney cited fifty cases of charities supported by that court prior to the statute of 1601.[62] It appeared quite clear that the common law rule had been different from that stated by Marshall and now by plaintiffs' counsel. Since Pennsylvania had adopted the common law, it did not matter that she had not also adopted the statute of 43 Elizabeth. There was, moreover, a very able opinion by Justice Henry Baldwin at the United States Circuit Court of Pennsylvania in *Magill* v. *Brown* (1833).[63] Baldwin had upheld a bequest by a Pennsylvania citizen to Quaker meetings on the ground that the common law of England and of America had always been liberal toward charities. This learned opinion was all the more relevant to the *Girard* case, because it came from the Pennsylvania circuit and concerned the law of that state. And a nearly conclusive case on this point was *Zimmerman* v. *Anders*, decided the previous month by the Supreme Court of Pennsylvania and upholding a devise to an unincorporated society for the benefit of poor orphans.[64]

Binney and his colleague, John Sergeant, gave less attention to other questions.[65] The city charter of Philadelphia empowered it to hold property, they insisted, and this was sufficient authority for it to take this trust. In addition, the state constitution and especially statutes enacted in 1832 to implement the provisions of Girard's will supported the charity. Anticipating Webster's argument, they also contended that the bequest was not anti-Christian, because *lay* teaching of Christian principles was entirely possible, and indeed probable, despite the exclusion of *clerical* teachers.

The last three days of the hearing were Webster's. Always responsive to popular interest and excitement on such oc-

---

[62] The calendar of chancery proceedings was published in 1827. Thus it was unnecessary for Binney to travel to England to study the manuscript rolls as erroneous accounts said he did. See, for example, Henry Wise, *Seven Decades of the Union* (Philadelphia, 1881), 216.

[63] 16 *Federal Cases* 408.

[64] 6 Watts and Sergeant 218 (Pa., 1844).

[65] Sergeant's argument is in 2 Howard 164–72. It was a strong argument but not as eloquently delivered as Binney's. Sargent, *Public Men and Events*, II, 213.

casions, he now mustered all his oratorical skill. No doubt an equally strong stimulus was the possibility of a very large fee, should he be successful in breaking Girard's will. But he had a hard case, and he must have realized it. The prospect of winning over the Court on the common law question was decidedly dim, and so Webster quite wisely took the path more promising of victory. Most of his argument related to the will's provision excluding clergymen from the school, whereas his treatment of other points was perfunctory.[66]

Only a court of equity, Webster began, not a court of law, could sustain such a bequest, because the beneficiaries were an indefinite, general class of poor orphans. "No individual can acquire any right or interest," he continued, and "nobody, therefore, can come forward as a party, in a court of law, to claim participation in the gift." Consequently the special rules of equity on charities must support the trust, if it was supportable at all. Was this devise, he asked, truly a charity "in the eye of equitable jurisprudence?"[67]

Of course his answer was that it was not. The exclusion clause would establish a system of education "derogatory" to the Christian religion. Indeed the will attached an "opprobrium to the whole profession of the clergy," in whose defense the lawyer thereupon delivered an extended encomium. No other body of men had done more for humanity than the Christian ministry, but Girard would heartlessly exclude them from his school, even to offer consolation to the sick and dying. To say that laymen could teach the Christian principles of morality was completely untenable, thought Webster, since many churches forbade lay preaching. And more to the point, it would violate the testator's intention to shield young and tender minds from clashing doctrines of conflicting sects. What Girard really desired was the total exclusion of Christian knowledge, and he would justify this course of action with the old "infidel" argument that there were too many differences among the sects. Actually the theory behind Girard's system, he asserted, was exactly like Thomas Paine's in the *Age of Reason*. But a school of learning to be a charity,

---

[66] A full report of Webster's argument is in *WS*, XI, 133–84. A shorter summary is in 2 Howard 172–83.

[67] *WS*, XI, 138.

the attorney insisted, must be founded on those principles which Girard would shut out. Courts of equity could not be called upon to uphold such an insidious project, for it was no charity.[68]

Repeatedly Webster attacked Girard's reasons for prohibiting the ministry from his school. Notwithstanding differences of theological opinion among the churches, he contended, there were great basic truths upon which all agreed: the existence of God, the divine authority of the Bible, and man's responsibility in another world for his conduct in this world. Just because the tree may be twisted and twined, Girard ought not lay the axe to the tree's roots. Far better permit some religious doubts and controversies than deny these young people any opportunity to learn the precepts of Christianity. Webster warmed to the subject as he outlined the evils he foresaw: "Why Sir, it is vain to talk about the destructive tendency of such a system; to argue upon it is to insult the understanding of every man; it is mere, sheer, low, ribald, vulgar deism and infidelity!"[69] At that moment applause broke the tense quiet of the Courtroom.

Toward the end of his argument, Webster felt obliged to counteract as best he could the telling effect of Binney's discussion of charitable uses at common law. One of his assistants, ironically Binney's son-in-law, had drafted a hurried note on early charities in the Chancellor's Court. Obdurately Webster still maintained that equity had not protected charities until the passage of the statute of 1601 and that Pennsylvania, not having adopted that statute, could not now so protect them.[70] But he more heavily emphasized the view that Girard's bequest was contrary to the state's public policy, founded, he said, on Christianity. Though Pennsylvania had always been tolerant of all religions, it had not permitted blasphemy or scoffing at religion. Thus the objectionable feature of the will was *exclusion* of the ministry instead of omission of a positive provision for teaching Christianity. Or it might have been acceptable for Girard in his lifetime to establish a school of this sort, but he

68 *Ibid.*, 139–58.
69 *Ibid.*, 167–68.
70 2 Howard 178–81 (1844). Webster's assistant and Binney's son-in-law was John Cadwallader, "the principal *grubber* after facts and documents," according to the New York *Herald*, Feb. 7, 1844.

could not do it by a devise, since a court of equity would then have to execute it.[71]

The lawyers' peroration was a mixture of vehemence and hope.

I believe this plan [he concluded], this scheme, was unblessed in all its purposes, and in all its original plans. Unwise in all its frame and theory, while it lives it will lead an annoyed and troubled life, and leave an unblessed memory when it dies. If I could persuade myself that this court would come to such a decision as, in my opinion, the public good and the law require, and if I could believe that any humble efforts of my own had contributed in the least to lead to such a result, I should deem it the crowning mercy of my professional life.[72]

There is more than the ordinary information on reactions to Webster's argument. His opponent Binney, well aware of his courtroom skills, followed the argument quite carefully, anxious to repel any unfair or unfounded statement and ready to interject a question or comment. At times, the two lawyers exchanged animated remarks, for example when the two disagreed about the distinction between religious "tenets" and religious "opinions."[73] Yet Webster also respected Binney's prowess and gave the Philadelphian close attention.[74] Understandably, counsel on both sides felt the nervous excitement of such a case involving a highly important legal question, not to mention millions of dollars.[75]

Accounts by those present in Court tell of a deep emotional response by the audience to Webster's oratory. His defense of the power and influence of the Christian religion, said the New York *Herald's* reporter, caused many to shed tears. A

[71] 2 Howard 178 (1844); *WS*, XI, 174–76.

[72] *WS*, XI, 177.

[73] *Ibid.*, 165–67.

[74] The New York *Herald* reporter, much more favorable toward Binney than Webster perhaps because the paper was Democratic, wrote that Webster and the others in Court were sometimes taken into deeper water by the Philadelphian than "they commonly swim in." Now and then during his argument Binney spoke directly to Webster. "In quoting from one of Mr. Webster's own arguments in 13 Peters," Binney begged Webster "to answer his own authorities. Webster answered 'That was a *bad* case, and I had to make my arguments to suit my case!' This raised quite a laugh." *Herald*, Feb. 8, 1844.

[75] Jones and Sergeant had a lively dispute, according to an observer, about the former's remarks on the "anti-Christian" will of Girard. Wise, *Seven Decades*, 217–18.

particularly touching passage was the lawyer's allusion to the story of Jesus and the children: " 'Suffer little children to come unto me.' Unto *me;* he did not send them first for lessons in morals to the schools of the Pharisees. . . . He said nothing of different creeds or clashing doctrines; but he opened at once to the youthful mind the everlasting fountain of living waters, the only source of eternal truths."[76] Altogether, Webster's private secretary later wrote, he unfolded "a splendid sermon on the Christian ministry, as well as the religious instruction of the young."[77]

At Washington on the last day of Webster's argument churchmen of several denominations held a meeting and resolved to ask the attorney to prepare that part of his remarks on the exclusion clause for publication. They proposed to distribute it throughout the country to demonstrate "the vital importance of Christianity to the success of our free institutions, and its necessity as the basis of all useful moral education."[78] Webster consented to give the newspaper report of his argument a cursory reading to correct "material errors," and afterwards a pamphlet edition was circulated widely.[79] After reading the *Herald's* report, a friend enthusiastically requested him to prepare it also for publication in the religious journals.[80]

Some reactions were less enthusiastic. Unfriendly observers suspected Webster of striking an insincere pose as he sermonized. It was the "greatest novelty of the season," said one newspaper, to see him "working himself up into such a fervor of piety as to shed tears while contemplating the malign influence which the bequest would exercise upon the destinies of the rising generation." Another paper said, "It is not known when he will 'take orders.' "[81] Years later Webster's biographer, Henry Cabot

[76] *WS*, XI, 153–54.

[77] Charles Lanman, *The Private Life of Daniel Webster* (New York, 1853), 110.

[78] P. R. Fendall et al. to Webster, Feb. 13, 1844, *WS*, XI, 133–34.

[79] Webster to Fendall et al. Feb. 13, 1844, *ibid*. The pamphlet is entitled *Mr. Webster's Speech in Defence of the Christian Ministry, and in Favor of the Religious Instruction of the Young. Delivered in the Supreme Court of the United States, February 10, 1844, in the Case of Stephen Girard's Will*. Washington: Gales and Seaton, 1844. 60 pp.

[80] Hiram Ketchum to Webster, Feb. 21, 1844, Webster Papers (New Hamp. Hist. Soc.).

[81] Boston *Post*, Feb. 16, 1844, and the *Pennsylvanian*, Feb. 14, 1844, quoted in Warren, *Sup. Ct. in U.S. Hist.*, II, 406.

Lodge, ever doubtful of his subject's moral strength, declared, "If he had flourished in the Middle Ages he would have been a staunch and honest supporter of the strongest government and the dominant church."[82] John Quincy Adams, who attended Court during argument, was convinced that Girard had inserted an "infidel" provision in his will, but he suspected the motives of everybody, including Webster. Adams believed the report that if Webster won the case, he would receive fifty thousand dollars "for his share of the plunder."[83] Webster's anticipation of a handsome fee, he implied, may have generated his religious fervor. There were others who thought that the attorney's object went beyond this judicial case. He had recently extricated himself from Tyler's cabinet, this was a presidential election year, and his part in the great will case might promote him for the Whig nomination and election. This pleasant possibility was suggested by a friend who assured Webster that he was now "the man for the clergy, and all the clergy of the country."[84]

The effects upon the judges were what mattered most. Although only Story's reactions are now known, those of his associates were probably similar. "I was not a little amused," the Justice remarked, "with the manner in which, on each side, the language of the Scripture, and the doctrines of Christianity, were brought in to point the argument; and to find the Court engaged in hearing homilies of faith, and expositions of Christianity, with almost the formality of lectures from the pulpit."[85] On the whole, Binney's "masterly" argument impressed Story much more than Webster's, which seemed to him to be "an address to the prejudices of the clergy" and largely irrelevant to the law of the case.[86]

Story's views were especially important, because it was he who delivered the Court's unanimous opinion, upholding the

[82] Henry C. Lodge, *Daniel Webster* (Boston, 1883), 104.

[83] *Memoirs of J. Q. Adams*, XI, 507, 510.

[84] Hiram Ketcham to Webster, Feb. 21, 1844, Webster Papers (New Hamp. Hist. Soc.).

[85] Story to Mrs. Story, Feb. 7 and 10, 1844, Story (ed.), *Story*, II, 467–68.

[86] Story to James Kent, Aug. 31, 1844, *ibid.*, 469. That the other justices reacted similarly is indicated by Story's remark to Kent that "the Court was unanimous, and not a single sentence was altered by my brothers, as I originally drew it."

validity of the Girard will.[87] There was no reason to doubt, Story said, that the city of Philadelphia could take as a trust the property bequeathed to it. To support his holding, he cited the city's charter and Pennsylvania statutes of 1832 enacted to give effect to the trust. Then with characteristic penetration, he inquired into the question whether the uses of the trust were charitable and capable of execution at equity. He adopted Binney's line of reasoning but explored some new ground as well. Much weight was given to Baldwin's circuit opinion in *Magill* v. *Brown* (1833), holding a charity good under equity. And the cases drawn from the calendar of English Public Record Commissioners, continued the Justice, shed new light on the subject. Very recent cases in England and in Pennsylvania itself were conclusive expositions of the common law of charitable uses, he ruled. Binney had overlooked the English cases,[88] but had cited the Pennsylvania decision of *Zimmerman* v. *Anders* (1844). Story was somewhat hesitant as he faced Marshall's decision against equitable jurisdiction in *Baptist Association* v. *Hart* (1819). Though distinguishing the facts of the present case from *Hart,* the total effect of his opinion was to overrule it.[89] Finally, he rejected Webster's contention that excluding the clergy invalidated the will. He did not agree that this provision forbade religious teaching of any kind in the school. Laymen could still instruct the children in Christian morality, he thought; and if this were an imperfect system, it was not a matter for this Court to decide.

Vidal v. *Girard's Executors* was more than a colorful, entertaining episode in the history of the Supreme Court. The case represented the culmination of the development over many years of a liberal law of charity. The legal precedents reaching back to earlier days and extending through the first part of the nineteenth century obviously had not emerged from a vacuum or

[87] 2 Howard 183–201.

[88] *Incorporated Society* v. *Richards,* 1 Drury and Warren 258.

[89] In the *Hart* case the devisee was an *unincorporated* society, but in this case it was the corporation of Philadelphia. Virginia had expressly repealed the statute of 43 Elizabeth, while Pennsylvania had made no such explicit declaration of policy. The Court had distinguished the facts and thus sidestepped but not overruled the *Hart* precedent in *Inglis* v. *Trustees of Sailor's Snug Harbor,* 3 Peters 99 (1830).

even from sheer logic of jurisprudence. They reflected a deep social belief in America that benevolence was highly desirable and must receive maximum encouragement. The *Girard* decision was a large forward step in encouraging the whole field of philanthropy that would be significant throughout the next century.[90]

By mid century Webster could feel assured by the steadily expanding body of precedents available for the protection of property. In the cases he and his colleagues had argued they had asked the Court to go very far toward that end. Often it had consented. Not only did the contract clause of the Constitution become a trustworthy shield for private rights of many kinds against state power, but the common law and principles of natural justice were valuable supplements. Inherent judicial power, exclusive of constitutional and statutory authority, was also a possible instrument for the purpose. But usually there were laws and public policy, state or national, upon which to rely. Thus though the Court announced a Federal common law on commercial transactions in *Swift* v. *Tyson,* it did not go beyond the statutes on copyrights in *Wheaton* v. *Peters.* Where exercising a private right, such as a philanthropic devise, promoted the public good, the judges quite willingly approved. Basically bench and bar believed that private rights were consistent with the public good, and it was on that ground that the *Girard* decision stood.

[90] Irwin G. Wyllie, "The Search for an American Law of Charity, 1776–1844," *Mississippi Valley Historical Review,* XLVI (Sept., 1959), 203–21; Howard S. Miller, *The Legal Foundations of American Philanthropy, 1776–1844* (Madison, 1961).

Since its opening in 1848 Girard College has grown into the very successful institution it is today. In 1957 the Supreme Court held that Philadelphia could not exclude Negro students because the will violated the Fourteenth Amendment. But the city was then divested of all connections with the school, and the Court at its next term accepted this evasive tactic making the institution private instead of public. *Pennsylvania* v. *Board of Trusts of Philadelphia,* 353 U.S. 230 (1957); 391 Pennsylvania Reports 434–86 (1958); 357 U.S. 570, 358 U.S. 858 (1958).

VII

THE NATIONAL BANK

Webster was very interested in the Second Bank of the United States from the time Congress chartered that corporation until it closed its doors over twenty years later. As a member of the House in 1815 and 1816, he participated actively in the debates on establishing the Bank. He thought the nation's experience during the War of 1812, when unrestrained state-chartered banks threw currency and credit into confusion, unquestionably dictated Congressional legislation. But he did not much like the kind of corporation created in April, 1816, because the government subscribed one-fifth of the stock, the President appointed one-fifth of the directors, and there were no requirements for redemption of notes in specie. He preferred a completely private, basically conservative bank and therefore voted against the bill. Nevertheless he and others of a similar mind had gained a partial victory by defeating a proposal to set up essentially a governmentally owned bank free to issue large amounts of inflated paper.[1] Predominantly private in its capitalization and management, the Second Bank of the United States not only performed all the usual banking functions but also served as a depository for the government's funds and as a note-issuing agency for the circulation of currency. Notwithstanding his initial reservations, Webster became a warm friend of this corporation in the years ahead.

[1] Claude M. Fuess, *Daniel Webster* (2 vols., Boston, 1930), I, 180–84.

Hostility toward the Bank pervaded the South and the West. Local interests seemed endangered by this economic giant of Philadelphia, extending its numerous branches into these states with no obligation of obtaining their consent. By their constitutions of 1816 and 1818, Indiana and Illinois excluded branches of the Bank, while Georgia, North Carolina, Maryland, Tennessee, Kentucky, and Ohio laid heavy taxes upon those branches within their jurisdictions. Further animosity arose when the Bank suddenly reversed its overly generous loan policy and demanded that inflationist state banks redeem their paper. The "Eastern Monster" incurred blame for precipitating the Panic of 1819 and the consequent severe depression. An unsuccessful effort in Congress to repeal the corporation's charter reflected continuing opposition to the Bank.[2]

Maryland's tax upon the Baltimore branch occasioned the first Supreme Court case involving the constitutionality of the 1816 charter. The state brought an action against Cashier James W. McCulloch for violating the statute requiring banknotes to be issued on stamped paper. McCulloch had refused to purchase stamps from the state or to pay a heavy tax. Recognized as a test case, *McCulloch* v. *Maryland* quickly went through the state tribunals, where the Bank lost, up to the Supreme Court at the February term of 1819.[3]

Dispensing with its general rule that permitted only two attorneys for either party, the Court heard three arguments on each side from February 22 to March 3. Webster, Attorney General William Wirt, and William Pinkney appeared for the Bank; and Joseph Hopkinson, Walter Jones, and Luther Martin represented the state. Counsel exhaustively discussed every aspect of the controversy before a mass of spectators crowded into the temporary Courtroom in the Capitol basement.[4]

Webster opened the case with a succinct, lucid examination of two questions: (1) can Congress establish a bank; and

[2] Ralph C. H. Catterall, *The Second Bank of the United States* (Chicago, 1903), 60–65; Charles Warren, *The Supreme Court in United States History* (3 vols., Boston, 1923), I, 505–06; *Annals of Congress,* 15 Cong., 2 sess., Vol. II, pp. 1240–71, 1283–1328, 1330–93, 1394–1402, 1411–15.

[3] 4 Wheaton 317–22.

[4] Albert J. Beveridge, *The Life of John Marshall* (4 vols., Boston, 1916–19), IV, 283–85.

(2) can the states tax it? On the first point, he drew upon Secretary of the Treasury Alexander Hamilton's opinion of 1791 defending the constitutionality of the first national bank bill. Feigning surprise that anyone should now raise the question after thirty years of acquiescence by all three branches of the national government, Webster proceeded to elaborate the now well-known theory of implied powers. To accomplish an end within the scope of a delegated power, Congress must have discretion to select appropriate means. The framers of the Constitution, he said, did not intend "to enumerate particulars," since social progress brings on new means that may be suitable unless specifically prohibited. Then he cited the clause authorizing Congress to pass all laws necessary and proper for carrying into execution the delegated powers. Accordingly, Congress determined that the Bank was useful to assist the government in raising a revenue, in levying taxes, and in regulating the currency. The Court could not decide whether this corporation was the best possible means of accomplishing these ends, Webster contended, but could only judge whether there was a fair connection between the means and the ends. Nor was granting a charter of incorporation a power that the Constitution must specify, he concluded, because it was a universally accepted means, available to all governments, to accomplish various legitimate ends.[5]

Concerning the second question, the states' power to tax the Bank, Webster began with the premise that Congressional statutes were the supreme law of the land, as provided in Article Six of the Constitution. Consequently if Maryland's tax impeded the execution of the national law creating the Bank, it was void, and the Court must declare it so.

If the States may tax the bank [he asked], to what extent shall they tax it, and where shall they stop? An unlimited power to tax involves, necessarily, a power to destroy; because there is a limit beyond which no institution and no property can bear taxation. A question of constitutional power can hardly be made to depend on a question of more or less.[6]

Essentially, the argument here was *ad extremum*. The state must have an unrestricted taxing power, or it must have none. Other-

[5] *WS*, XV, 262–64.
[6] *Ibid.*, 265.

wise Congressional powers would be at the mercy of fluctuating state legislation. In the present instance, the lawyer asserted, Maryland was even taxing the pecuniary interest of the national government in Bank stocks. Her policy affected both the property and the fiscal operations of the United States. If the states could do this, what would prevent them from taxing, and thereby destroying, any Federal function? To Webster, the answer was obvious: such power in any degree was intolerable.[7]

Counsel for Maryland attacked the constitutionality of the Bank's charter.[8] They expounded familiar states' rights theory, strict construction of the Constitution, and narrowly defined Congressional power. Current circumstances ought to determine the necessity of a national bank, they contended. Though there were only three banks in the young nation of 1791, when Congress chartered the First Bank of the United States, there were many institutions competent to assist the government in its fiscal operations in 1816. What was constitutional when Hamilton proposed a bank might not be so twenty-five years later. To challenge the law of 1816 further, the lawyers cited the Tenth Amendment[9] and referred to the absence of a delegated Congressional power to charter corporations. The argument was carefully selective, as it had to be in an era of nationalism before a nationalistic court.

A persuasive point advanced by Joseph Hopkinson was his denial of the Bank's discretionary power to set up branches in those states not giving their consent. Even if Congress had such dubious authority, why should a mere "trading corporation" also tread upon state sovereignty? As a matter of fact, said Hopkinson, branches were unnecessary, since the parent bank could perform all essential financial functions.[10] Oddly, other counsel and the Court gave little notice to this question.[11]

Finally, Hopkinson and his colleagues defended state

[7] *Ibid.*, 265–67.

[8] Hopkinson's argument is in 4 Wheaton 330–52; Jones', *ibid.*, 362–71; Martin's, *ibid.*, 372–77.

[9] The Tenth Amendment provides: "The powers not delegated to the United States by the Constitution, nor prohibited by it to the States, are reserved to the States, respectively, or to the people."

[10] 4 Wheaton 335–37.

[11] See Marshall's brief consideration of the point in *ibid.*, 424.

power of taxation. States could tax a corporation if the national government owned all its stock, asserted counsel, and they could certainly tax a *private* institution such as this. Each of the three attorneys representing the state insisted that the taxing power was concurrent, except for the constitutional limitation on state imposts on imports (Article I, section 10).[12] Both the nation and the states, they argued, must practice restraint and forbearance. "Mutual confidence" was their formula for harmony within the Federal Union.

Closing for the Bank, Pinkney made by far the most extensive and eloquent argument.[13] Over a period of three days the attorney fascinated both visitors and judges in the packed Courtroom. Here was an example of the role lawyers of that day played in the business of the Court. Such well-built arguments, embellished by flights of oratory, often foreshadowed judicial opinions.

In his exordium Pinkney paid his respects to both justices and opposing counsel. He had fulsome praise for the Court, presenting "the proud spectacle of a peaceful judicial review of these conflicting sovereign claims by this more than Amphictyonic council." Then he awarded compliments to his opponents for their "polished elocution" and to Martin, in particular, for his "robust and hardy wit." Yet he pretended weariness with the "endless repetition" of the discussion concerning the Bank's constitutionality. Men had worn that "threadbare" topic into "tatters," he said.[14]

[12] They cited Hamilton's Federalist 32, but it should be remembered that Hamilton was writing as a propagandist for the ratification of the Constitution and therefore attempting to allay state suspicion of the new document. Any concurrent state power might still conflict with some *other* constitutional provision, such as the financial or commerce powers of Congress.

[13] Wirt went over much the same ground that Webster had, adding little worthy of note except brief reference to the contract clause of the Constitution, which he said was violated by the state. 4 Wheaton 352–62.

[14] Pinkney's exordium is printed in Henry Wheaton, *Some Account of the Life, Writings, and Speeches of William Pinkney* (New York, 1826), 161–66. The main body of his argument is in 4 Wheaton 377–400.

Pinkney had written to Webster on December 28, 1818, saying: "In the affair of the Bank of the United States (relative to the power of the Legislature of Maryland to tax it) I understand that we are on the same side. It was my intention to have asked from you an interchange of Ideas in this Cause; but I now suppose it will not be necessary, since it is said that little else than the threadbare topics connected with the constitutionality of the establishment of the Bank will be

Pinkney, nevertheless, investigated the subject at some length. In expounding the supremacy and flexibility of national power he stated a view of the Constitution that Marshall, Webster, Lincoln, and many others would reiterate in the future:

But the constitution acts directly *on* the people, by means of powers communicated directly *from* the people. No State, in its corporate capacity, ratified it; but it was proposed for adoption to popular conventions. It springs from the people, precisely as the State constitutions spring from the people, and acts on them in a similar manner. It was adopted by them in the geographical sections into which the country is divided.[15]

Like Webster, Pinkney developed the implied-powers theory and also relied upon the necessary and proper clause to justify the Bank's charter. The word "necessary," he contended, could be "qualified by the addition of adverbs of diminution or enlargement, such as very, indispensably, more, less, or absolutely."[16] Since the Constitution did not qualify it, the word deserved the most liberal interpretation.

Pinkney repeated Webster's objection that the state tax could be destructive. When a state undertakes to tax such a vital instrument of the national government, he declared, a part of the Union is taxing the whole Union. This, he thought, was entirely inadmissible, and therefore the Court must prohibit any degree of taxation.[17]

Pinkney's performance impressed no one more than Justice Story.

---

introduced into the argument, which is expected to take place early in the next term of the Supreme Court." Webster Papers (New Hampshire Historical Society), Box (1803–1840).

[15] 4 Wheaton 377. Webster's "Reply to Hayne" in the Senate debates of 1830 and Lincoln's First Inaugural Address expressed this theory of the Union. In the Gettysburg Address Lincoln asked that "we here highly resolve . . . that government of the people, by the people, for the people, shall not perish from the earth." See also the following discussion of Marshall's opinion in this case.

[16] 4 Wheaton 388. Pinkney referred to Article I, section 10 of the Constitution prohibiting states, without the consent of Congress, from laying "imposts or duties on imports or exports, except what may be *absolutely* necessary for executing [their] inspection laws." (Italics added.) Again compare the argument with Marshall's opinion.

[17] 4 Wheaton 390–99. Striking similarities of Pinkney's argument and Marshall's opinion concerning the states' taxing power are apparent. This is true even of the concession by both that Maryland could tax the bank stock owned by her own citizens in common with other property within her jurisdiction.

I never in my whole life, [wrote Story] heard a greater speech; his elocution was excessively vehement, but his eloquence was overwhelming. His language, his style, his figures, his arguments, were most brilliant and sparkling. He spoke like a great statesman and patriot, and a sound constitutional lawyer. All the cobwebs of sophistry and metaphysics about State rights and State sovereignty he brushed away with a mighty besom. . . . Mr. Pinkney possesses, beyond any man I ever saw, the power of elegant and illustrative amplification.[18]

The decision in *McCulloch* v. *Maryland,* as Webster confidently believed it would,[19] unanimously invalidated the state tax. On March 7, 1819, only four days following the argument, Chief Justice Marshall delivered his opinion after what he perplexingly said was the "most deliberate consideration" of the Court.[20] This case is a landmark in constitutional history because of the opinion's sweeping character and its frequent application afterward.

Congress could incorporate the Bank of the United States, the Chief Justice held. In arriving at this conclusion, he set forth in the broadest terms his view of the nature of the Union and of the extent of national sovereignty. Characteristically, he launched into a refutation of the position of Maryland's counsel. National legislative powers were not delegated by sovereign states, he declared, but derived from popular ratifications of the Constitution. Thus the state conventions of 1787–1789 expressed the will of the people and met in the several states simply because of geographical convenience. "The government of the Union, then, (whatever may be the influence of this fact of the case,) is, emphatically, and truly, a government of the people. In form and in substance it emanates from them. Its powers are granted by them, and are to be exercised directly on them, and for their benefit."[21] Though the Constitution does not enumerate the power to create a banking corporation, several clauses (such as those concerning taxes, commerce, and war)

[18] Story to Stephen White, Mar. 3, 1819, William W. Story (ed.), *Life and Letters of Joseph Story* (2 vols., Boston, 1851), I, 325.

[19] In letters to Jeremiah Mason on February 15 and 23, 1819, Webster said he had "no doubt" of the outcome. Webster Papers (New Hamp. Hist. Soc.).

[20] 4 Wheaton 436. The whole opinion is in *ibid.,* 400–37.

[21] *Ibid.,* 404–05.

imply it, he said. Marshall also accepted the interpretation of the necessary and proper clause put forward by the Bank's attorneys. There are various degrees of necessity, he asserted, and the authors of the Constitution did not intend to limit Congress to those measures absolutely or indispensably necessary. Reminiscent of Hamilton's opinion on the bank bill of 1791, his classic statement of the matter was: "Let the end be legitimate, let it be within the scope of the constitution, and all means which are appropriate, which are plainly adapted to that end, which are not prohibited, but consist with the letter and spirit of the constitution, are constitutional."[22]

The second part of Marshall's opinion, considering state taxing power, was less exhaustive than the first. Though he conceded that this was, in general, a concurrent power, he would restrain it wherever it conflicted with a supreme law of the Union. Searching for a standard for gauging the boundaries of state power, he approved Pinkney's formula of prohibiting a part of the Union from interfering with the whole, from taxing resources outside its own sphere of jurisdiction. As both Webster and Pinkney had insisted, the Chief Justice quite agreed

that the power to tax involves the power to destroy; that the power to destroy may defeat and render useless the power to create; that there is a plain repugnance, in conferring on one government a power to control the constitutional measures of another, which other, with respect to those very measures, is declared to be supreme over that which exerts control, are propositions not to be denied.

These inconsistencies could not be reconciled, he thought, "by the magic of the word CONFIDENCE."[23] Any *degree* of taxation of the bank notes would consequently be dangerous, and Maryland's statute was void.[24]

Because Marshall delivered his opinion so soon after

---

[22] *Ibid.,* 421.

[23] *Ibid.,* 431.

[24] Denying to the Court the vast power of deciding what degree of state taxation was admissible, Marshall declared such a function was "unfit for the judicial department." *Ibid.,* 430. Later commentators criticize Marshall for not differentiating between discriminatory and non-discriminatory taxes as a rule of decision. See, for example, Thomas R. Powell, *Vagaries and Varieties in Constitutional Interpretation* (New York, 1956), 90. But, as mentioned in note 17 above, Marshall did not extend his holding to forbid taxation of bank stock and property in common with other property throughout the state. 4 Wheaton 436.

argument, his biographer infers that he drafted it during the preceding winter and thus gave little weight to the arguments.[25] But evidence to the contrary stands out. As previously shown, Marshall borrowed extensively from Pinkney—relative to the nature of the Union, to the meaning of the necessary and proper clause, and to the limits of the states' taxing power. Similarities not only of concepts but also of specific expressions in Pinkney's argument and Marshall's opinion are obvious. To a lesser degree, the same is true of Webster's argument, the most striking example being the declaration that the power to tax involves the power to destroy. And typically, counsel of the losing party stimulated the Chief Justice as he undertook to refute point after point they had put forward. Especially did he do so against Hopkinson's argument.

Undeniably, there were other sources for the opinion. The full-blown nationalistic, loose-constructionist interpretation of the Constitution here voiced by Marshall is of course traceable back to the first days of the republic. No better statement of that philosophy exists than Secretary of the Treasury Alexander Hamilton's advocacy of chartering the first national bank in 1791.[26] That this was public intellectual property is immediately recognizable in the lawyers' briefs as well as in the opinion of the *McCulloch* case. The contention that Congress can employ appropriate means to secure ends stated in the Constitution is well-known Hamiltonian doctrine. Years earlier, in 1805, Marshall had stated the idea in *U.S.* v. *Fisher:*

In construing this clause [necessary and proper] it would be incorrect, and would produce endless difficulties, if the opinion should be maintained that no law was authorized which was not indispensably necessary to give effect to a specific power. . . . Congress must possess the choice of means, and must be empowered to use any means which are in fact conducive to the exercise of a power granted by the constitution.[27]

The principal lines of Marshall's opinion were no doubt predetermined when the *McCulloch* case came on for argument, but

---

[25] Beveridge, *Marshall,* IV, 290. See also Fuess, *Webster,* I, 253.

[26] John C. Hamilton (ed.), *The Works of Alexander Hamilton* (7 vols., New York, 1851), IV, 104–38.

[27] 2 Cranch 501–02. The *Fisher* case was not cited either by counsel or Court. Marshall's familiarity with Hamilton's language doubtless came not only from his own experience in politics but also from the detailed treatment of Hamilton's career in his biography of Washington.

in several respects the lawyers contributed to the final form which that opinion assumed.

Through the years in reliance upon the *McCulloch* precedent, courts erected additional restrictions against both national and state taxing powers. Intergovernmental immunity from taxation expanded to protect private as well as public activities, local as well as national agencies, merely useful as well as vital functions.[28] One should not forget that the decision in 1819 only invalidated state taxation of national bank notes. Good and sufficient reasons for protecting this circulating currency abounded, but Marshall did not express himself as carefully as he might have. As a result others found reasons to apply loosely the doctrine he and Webster and Pinkney had stated.[29] Justice Holmes once aptly criticized this inability to distinguish between degrees and nuances of factual circumstances when he said, "The power to tax is not the power to destroy while this Court sits."[30] In the main, the Court of the present generation has retreated from its former extreme positions built upon *McCulloch* and permits a substantial amount of intergovernmental taxation unless it cripples a governmental activity or unless Congressional legislation prohibits it.[31]

Antagonism toward the Bank did not diminish in the slightest after the decision of 1819, and in some states angry determination to kill the "Monster" mounted. Ohio forcibly collected a paralyzing tax on the branches at Cincinnati and Chillicothe. The Bank obtained injunctions from the United States Circuit Court forbidding collection for an unconstitutional tax and secured decrees ordering return of funds the state had seized. The case of *Osborn* v. *Bank of the United States* then came up to the Supreme Court.[32] Resentment toward the Bank's

28 Thomas R. Powell, "Intergovernmental Tax Immunities," *Harvard Law Review,* LVIII (May–July, 1945), 633–74, 757–805.

29 Bray Hammond, *Banks and Politics in America: From the Revolution to the Civil War* (Princeton, 1957), 265–66, deplores Marshall's failure to base the decision on the specific ground of state interference with a national circulating currency. In his argument Webster lightly touched this topic. *WS,* XV, 266.

30 *Panhandle Oil Co.* v. *Mississippi ex rel. Knox,* 277 U. S. 223 (1928).

31 Edward S. Corwin (ed.), *Constitution . . . Analysis and Interpretation,* 729–36.

32 9 Wheaton 739–44; R. Carlyle Buley, *The Old Northwest: Pioneer Period, 1815–1840* (2 vols., Bloomington, Ind., 1951), I, 588–94.

policy of retrenchment occasioned another suit in Georgia. Here the Federal Circuit Court refused to grant a remedy when the two state banks did not redeem their inflated notes held by the national corporation. This controversy, *B.U.S.* v. *Planters' Bank of Georgia,* was also appealed to the Supreme Court and decided coincidentally with the *Osborn* case in 1824.[33]

The principal questions raised by these cases were jurisdictional. Had the Bank action been brought against Ohio's auditor, Ralph Osborn, or really against the state itself? Could Osborn claim immunity on the ground of the Eleventh Amendment, which prohibits suits in Federal Courts against a state by citizens of another state? Did the Bank's charter of 1816 authorize it to sue in the circuit courts; and, if so, had Congress acted in conformity with Article III of the Constitution concerning Federal jurisdiction? Greatly discontented with the *McCulloch* decision, Ohio also sought a reversal of the holdings in that case. At the 1823 term Charles Hammond and John C. Wright represented Osborn; and Henry Clay, the Bank. Wishing to consider the jurisdictional questions more fully, the Court heard additional arguments the following year, this time in conjunction with the Georgia case. Now the Bank brought in its most effective counsel, John Sergeant and Webster.

A separate brief of Webster's argument is not available, but one that he and his associates filed jointly is in the official reports.[34] As Clay, Sergeant, and Webster interpreted Article III of the Constitution, the jurisdiction of the national courts extended both to cases involving the Constitution, Federal laws, or treaties (dependent upon the nature of the subject matter) and to cases involving diversity of citizenship (dependent upon the character of the parties to the suit).[35] For either category, but not necessarily for both in the same case, Congress could distribute jurisdiction as it saw fit.[36] Consequently, by the charter

[33] Hammond, *Banks and Politics in America,* 272–73; Catterall, *Second Bank of U. S.,* 89–91.

[34] 9 Wheaton 805–11.

[35] The relevant words of the Constitution, Article III, section 2, are: "The judicial power shall extend to all cases, in law and equity, arising under this Constitution, the laws of the United States, and treaties made, or which shall be made, under their authority; . . . to controversies . . . between citizens of different States. . . ."

[36] Webster and his associates were well supported by Marshall's opinion on this point in *Cohens* v. *Virginia,* 6 Wheaton 383 (1821).

of 1816 Congress conferred upon that institution the right to sue in any Federal circuit court. The purpose was, the lawyers asserted, to prevent a handicap such as the Supreme Court placed upon the First Bank of the United States a few years earlier when it decided that a corporation was not a citizen for purposes of Federal jurisdiction.[37] Thus the privilege of original actions in the circuit courts rested on the subject matter of the case—the Bank's charter, a United States law—and it was unnecessary also to show diversity of citizenship. What Congress had done, therefore, was to supersede the Judiciary Act of 1789 as far as Bank cases were concerned, since that earlier law had provided for appeals to the Supreme Court from the *state* courts, not the circuits, in civil cases involving Federal questions.[38] Broadly construing the constitutional boundaries of national jurisdiction, the argument contended that it must be possible for Congress to vest judicial power in the nation's courts "coextensive" with its legislative power.[39]

With regard to these technical but highly important points, Marshall's opinion for the Court approved all that the Bank's lawyers had said.[40] The benefits to the Bank were substantial, since it could now resort to the Federal courts whenever need arose and did not have to throw itself initially upon the mercy of state tribunals, which were often unfriendly. In a period when public opinion toward corporations was still in a formative, suspicious stage, there were obvious advantages in the *Osborn* decision.[41] On the question of violation of the

[37] *Bank of U. S.* v. *Deveaux,* 5 Cranch 61 (1809).

[38] Section 25 of the law. *U. S. Statutes at Large,* I, 85–87.

[39] Counsel for neither party discussed at any length the pertinence of the Eleventh Amendment, prohibiting suits in the Federal courts against states by citizens of other states. Charles Hammond, representing Osborn, contended the action was really against the state of Ohio and thus not within the jurisdiction of the Federal circuit courts, but he did not specifically cite the Eleventh Amendment and relied upon Article III and the Judiciary Act of 1789. 9 Wheaton 755–65. John C. Wright briefly referred to the Eleventh Amendment. *Ibid.,* 803–04. Webster, Clay, and Sergeant seemingly gave it little attention. *Ibid.,* 795–800, 804–11. The focus of all arguments was upon the Bank's charter of 1816—whether it could and did confer to the corporation the right to sue in the Federal courts. This fact may explain the weakness of the part of Marshall's opinion concerning the Amendment, as noted below.

[40] The whole opinion is in 9 Wheaton 816–71.

[41] For illustrations, see the cases discussed and cited below. Grounded on the charter of 1816, the decision applied only to the Bank of the United States, as distinguished from other corporations. *Deveaux* was not overruled until 1844. See note 37 above.

Eleventh Amendment if this were actually a suit against the state, not against Osborn as an individual, the Chief Justice held that Ohio was not a party in the record and that the state's auditor must assume personal responsibility for enforcing an unconstitutional statute. Although this phase of the case came to be an important precedent for general application, it was less significant to the Bank at the moment, and Marshall treated it less satisfactorily by such an undiscriminating dependence upon the face of the record. The opinion concluded, as anyone could have predicted, with an affirmation of the *McCulloch* holdings that the Bank charter was constitutional and that the state tax was not.

Through the years Webster maintained a close connection with the Bank. At times, his professional services for that corporation kept him busy; and altogether from 1819 to 1839, he appeared as its counsel before the Supreme Court in ten cases but opposed it in only two.[42] He and Nicholas Biddle, the Bank's president, were on friendly terms, as the active correspondence between them shows. Their communications were confidential and candid on a variety of matters, many of them on politics.[43] When the Bank struggled for its life against the Jacksonians during the 1830's, Webster was its ardent champion. Even after the Bank ceased to be the fiscal agent of the national treasury, the lawyer represented it in a very important suit involving interstate comity.

There were those who complained that such a relationship was unethical, that by employing Webster's legal talents the Bank purchased his political support as well. Excessive fees and unwarranted personal loans, said Webster's enemies, nourished his steady loyalty to the institution.[44] In reply to the charge that he had received special treatment by the Bank, he said that

I never had any particular or unusual accommodation from the bank to the amount of a single dollar; that since I went to Boston, in 1817, I have

[42] Warren, *Sup. Ct. in U.S. Hist.*, I, 157 n. 2, says that there were forty-four Supreme Court cases involving the Bank from 1815 to 1830. By 1830, banking questions constituted a significant share of the Court's business.

[43] Reginald C. McGrane (ed.), *The Correspondence of Nicholas Biddle Dealing with National Affairs, 1807–1844* (Boston, 1919), *passim;* Webster Papers (Library of Congress), *passim.*

[44] George T. Curtis, *Life of Daniel Webster* (2 vols., New York, 1870), I, 495–97.

kept my account and done my necessary banking business at the Boston office; and notes, bills of exchange, &c. &c. with my name on them, have been collected and discounted, &c. as often as occasion required, precisely as would have been done in the case of any other person, and not otherwise. I hear reports of mortgages, standing loans &c. &c. between the bank and myself, in all of which there is not a single word of truth. I never gave the bank any mortgage, and never had any standing loan, or any other accommodation, except in the way of discount of bills and notes, as at other banks.[45]

Despite Webster's disclaimer, he found the Bank a convenient fountainhead of credit, for which he had insatiable need. At one juncture, around 1830, his indebtedness to the Bank amounted to $17,782. But other politicians of both parties were also debtors —Jacksonians, such as Isaac Hill, William B. Lewis, and Amos Kendall, as well as National Republicans, J. Watson Webb and Henry Clay.[46] Fees for representing the Bank in Court were apparently quite liberal, in a couple of cases amounting to two thousand dollars each.[47] Occasionally the Bank paid sums to Webster as standing counsel;[48] and once he reminded Biddle that his retainer had not been "renewed, or *refreshed* as usual."[49]

At the 1826 term Webster had charge of several cases when the Bank's leading attorney, John Sergeant, departed on a diplomatic mission to the Panama Congress.[50] The Bank defended against appellants from the Federal circuit courts in controversies involving points of practice and rules of commercial law. In reading the reports of these cases, all of which the Bank won, one has the impression that the Court, including

45 Webster to Edward Everett, Apr. 26, 1834, *WS,* XVIII, 6. See also another letter to the same effect: Webster to Henry Hubbard, Nov. 18, 1834, quoted in Curtis, *Webster,* I, 499.

46 Memorandum of Biddle, McGrane (ed.), *Biddle Correspondence,* 357.

47 Information from Webster's account books in *WS,* XVII, 291-96; Peter Harvey, *Reminiscences and Anecdotes of Daniel Webster* (Boston, 1878), 84-85. In *McCulloch* v. *Maryland* his fee was two thousand dollars, of which fifteen hundred was "an additional fee" with the "respectful thanks" of Bank President Langdon Cheves and the directors of the Bank. Cheves to Webster, Apr. 2, 1819, Webster Papers (New Hamp. Hist. Soc.). Wirt received the same. Wirt to Webster, Apr. 28, 1819, Webster Papers (Lib. Cong.). And Pinkney probably was paid considerably more.

48 Webster to Biddle, Feb. 24 and 26, 1827, *WS,* XVI, 142, 144.

49 Webster to Biddle, Dec. 21, 1833, McGrane (ed.), *Biddle Correspondence,* 218.

50 Biddle to Webster, Feb. 10, 1826, Webster Papers (Lib. Cong.); Webster to Biddle, Mar. 1 and 15, 1826, *WS,* XVI, 121-22, 123.

not only Marshall but the other justices as well, was sympathetically aware of the Bank's economic role during this dynamic era. And it is evident that the Bank's rights and privileges were well protected in the circuit courts, where the suits originated, now that the *Osborn* decision had opened these tribunals to the institution.[51]

One of the rare cases in which Webster appeared in Court against the Bank was *Etting* v. *Bank of U.S.* (1826).[52] Another peculiarity of the case is that Taney was his associate. James W. McCulloch, cashier of the Baltimore branch and one of the parties in the famous cause of 1819, had manipulated stock and borrowed heavily from the Bank. Together with the president of the branch and a director, McCulloch owed the institution three and a half million dollars. The transaction seemed to be a plain example of fraud and embezzlement. When the parent Bank came under the efficient management of President Langdon Cheves in early 1819, the board discovered these peculations and insisted that McCulloch seek additional security, besides the Bank's own stock. Meanwhile the board retained McCulloch in office. Sixteen Baltimore merchants, including Solomon Etting, endorsed McCulloch's note, whereupon the Bank then dismissed the young cashier. Later the note fell due, and since McCulloch could not begin to meet his obligation, the Bank demanded that Etting and the others deliver their securities of $12,500 each. When they refused, the Bank sued them and won the case in the circuit court.[53]

In the Supreme Court Webster and Taney represented Etting. By keeping McCulloch in office after it had discovered his frauds, the lawyers argued, the Bank had concealed circumstances, deceived Etting, and therefore voided the contract. For the Bank Wirt and Emmet contended that there was a right in this instance to remain silent. The Court divided on the question, however, and thus affirmed the lower court's judgment for the

[51] *Finley* v. *B. U. S.*, 11 Wheaton 304 (1826); *Williams* v. *B. U. S.*, *ibid.*, 414; *Mills* v. *B. U. S.*, *ibid.*, 431. See also *McGill* v. *B. U. S.*, 12 Wheaton 511 (1827); Webster to Biddle, Feb. 20, 1827, *WS*, XVI, 140–41; *Winship* v. *B. U. S.*, 5 Peters 529 (1831); *B. U. S.* v. *Hatch*, 6 Peters 250 (1832).

[52] 11 Wheaton 59 (1826). The only other Bank case in which Webster represented the opposing party was *B. U. S.* v. *Martin*, 5 Peters 479 (1831).

[53] 11 Wheaton 59–65; Hammond, *Banks and Politics in America*, 260–62; Carl B. Swisher, *Roger B. Taney* (New York, 1936), 88–90.

Bank. Unable to resist a broad hint of his own position, Marshall referred to the "deservedly high character of the individuals who were engaged on the part of the bank."[54] The parties later agreed to a retrial, the Bank again won a judgment, and after much delay the parties compromised out of court at half the amount of the securities. Ironically, McCulloch himself escaped punishment following futile prosecutions in the Maryland courts.[55]

Other cashiers caused the Bank difficulty. At the Richmond branch Cashier Dandridge committed various breaches of his bond, and the Bank sued him in Marshall's circuit court. Dandridge defended on the ground that the board of directors had never accepted his bond formally in writing. On the question whether a corporation, unlike a natural person, had to show written acceptance for a bond to be valid, Marshall ruled that it did. He relied upon the Congressional statute of incorporation as well as upon English and American state cases to arrive at a rather strict rule for the conduct of the Bank's business.[56] The determination of the controversy, now appealed to the Supreme Court, would have wide implications in the whole field of corporate enterprise.

During the 1826 term, in the absence of John Sergeant, Webster prepared to argue *B.U.S.* v. *Dandridge* and arranged for Wirt to help him.[57] He built his brief upon one supplied by his friend Jeremiah Mason, with whom he shared his large fee.[58] But the Court did not hear the case until the following term. In the three-week interval between argument and decision Webster corresponded frequently with President Biddle.[59] The Court would reverse Marshall's circuit ruling, the lawyer assured him. "I have some little spice of *professional* feeling in the case, having spoken somewhat more freely than usually befits the mouth of an humble Attorney at law, like myself, of the

54 11 Wheaton 73.

55 Hammond, *Banks and Politics in America,* 268–72; Swisher, *Taney,* 91–92.

56 2 *Federal Cases* 691 (1824).

57 12 Wheaton 64.

58 Webster to Mason, Apr. 10, 1827, quoted in Warren, *Sup. Ct. in U. S. Hist.,* II, 159 n. 1.

59 Biddle to Webster, Feb. 4, 1826, Webster Papers (Lib. Cong.); Webster to Biddle, Mar. 21, 1826 and Feb. 24 and 25, 1827, *WS,* XVI, 123–24, 142, 143.

'manifest errors' in the opinion of the great Chief."[60] Marshall himself had recognized the probability of reversal as soon as he had tried the case in Richmond and had privately conceded in a letter to Story that "the practice of banks has not conformed to my construction of the law. The Judge, however, who draws the opinion must have more ingenuity than I have if he draws a good one."[61]

The ingenious judge was Story. Not only did he find other state cases holding the opposite of Marshall's decision, but he also interpreted the statute of incorporation differently. Since the Bank's directors acted as *agents* of the corporation and not as the corporation itself, concluded Story, the Court must apply the same rule of evidence to them that it would to private individuals.[62] To this generous view of the question Marshall could not assent and wrote one of his rare minority opinions. "I should now, as is my custom," he wrote, "when I have the misfortune to differ from this Court, acquiesce silently in its opinion, did I not believe that the judgment of the Circuit Court of Virginia gave general surprize to the profession, and was generally condemned."[63] After restating his reasoning, he conceded that "the law is now settled otherwise, perhaps to the advancement of public convenience. I acquiesce, as I ought, though I could not concur in it."[64]

Webster did not conclude his professional connections with the Bank of the United States when the institution's national charter expired. In fact, he argued one of his most important banking and corporation cases in 1839, when Biddle's bank was operating under a Pennsylvania charter. This was *Bank of U.S.* v. *Primrose,* coming up to the Supreme Court from the Federal circuit in Alabama with two other cases, *Bank of Augusta* v. *Earle,* and *New Orleans and Carrollton Railroad* v. *Earle.*[65] The three were known as the *Alabama Bank Cases.* In

---

[60] Webster to Biddle, Feb. 20, 1827, *WS*, XVI, 141.

[61] Marshall to Story, July 2, 1823, *Proceedings of the Massachusetts Historical Society* (Boston, 1900–01), Second Series, XIV, 332–33.

[62] 12 Wheaton 64–90. The case was illustrative of the steady trend of this time toward placing corporate rights on the same legal footing as the rights of natural persons.

[63] *Ibid.,* 90.

[64] *Ibid.,* 116.

[65] 13 Peters 519 (1839).

her constitution Alabama had prohibited the legislature from establishing any bank except one in which the state held part of the stock and shared the directorship. The effect was to create a monopoly of the banking business in the state. All three corporations involved in these cases held charters from other states and had purchased bills of exchange in Alabama. The endorsers of the bills, Earle and Primrose, refused to pay on the ground that the state's policy forbade these companies to deal in exchange. Several fundamental questions arose. Were the acts of buying and selling such bills exclusively *banking* operations? If not, any individual or any kind of corporation would be free to do so, since there was no explicit statement in the Alabama constitution concerning exchange. Could foreign corporations (those chartered by other states) make contracts in Alabama without her positive consent? Was Alabama's consent implied? Did Alabama have the power to exclude these corporations from doing business within her jurisdiction?[66]

From an economic viewpoint the questions were critical because in the South many transactions, such as the sale and shipment of cotton, were made in exchange. And for the whole nation the interstate operations of all sorts of corporations were increasingly significant. Thus these cases might affect the commercial harmony of the Union. From a political viewpoint the controversy was a continuation of the Jacksonian bank struggle. Hatred toward the Bank persisted, though it no longer held a national charter. A good many states' rights Democrats, but not all of them, still suspected corporations *per se;* and many more detected the sinister manipulations of the "money power" thriving upon special chartered privileges. To Whigs like Webster these were foolish delusions, but men of both parties recognized the authority and responsibility of states to govern their own internal concerns.[67] Was this an instance where state interest should prevail?

In true alignment with prevailing local sentiment, Justice John McKinley decided the cases on his circuit for the defendants. He held that Alabama had specifically and rightfully pro-

66 *Ibid.*, 519–23.

67 George R. Taylor, *The Transportation Revolution, 1815–1860* (New York, 1951), 240–43; Glyndon G. Van Deusen, *The Jacksonian Era, 1828–1848* (New York, 1959), 22–25, 96–98, 122; Warren, *Sup. Ct. in U. S. Hist.*, II, 324–30.

hibited foreign banking corporations from doing business within its jurisdiction. Alarmed at the damaging consequences of such doctrine if applied throughout the land, conservatives realized the crucial nature of what the Supreme Court might hold when the cases came up at the 1839 term. Both Whig and Democratic newspapers gave the controversy more than the usual amount of coverage, but from opposing positions.[68]

The banks' counsel were David B. Ogden, John Sergeant, and Webster. Staunchly they maintained the rights of the corporations to buy and sell exchange in Alabama.[69] The three lawyers emphasized the rule of comity obligating all nations, and in this instance the states, to permit foreign citizens to trade, to travel, to sue, to do many things that domestic citizens could do. Under international law, Webster declared, denial of these rights was just ground for war. In this country, he contended, comity bound each state to safeguard the privileges of citizens of every other state, because the members of the Union still possessed some attributes of national as well as municipal sovereignty. Indeed there was all the more reason for comity to apply to American states because of their common historical experience and large dependence upon one another.[70] Sergeant advanced a strong argument that comity had been received by the common law, which in turn was a part of state law.[71]

On a constitutional basis, said Webster, the provision in Article IV that "the citizens of each State shall be entitled to all privileges and immunities of citizens in the several States" required comity. A forerunner of this clause had been the common allegiance of all colonists to the British crown. And later there had been an obligation of the states to each other under the Articles of Confederation (Article IV), which had specified that "the free inhabitants of each of these states . . . shall be entitled to all privileges and immunities of free citizens in the several states; and the people of each state shall have free ingress and regress to and from any other state, and shall enjoy therein all the privileges of trade and commerce, subject to the same

[68] Washington *Globe,* Feb. 1, 1839; Warren, *Sup. Ct. in U. S. Hist.,* II, 324–30.

[69] The arguments for the corporations are printed in 13 Peters 523–67.

[70] *WS,* XI, 117–23.

[71] 13 Peters 534–45.

duties, impositions and restrictions as the inhabitants thereof respectively." As Webster said, this was "the expounder" of the privileges and immunities clause in the Constitution of 1787.[72] If the constitutional provision applied to these cases, the Court would not merely infer a state's consent for foreign corporations to do business within its jurisdiction when the legislature was silent but would protect such corporations despite any state statute to the contrary. More than his associates, Webster pressed the point hard, extreme and ominous though it was.[73]

An indispensable condition for the application of the privileges and immunities clause to the Alabama cases was the definition of a corporation as a citizen. To arrive at such a definition, Webster turned to Article III of the Constitution, conferring jurisdiction upon the Federal courts in cases between citizens of different states.[74] Many years ago, the attorney observed, Chief Justice Marshall had held in *Bank of U.S. v. Deveaux* (1809)[75] that if members of a corporation were citizens of states other than the one of the other party, they might sue under their corporate name in the United States courts. This approached but did not technically lay down the rule that a corporation was a citizen. If a corporation, or at least agents in the name of that corporation, could sue in the courts throughout

---

[72] *WS,* XI, 111–12.

[73] In early American history the meaning of the privileges and immunities clause of the Constitution was uncertain. The silence of the Constitutional Convention, the brevity and generality of the constitutional provision, and the infrequency of judicial interpretation accounted for this uncertainty. In a circuit court case, *Corfield* v. *Coryell,* 6 *Federal Cases* 3230 (1823), Justice Bushrod Washington said that the clause protected "fundamental" rights of citizens of "all free governments," implying that there was a natural-law basis for protecting out-of-state citizens against state legislation which might still be valid as to in-state citizens. On the other hand, another possible interpretation of Washington's language was that the clause simply protected out-of-state citizens from suffering discrimination because of their residence and guaranteeing rights *equal* to those of in-state citizens. With modifications, the present interpretation of the clause is closer to the latter version than to the former. Had the natural-law theory prevailed in the Alabama bank cases, foreign corporations might have been able to trade in exchange even though Alabama citizens might not. Webster did not cite *Corfield* v. *Coryell.* In the main, his argument seems to have been based on the nondiscrimination rather than the natural-law theory, but there was a suggestion of the second when he said: "[the state] cannot create a monopoly to the prejudice of citizens of other States, or to the disparagement or prejudice of any common commercial right." *WS,* XI, 117.

[74] Article III, sec. 2, par. 1.

[75] 5 Cranch 61.

the states, why could it not also make contracts, asked Webster. The present cases were an excellent example, since the United States Circuit Court of Alabama, on the principle of *Deveaux,* entertained suits by these corporations. There would be small comfort for a corporation to sue on the non-performance of a contract if it could not collect judgment because every contract that it entered was illegal.[76]

Webster and his fellow counsel developed additional arguments of narrower dimensions.[77] No matter if the state constitution did confer a monopoly of banking, they contended, this did not prevent others from buying bills of exchange. For one thing, agents of the out-of-state banks were simply acting as individuals, not as bankers, and had the same rights as all other individuals. Besides, dealing in exchange was not necessarily a banking operation—any type of corporation or any individual could do this.[78] The identifying characteristic of banking was issuing notes for circulation as currency, said Webster, and the plaintiffs had not done this.[79] In order to limit the privilege of purchasing and selling bills only to the state chartered bank, Alabama would therefore have to enact a statute to that effect.

The leading lawyer for the defendants was Charles J. Ingersoll of Philadelphia, accomplished author, district attorney for many years, and fiery crusader against the Bank of the United States. Opposing excessive corporate privileges in any form, Ingersoll spoke with great feeling in behalf of the state's power to exclude foreign corporations.[80] At several junctures he warned the Court of political manipulations by these threatening combinations of power, and his remarks were now

[76] *WS,* XI, 112–15.

[77] *Ibid.,* 125–30; 13 Peters 529–31.

[78] One of the corporations involved in these cases was a railroad.

[79] Hammond, *Banks and Politics,* 688–90, criticizes Webster and others of his time for believing that note issue was the indispensable function of banking. He argues that creation of deposits was fast becoming more important. Ogden did refer to receiving deposits as a characteristic banking activity. 13 Peters 530.

[80] Ingersoll's argument is in 13 Peters 567–82. A flattering commentary appeared in the Washington *Globe,* Feb. 1, 1839. Justice McKinley arrived at Court late, but in time, said the *Globe,* "to hear a complete vindication of his positions and a conclusive argument against the right of these money-mongering monsters to stray from their spheres, and invade the quiet regions of distant States, there to ravage, monopolize, and destroy."

all the more heated since he was doing battle with Webster, the national bank's champion in Congress during the recent recharter controversy.

Ingersoll rejected comity entirely. Within the Union, he insisted, the several states had a relationship to each other prescribed by the Constitution. The Court could not engraft a different rule derived from the common law. Consequently, for a corporation to operate outside its chartering state, other states must explicitly admit it to do business within their jurisdictions. Ingersoll would deny it all extraterritorial privileges. In closing, the Philadelphian declared he was cheered by an assurance that his country was his client—to which Webster objected as an inappropriate manner of addressing the Court.[81]

Chief Justice Taney delivered the Court's opinion upholding the rights of the corporations to make contracts in Alabama.[82] But Webster's victory was not complete, for the opinion assumed a position between the extremes of the opposing arguments. Actually, the Jacksonian judge made a realistic accommodation of law to current economic conditions. Early in his opinion Taney noticed the importance of this question to the nation, when he said, "Contracts to a very great amount have undoubtedly been made by different corporations out of the particular state by which they were created."[83] Clearly he was thinking of the difficulties that might follow a decision supporting complete state power. On the other hand he also saw the folly of attempting to deprive states of all authority to regulate corporations. As a result, he ruled that by comity a state implied its consent for foreign corporations to make contracts unless it enacted prohibitory legislation.

Taney quickly came to grips with the most explosive branch of Webster's argument, the privileges and immunities clause in the fourth article of the Constitution. He refused to consider corporations as citizens within the meaning of that clause and cut off a promising line of defense for corporations against state power. If he had accepted Webster's point of view, there would have been little, if any, opportunity for the states

[81] *WS*, XI, 131.
[82] 13 Peters 584–97.
[83] *Ibid.*, 585.

to adopt discriminatory legislation against foreign corporations.[84] Taney differentiated the rights of natural persons to sue
in Federal courts in their corporate name, claimed under Article
III, from the rights of corporations to make contracts, claimed
under Article IV. The status and powers of corporations, he
said, were unlike those of individuals, since the former depended
upon the statutes that created them as legal entities. Thus it was
impossible to identify any body of privileges uniform for all
corporations, regardless of domicile, such as for natural persons.

Proceeding then to the question whether comity operated
in the present controversy, the Chief Justice found that it did.
He cited various English and American precedents to show that
custom, judicial decisions, and legislation had universally received
the principle of comity from the common law. Inasmuch as the
states chartering these corporations had granted them the right
to deal in exchange, the Court would presume that Alabama had
implied its consent for them to do so within its jurisdiction unless there was a specific statute or policy to the contrary. None
existed, Taney said.[85] Here the opinion followed the arguments
of Webster, Ogden, and Sergeant very closely, even to the point,
interestingly enough, of saying that the right to sue and the right
to make contracts were parallel under comity. As explained
above, Taney did not think they were parallel, however, under
Articles III and IV of the Constitution. The right to sue therefore derived from both the Constitution and comity, while the
frailer right to make contracts derived only from comity and
could be prohibited by the declared will of the state.[86]

In expected quarters the decision in the *Alabama Bank
Cases* kindled anger. Some states' rights advocates noticed only
the part of Taney's opinion favoring corporations and not that
part upholding the power to pass regulatory legislation. But in
Alabama itself the immediate reaction of the irritated governor
and legislature was to enact a law forbidding agents of foreign

[84] See note 73 above.

[85] Thus Taney thought that the Alabama policy setting up a banking monopoly did not preclude such transactions as these. Buying and selling exchange, he
implied, were not necessarily *banking* operations.

[86] Justice Baldwin wrote a concurring opinion, not printed in the official reports, which apparently accepted Webster's argument relative to the privileges and
immunities clause. *Niles' Register*, LVI (Mar. 23, 1839), 50. Justice McKinley re-
affirmed his circuit court decision with great vigor. See the discussion below.

corporations to deal in exchange, thereby dampening the particular victory won by the plaintiffs.[87]

The general, long-range result of the decision, however, was decidedly to encourage corporate expansion. It was one of a series of adjustments of the law at a time when the corporation became an increasingly effective means of conducting the nation's business. Many of these corporations operated beyond the boundaries of the chartering state. Seen against this background, the Alabama cases stand out as a long step away from the earlier restrictive theory of corporation law toward a liberal theory.[88] Another step taken by the Taney Court was its decision in *Louisville, Cincinnati, and Charleston Railroad Co.* v. *Letson* (1844),[89] overruling *Bank of U.S.* v. *Deveaux*. Afterward, for purposes of jurisdiction of the Federal courts, it was no longer necessary that all members of a corporation be citizens of states other than the one of the opposing party in a suit. The judicial presumption would be (obviously a legal fiction to recognize economic facts) that a corporation was a citizen of the state creating it. Later this was modified to presume that all the *shareholders* of the corporation were citizens of the incorporating state.[90] Though the Court did not then or subsequently adopt Webster's argument that a corporation was a citizen within the meaning of Article IV of the Constitution, the privileges and immunities clause, it did in time find other protections in the due process clause of the Fourteenth Amendment (ratified in 1868) and in the commerce clause. So the Court materially altered Taney's rule which permitted positive state legislation regulating corporations.[91] Remnants of that rule have nonetheless survived,

[87] Charles G. Haines and Foster H. Sherwood, *The Role of the Supreme Court in American Government and Politics, 1835–1864* (Berkeley, 1957), 69, 72; Warren, *Sup. Ct. in U. S. Hist.*, II, 331–36.

[88] An excellent treatment of the whole subject is "The Adoption of the Liberal Theory of Foreign Corporations," *University of Pennsylvania Law Review*, LXXIX (1931), 956–72, 1119–38. See also Gerald C. Henderson, *The Position of Foreign Corporations in American Constitutional Law; A Contribution to the History and Theory of Juristic Persons in Anglo-American Law* (Cambridge, 1918).

[89] 2 Howard 497.

[90] *Marshall* v. *Baltimore and Ohio Railroad Co.*, 16 Howard 325 (1853).

[91] Taney himself recognized such possibilities when he said: "Nor do we mean to say whether there may not be some rights under the Constitution of the United States, which a corporation might claim under peculiar circumstances, in a state other than that in which it was chartered." 13 Peters 597.

and at present a state can impose some conditions upon a foreign corporation wishing admission to do business.

These very cases provided an opportunity to invoke the commerce clause as a limitation on state power. Ogden in his argument for the Bank of Augusta contended that the purchase and sale of exchange related in an important way to interstate commerce and that Alabama's policy conflicted with the constitutional grant of the commerce power to Congress.[92] Surprisingly, Webster did not develop the point but only suggested that the state had created an obstacle to commerce.[93] In behalf of state power, Ingersoll briefly countered Ogden's argument by asserting that exchange, though a medium of commerce, was subject solely to state regulation.[94] Although Taney did not rest his opinion on the commerce clause, the dissenting Justice McKinley seemed very disturbed by the possibility that the majority was taking that ground implicitly. When the Court assumed that comity applied here, McKinley complained, it could only justify this unwarranted use of judicial power by the doctrine that Congressional commerce power

deprives Alabama of the power to pass any law restraining the sale and purchase of a bill of exchange; and by consequence, the whole power belongs to Congress. The Court, by the opinion of the majority, does not recognize this doctrine, in terms. But if the power which the Court exercised is not derived from that provision of the Constitution, in my opinion it does not exist.

If ever Congress shall exercise this power to the broad extent contended for, the powers of the States over commerce, and contracts relating to commerce, will be reduced to very narrow limits.[95]

Taney did not go so far in this case as McKinley suspected, nor did the Court later inflate the commerce power as much as he feared.

As an attorney for the Bank of the United States over a twenty-year period, Webster participated in each of its great constitutional cases and many others as well. He and his as-

[92] *Ibid.*, 531–32.
[93] *Ibid.*, 556.
[94] *Ibid.*, 572–73.
[95] *Ibid.*, 600.

sociates surveyed a number of important questions: the scope
of national and state powers within the federal system; the
authority of Congress to charter corporations, and in particular
a national bank; the jurisdictional boundaries of the national
courts; the right to sue a state official; the characteristics of
American corporations; and the extent of state power to regulate
foreign corporations. Webster spoke for nationalistic answers to
the questions, as he consistently did in law and politics. This is
a commonly known fact. But the ways in which he spoke for the
corporate form of business, generally, are not so well-known.
The effects were far-reaching. The Bank's victories were often
also victories for other corporations—standing in the courts,
operations across state lines, and favorable legal status. In these
successes Webster was an advocate not only for the national bank
but for all American corporations.

VIII

THE COMMERCE CLAUSE

Today a fertile source of national power is the constitutional provision authorizing Congress "to regulate commerce with foreign nations, and among the several states." On the basis of this brief clause Congress enacts measures affecting virtually every part of the nation's economy—transportation, communications, industrial production, agriculture, labor relations, and numerous others. Notwithstanding the breadth of this national power, the states concurrently exercise a good deal of power over many of the same subjects. They do so for their own jurisdictions, within their own boundaries, it is true; nevertheless they materially regulate commerce "among the states," and the courts usually approve unless there is some compelling reason to the contrary.[1]

This was not always so. Up to the 1930's the extent of permissible state power remained quite limited indeed, limited not only by the operation of Congressional statutes but often by the mere constitutional delegation of power as well. It was during the second quarter of the nineteenth century that the Court first considered this question of the division of state and national powers over commerce. In a series of cases from 1824 to 1849 the bar fully discussed the matter, though the bench did not conclusively decide it. Finally in *Cooley* v. *Board of Wardens*

[1] Much weight is given to the provisions of relevant Congressional statutes, which may be construed to permit or prohibit concurrent legislation.

(1852) the Court arrived at a formula compromising the doctrines of exclusive-national and of concurrent-state power.[2] Thereafter this formula, laid down only in general terms, meant different things to different judges. Not until recent years, however, did the Court apply it in a manner that allowed much state legislation "directly" affecting interstate commerce.[3]

Webster was counsel in several of these early cases. As one might expect, he was a vigorous advocate of maximum national power, preferably exclusive but otherwise as nearly so as possible. Although the *Cooley* formula was not all he would have liked, neither was it all the exponents of states' rights had demanded. Webster did not participate in *Cooley* v. *Board of Wardens;* yet odd as it may seem, in the initial commerce case he himself had suggested the rule later laid down. This case was *Gibbons* v. *Ogden* (1824), opening up issues later repeatedly examined.[4]

The origins of the *Gibbons* case are traceable to the time when Americans were developing the steamboat as a means of transportation. In order to encourage this form of navigation, the New York legislature enacted several statutes granting an exclusive right to Robert R. Livingston and Robert Fulton or their assignees to operate steamboats on the state's waters. In *Livingston and Fulton* v. *Van Ingen* (1812)[5] the highest state court upheld the constitutionality of these laws on the grounds that the legislature had power concurrent with Congress to regulate commerce, that the monopoly applied only to internal commerce of New York, and that the state statutes did not conflict with a Federal enactment. Chief Justice James Kent, writing one of the three opinions,[6] emphasized Hamilton's *Federalist 32* as a proper rule for construing the commerce clause. Accordingly, since the Constitution had neither expressly delegated exclusive power to Congress nor explicitly prohibited

---

[2] 12 Howard 299. The case will be discussed below. Those subjects of commerce requiring a "uniform rule" were to be exclusively regulated by Congress.

[3] The terms "interstate commerce" and "commerce among the several states" —the latter is the language of the Constitution, Article I, section 8—are used in this chapter interchangeably. As it will appear below, there have been others who would not use "interstate" because they believe its scope is not as broad as "among the states."

[4] 9 Wheaton 1.   [5] 9 Johnson 507 (New York).

[6] Kent's opinion is in *ibid.,* 572–90.

state power, it was necessary, Kent held, to show that concurrent state authority "would be absolutely and totally *contradictory* and *repugnant*" to national authority. Kent did not believe that this was demonstrable. Of course if the two sovereignties had passed statutes which conflicted, the supremacy clause of the Constitution (Article VI) would have forced the state to give way.[7] But the present controversy concerned traffic from New York City to Albany, wholly within the state's jurisdiction, and Van Ingen did not rely upon a right conferred by Congressional law.

In 1819 and 1820 Kent, now presiding in the New York Court of Chancery, had to decide a number of other cases relating to the steamboat monopoly. On the basis of the *Van Ingen* precedent he granted injunctions on two occasions against Thomas Gibbons,[8] who persisted even after the restraining orders in running boats from New Jersey to New York City. Gibbons' associates, young Cornelius Vanderbilt and Vice President Daniel D. Tompkins, were also targets of determined litigation before the Chancellor.[9] In the case of Aaron Ogden, an assignee of the Livingston-Fulton monopoly, against Gibbons, Kent considered a new and important question. Gibbons claimed the right of navigation because he held a license under the Federal Coasting Act of 1793. Kent ruled that this statute merely set up standards in certifying the American ownership of coasting vessels for privileges within the revenue system and that it did not authorize the licensee to navigate in New York waters contrary to that state's laws.[10] The Court of Errors affirmed the Chancellor's decree,[11] and an appeal in *Gibbons* v. *Ogden* went to the United States Supreme Court.

After delay over technicalities,[12] the Court heard the lawyers' arguments from February 4 to 9, 1824. Opposing the

---

[7] "This Constitution and the laws of the United States . . . shall be the supreme law of the land . . . any thing in the constitution or laws of any state to the contrary notwithstanding." Const., Art. VI.

[8] *Livingston* v. *Ogden and Gibbons,* 4 Johnson Ch. 48 (New York, 1819); *Ogden* v. *Gibbons, ibid.,* 174.

[9] *In the matter of Vanderbilt, ibid.,* 57; *Livingston* v. *Tompkins, ibid.,* 415 (1820).

[10] *Ogden* v. *Gibbons, ibid.,* 150–65 (1819).

[11] *Gibbons* v. *Ogden,* 17 Johnson 488 (1820).

[12] The record was incomplete. 6 Wheaton 448 (1821).

steamboat monopoly were Webster and William Wirt. Thomas J. Oakley, Attorney General of New York, and Thomas A. Emmet, veteran representative of the Livingston-Fulton interests, were Ogden's counsel. William Pinkney, initially retained by Ogden, had died two years earlier.[13] Webster and Wirt apparently were not ready when the Chief Justice called up the case several days before they had anticipated.[14] But the often repeated story that Webster made all his preparation the night before his appearance is erroneous.[15] He had doubtless studied the record and drafted a brief when *Gibbons* v. *Ogden* was first docketed three years previously, although he may have reshaped the plan of his argument by laboring throughout the night of February 3.[16]

With an impressive performance of two and a half hours Webster opened for the appellant.[17] Typically he moved directly to the vital question, the nature of the commerce power. "I shall contend," he said, "that the power of Congress to regulate commerce is complete and entire, and to a certain extent, necessarily exclusive; that the acts in question are regulations of commerce, in a most important particular, affecting it in those respects in which it is under the exclusive authority of Congress."[18] It is noteworthy that Webster invoked the same rule of constitutional construction found useful by Chancellor Kent, to whom he paid an introductory compliment. This was *Federalist 32* (not identified by the lawyer), which accorded exclusive power to Congress when a similar authority by the states would be, in Hamilton's words, "totally contradictory." Thus Webster

---

13 Albert J. Beveridge, *The Life of John Marshall* (4 vols., Boston, 1916–1919), IV, 423–24; Charles Warren, *The Supreme Court in United States History* (3 vols., Boston, 1923), II, 59–61.

14 Three days before arguments began, Wirt wrote, "I . . . have yet to study the cause; but I know the facts, and have only to weave the argument." Quoted in John P. Kennedy, *Memoirs of the Life of William Wirt, Attorney-General of the United States* (Philadelphia, 1860), 144. This letter has interesting comments by Wirt concerning the counsel in the case. Webster is said to be as "ambitious as Caesar . . . not to be outdone by any man." *Ibid.*, 143.

15 William Plumer, Jr. to George Ticknor, "Reminiscences of Daniel Webster," in *WS*, XVII, 552; George T. Curtis, *Life of Daniel Webster* (2 vols., New York, 1870), I, 216–17.

16 Beveridge, *Marshall*, IV, 424–25 convincingly argues against the credibility of the story.

17 Webster's argument is printed in *WS*, XI, 4–23.

18 *Ibid.*, 8.

found it necessary to "consider of what parts the grant [of the power to regulate commerce] is composed, and which of those, from the nature of the thing, ought to be considered exclusive." Conceding that commerce was complex and that some state regulations affecting it were valid, he classified grants of monopolies of trade or navigation, like those the New York laws had made, as "higher branches" of commercial regulation forbidden to the states and exclusively delegated to Congress.[19]

Shrewdly turning to the history of the Confederation, he reminded the Court of the commercial confusion caused by conflicting state legislation. This was an argument which would certainly appeal to John Marshall. In order to eliminate the "perpetual jarring and hostility of commercial regulation," the delegates at Annapolis in 1786 and at Philadelphia the following year intended to establish "a uniform and general system." With a characteristic flourish Webster declared, "Henceforth, the commerce of the States was to be a *unit*." The system by which it would be governed "was to be described in the flag which waved over it E PLURIBUS UNUM."[20]

A decisive reason for steamboat traffic to be free from state interference, he asserted, was the great importance of that form of transportation to the nation. Business was seriously embarrassed by the New York monopoly and by retaliatory legislation of neighboring Connecticut and New Jersey.[21] For example, the New Jersey courts had awarded Gibbons damages for restraints against him in New York. Such conflicts between states caused commercial intercourse to suffer. In many respects, this was Webster's strongest point.

The lawyer attacked the theory of *general* concurrent power of commercial regulation by the states, that they could act on any matter in the absence of Congressional legislation. "What confusion such notions lead to is obvious enough," Webster exclaimed. To say that Congress could supersede state laws was unsatisfactory, in fact dangerous to the states as well as to the nation. The two spheres of government must be kept as distinct and separate as possible. Furthermore, who was to judge whether Congress "has made a plenary exercise of its power?"

[19] *Ibid.*, 11.   [20] *Ibid.*, 9–11.
[21] *Ibid.*, 4–6

Webster's own answer resembled the doctrine later known as "the silence of Congress": "All useful regulation does not consist in restraint; and that which Congress sees fit to leave free is a part of its regulation, as much as the rest."[22]

Webster was perfectly aware of the mass of state legislation affecting commerce—pilot, health, quarantine, ferry, turnpike, and bridge laws. But these were not regulations of commerce "in the constitutional understanding of that term," Webster said, and did not prove there was a concurrent state power. They were "rather regulations of police," thus not possessing the "importance and elevation" of commercial regulations. In deference to states' rights sentiment he maintained that this vast scope of "internal legislation," subject to the states' police power, was forbidden to Congress.[23]

In contrast to his detailed discussion concerning the conflict of the New York laws with the Constitution, Webster's consideration of the incompatibility of state and national statutes was cursory. His client Gibbons held a license under the Federal Coasting Act of 1793, which Chancellor Kent had interpreted as merely certifying American ownership for privileges within the revenue system. Webster contended that this was an incorrect construction. The license, he said, conferred the right of navigating "freely the waters of the United States," state restrictions to the contrary notwithstanding.[24] Congress need not expressly overrule the state grant, for its inconsistency with the Coasting Act was sufficient to make it void.[25] Here he relied entirely upon an analysis of the Federal statute's language instead of inquiring into its background and application. By present-day standards, his version of the act is not convincing, but he seems to have persuaded Marshall and his associates.

Oakley and Emmet, counsel for the respondent (Ogden), justified the steamboat monopoly on the ground that the state possessed concurrent power over commerce.[26] After discoursing upon the relationship of the nation and the states, Oakley declared that there was "no necessary repugnancy" of their acts under this power, "since it clearly admits of a great variety of

22 *Ibid.*, 12–13.   23 *Ibid.*, 14.
24 *Ibid.*, 20.   25 *Ibid.*, 21–22.
26 Oakley's argument is in 9 Wheaton 33–79; Emmet's, on pp. 79–159.

regulations, which may operate together, without direct inter-ference."[27] Emmet's principal contribution was an exhaustive survey of present and past state laws with respect to the slave trade, health and quarantine, pilotage, light houses, inspection, trade with the Indians, and transportation. These were regula-tions of commerce, he maintained, and not, as Webster had said, simply police legislation. Emmet concluded with some florid oratory, including a quotation from the *Aeneid,* to show that New York had wisely fostered Fulton's genius and thereby pro-moted the interests of the nation.

Webster's colleague, William Wirt, closed the case.[28] He reiterated the exclusive-power argument, but he amplified Webster's suggestion of the divisibility of the commercial power as an alternative. Webster may have assisted him in composing this statement in order to counteract the thrusts of Oakley and Emmet. Supposing that the states could regulate commerce (which he did not concede), Wirt asked why the matter was not "susceptible of division," some "portions" of it being ex-clusively delegated to Congress.

Some subjects [he observed] are, in their nature, extremely multifarious and complex. The same subject may consist of a great variety of branches, each extending itself into remote, minute, and infinite ramifications. One branch alone, of such a subject, might be given exclusively to Congress, (and the power is exclusive only so far as it is granted,) yet, on other branches of the same subject, the States might act, without interfering with the power exclusively granted to Congress. Commerce is such a subject. It is so complex, multifarious and indefinite, that it would be extremely diffi-cult, if not impracticable, to make a digest of all the operations which belong to it. One or more branches of this subject might be given exclu-sively to Congress; the others may be left open to the States. They may, therefore, legislate on commerce, though they cannot touch that branch which is given exclusively to Congress.[29]

. . . It was viewing the subject in this light, that induced his learned associate [Webster] to assume the position which had been mis-conceived on the other side. This proposition was, not that all the com-mercial powers are exclusive, but that those powers being separated, there

[27] *Ibid.,* 63.

[28] *Ibid.,* 159–86. At some length Wirt contended that the state was interfering with the Congressional patent power. *Ibid.,* 166–77. Webster merely touched upon this point, and Marshall ignored it in his opinion.

[29] *Ibid.,* 165.

are some which are exclusive in their nature; and among them, is that power which concerns navigation, and which prescribes the vehicles in which commerce shall be carried on.[30]

Webster and Wirt were offering a formula that the Court finally accepted in 1852.

Fully satisfied with the progress of the case, Webster was confident of victory. The decision "can go but one way," he wrote to his brother Ezekiel.[31] "I have no doubt," he reported to Jeremiah Mason, "the Court will decide, that so far as respects commerce between different states (which is this case) the law of N. York is inoperative."[32] Of the six judges sitting,[33] Webster had reason to count on at least four to sustain his appeal. Marshall's general views on national power were clear. There was furthermore a circuit decision by the Chief Justice giving a broad construction to the commerce clause, though Webster may not have been familiar with the case.[34] Justice William Johnson had recently invalidated a South Carolina Negro seaman act because he found it conflicted with the commerce clause, not merely a Congressional statute.[35] Webster may have known about this case, but did not cite it. Both Marshall and Johnson appeared to believe that national power was exclusive. And on such questions Justices Bushrod Washington and Joseph Story were reliable nationalists.[36]

Marshall's opinion for the Court has become a classic in the literature of constitutional history, which would suggest that what he said is well understood. This is not altogether true. Differing versions have appeared from the 1820's to the present. Some persons have believed that the Chief Justice went the whole

[30] Ibid., 180–81.

[31] Letter of Feb. 15, 1824, Claude H. Van Tyne (ed.), The Letters of Daniel Webster from Documents Owned Principally by the New Hampshire Historical Society (New York, 1902), 102.

[32] Letter also of Feb. 15, WS, XVI, 81.

[33] Smith Thompson of New York, recently appointed to the bench, did not assume his judicial duties until after the completion of the argument and thus did not participate in the decision.

[34] The Brig Wilson v. U. S., 30 Federal Cases 239 (1820).

[35] Elkison v. Deliesseline, 8 Federal Cases 493 (1823).

[36] For Washington's dislike of concurrent state and national powers, see Golden v. Prince, 10 Federal Cases 542 (1814). Story's enthusiastic praise of Webster's argument can be found in the Webster Papers, XII, Nos. 18009–15 (Library of Congress). This is an undated review of Webster's Speeches and Forensic Arguments (Boston, 1830).

distance in upholding exclusive national authority over interstate commerce.[37] Webster thought so.[38] The author of a modern treatise thinks Marshall decided there was a plenary power over intrastate commerce too, leaving little to the states.[39] In the New Deal era liberals advocating Federal economic regulation went to *Gibbons v. Ogden* for a constitutional benediction,[40] while conservatives of an earlier generation had invoked it to strike down state regulations because they were barriers to the "freedom of commerce."[41] Others have thought that Marshall's expansive view of the commerce clause was pure dictum and that the actual decision did not in the least impair state concurrent power. Taney took this position.[42] And Kent did too.[43] Still

[37] Even Oakley and Emmet believed this. In *North River Steamboat Co. v. Livingston*, 1 Hopkins Ch. 149 (New York, 1824), again acting as counsel for the steamboat monopoly, they conceded that Marshall had decided that Congress had exclusive power concerning *interstate* commerce. In the New York Court of Errors, the judges gave this interpretation to the Chief Justice's decision. One of them, John Savage, thought that Congress, according to Marshall, also had broad power over *intrastate* commerce. "Commerce among the states," said Savage, referred to that commerce among the *people* of the states, which *concerned* more states than one. *North River Steamboat Co. v. Livingston*, 3 Cowen 713 (New York, 1825). This case is complex and confusing, probably because the lawyers and judges were themselves confused.

[38] Webster's interpretation will be discussed below in connection with the *License* and *Passenger Cases*.

[39] William W. Crosskey, *Politics and the Constitution in the History of the United States* (2 vols., Chicago, 1953), I, 253–59. In the course of his extensive analysis of the meaning of the commerce clause, Crosskey decidedly approves Savage's opinion, cited in note 37 above.

[40] Edward S. Corwin, *The Commerce Power versus States Rights* (Princeton, 1936), 5–13; Hugh E. Willis, "Gibbons v. Ogden, Then and Now," *Kentucky Law Journal*, XXVIII (Mar., 1940), 280–305; Robert L. Stern, "Problems of Yesteryear—Commerce and Due Process," *Vanderbilt Law Review*, IV (Apr. 1951), 447, 462.

[41] Illustrative cases are *Wabash, St. Louis & Pacific R. Co. v. Illinois*, 118 U.S. 557 (1886) and *Leisy v. Hardin*, 135 U.S. 100 (1890). Furthermore, as the boundaries of exclusive national commerce power were drawn and as state police and taxing powers were defined, the Federal government was denied authority to meet new national problems relative to manufacturing corporations, labor, and agriculture. This was done in the name of Marshall, the nationalist. See the provocative, amusing articles by Frank R. Strong, "John Marshall—Hero or Villain," *Ohio State University Law Journal*, VI (Dec., 1939, and Mar., 1940), 42–62, 158–89.

[42] Taney's opinions in *Groves v. Slaughter* (1841) and the *License Cases* (1847) to be discussed below.

[43] James Kent, *Commentaries on American Law* (4 vols., Boston, 1884), I, 436–38. At the New York State Library is Kent's copy of the Supreme Court Report for 1824, in which he wrote a memorandum characterizing Marshall's opinion as "involved & perplexed & contradictory & arrogant." Quoted by Charles Fairman in W. Melville Jones (ed.), *Chief Justice John Marshall: A Reappraisal* (Ithaca, New York, 1956), 96.

others have been dissatisfied with Marshall for leaving the matter in confusion by straddling the fence between the exclusive and concurrent interpretations.[44]

Marshall's loose-constructionism dominated the opening section of his opinion.[45] Government must not be crippled, he said, by reading the Constitution too narrowly. Each power enumerated in the document must therefore accomplish the great objects the framers intended. Turning to the commerce clause, he painstakingly defined the words, "regulate," "commerce," and "among the states." "Commerce," he asserted, "undoubtedly, is traffic, but it is something more; it is intercourse. It describes the commercial intercourse between nations, and parts of nations, in all its branches, and is regulated by prescribing rules for carrying on that intercourse." And commerce "among the states" connoted that which is "intermingled" with them, concerns more states than one, and does not stop at the states' external boundaries. It was then an easy task for him to sweep aside the contention of Oakley and Emmet that commerce included only the sale and exchange of goods. So far as they concerned more states than one, steamboat navigation and passenger traffic were branches of commercial intercourse, for which Congress could prescribe rules. This flexible concept was Marshall's principal contribution in the case.

Following his exposition of a comprehensive national power, he considered the extent of state authority. He would leave to the states other and different powers to regulate their own strictly *internal* trade and to enact laws of police (health, safety, and morals) if they did not interfere with an act of Congress. Marshall did not specifically say what his position would be if a state attempted to exercise the same power delegated to Congress to regulate commerce and if Congress had not yet legislated upon it. He did say enough to *imply* his preference for Webster's argument that Congressional power over many

[44] Felix Frankfurter, *The Commerce Clause under Marshall, Taney and Waite* (Chapel Hill, North Carolina, 1937), 15–18; James B. Thayer, *John Marshall* (Boston, 1901), 89; Joseph P. Cotton, Jr., (ed.), *The Constitutional Decisions of John Marshall* (2 vols., New York, 1905), I, introduction, xxxiii–xxxiv. Of the many studies of the early commerce cases, the best is Frederick D. G. Ribble, *State and National Power over Commerce* (New York, 1937).

[45] The opinion is in 9 Wheaton 187–221.

subjects was exclusive whether or not it had been exercised.[46] All this proved to be an unnecessary inquiry in the present case, and Marshall admitted as much, for he did not rest his decision on either the exclusive or the concurrent doctrine. He held the New York laws conflicted with the United States Coasting Act of 1793, which established Gibbons' right of transporting passengers across state boundaries. Under the "supremacy" clause (Constitution, Article VI), the state statutes were therefore invalid.

There has been a persistent notion, perhaps originated by Webster himself, that Marshall fully accepted the lawyer's argument when he drafted his opinion. "It has been often observed," Webster once remarked, "that the opinion of the court, delivered by Chief Justice Marshall, follows closely the track of the argument."[47] His early biographer Peter Harvey records Webster's recollection that the argument so impressed Marshall that he took it in "as a baby takes in his mother's milk."[48] A number of writers come to a similar conclusion, probably on the basis of Webster's testimony rather than upon a study of the case itself.[49]

The fact is the Chief Justice used the Coasting Act, and not the commerce clause, to demolish the steamboat monopoly. Had he adopted Webster's reasoning *in toto* or in large part, as some have asserted, he would have given slight notice to the Congressional statute that did not seem to interest Webster much. Selecting the course that he did, Marshall devoted the last third of his opinion to a consideration of the Federal law. The result was a weak, probably erroneous construction of that act.[50]

[46] Marshall referred to Webster's argument that the national power to regulate "produces a uniform whole, which is as much disturbed and deranged by changing what the regulating power designs to leave untouched, as that on which it has operated." He remarked, "There is great force in this argument and the court is not satisfied that it has been refuted." 9 Wheaton 209.

[47] Webster to Everett, Oct. 30, 1851, *WS*, XVIII, 482.

[48] Peter Harvey, *Reminiscences and Anecdotes of Daniel Webster* (Boston, 1878), 142.

[49] Charles W. March, *Reminiscences of Congress* (New York, 1850), 77; Warren, *Supreme Court*, II, 70–71; Fuess, *Webster* I, 261.

[50] The law set out the requirements for enrolling vessels "entitled to the privileges of ships or vessels employed in the coasting trade" and established procedures relative to their payment of duties. *U. S. Statutes at Large*, I, 305–18. It revised a similar act of 1789 (*ibid.*, 55–65). Licensees were eligible for discounted customs duties and lower tonnage rates, as provided in statutes passed by the First

Chancellor Kent had been closer to the truth when he held that the statute of 1793 merely certified the character of ownership of vessels for the purpose of granting privileges under the customs system. Justice Johnson, who wrote a concurring opinion holding the New York legislation invalid because it collided with an exclusively national commerce power, convincingly declared that "if the licensing act were repealed to-morrow, the rights of the appellant . . . would be as strong as it is under this license."[51] There was no specific provision in the Coasting Act conferring privileges upon licensees such as Marshall awarded them by his deductions.

Gibbons v. Ogden would have been a more satisfactory precedent if Marshall had stood firmly on broad national authority operating from the Constitution itself, regardless of Congressional action, instead of backing away from that position toward which he leaned in the first two-thirds of the opinion. If he had done so, he would then have been following Webster. He would have been on even better ground if he could have overcome his usual reluctance to divide political power and had adopted the option proposed by Webster and Wirt that only the "higher branches" of the power were exclusive. Surely interstate steamboat traffic, in those days very important economically, was a "higher branch" admitting only national legislation.

There are reasons to suppose that the Chief Justice shunned both the exclusive and the concurrent theories because of the practical difficulties he feared would attend either of them. He was quite aware of the troubles growing out of a recent circuit case in which Justice Johnson had declared unconstitutional a South Carolina Negro seaman act.[52] Johnson had excited the slavery interest to fiery anger by his unreserved statement of exclusive commercial power.[53] In a letter to Story, Marshall referred to the great irritation in the South at what it considered

---

Congress. Ibid., 24–28. The Annals of Congress, 2 Cong., 2 sess., provide no information on the purposes of the Coasting Act, but it seems certain that the primary object was to foster a mercantilistic system in foreign trade instead of superseding state laws.

[51] 9 Wheaton 231–32.

[52] Elkison v. Deliesseline, 8 Federal Cases 493 (1823).

[53] Donald G. Morgan, Justice William Johnson: The First Dissenter (Columbia, South Carolina, 1954), 196–202.

a "judicial usurpation." "We have its [the South Carolina statute's] twin brother in Virginia," he continued, "a case has been brought before me in which I might have considered its constitutionality had I chosen to do so; but it was not absolutely necessary, and as I am not fond of butting against a wall in sport, I escaped on the construction of the act."[54] In the light of such an explosive situation, it is understandable why he cautiously skirted around the formula of exclusive power in *Gibbons* v. *Ogden*.

Concurrent authority was an unattractive alternative, for Marshall preferred to classify powers as absolutes, indivisible between two sovereignties. The power to regulate commerce among the states therefore belonged either to the states or the nation, not to both. Concurrent power would raise the question of degree and thus openly require judicial discretion. Inconsistently, Marshall seemed quite willing to distinguish between national commerce power and state police power. This would also entail judicial subjectivity, for the Court would have to determine the nature of the powers and to identify them when exercised in the circumstances of the case.[55] But he now escaped even this embarrassment by relying on a Congressional statute, conveniently construed to answer the delicate question at hand.

In the other two commerce cases coming up to his Court, the Chief Justice continued to avoid a definite position. His opinion in *Brown* v. *Maryland* (1827) invalidated a state license tax on imports because it was an impost on goods still in the "original package" and because it regulated foreign commerce in a particular where Congress had acted. He again found a Federal law, supreme over the state statute, as an instrument more suitable than the commerce clause of the Constitution itself.[56] Two years later he gave some encouragement to exponents of the concurrent-power theory in *Willson* v. *The Blackbird Creek Marsh Company* when he upheld a state law authorizing a dam across a small creek that flowed into the Delaware River. He did so in a brief opinion which probably

---

[54] Marshall to Story, Sept. 26, 1823, Story Papers (Massachusetts Historical Society.

[55] Ribble, *State and National Power over Commerce*, 8–51.

[56] 12 Wheaton 419, 436–49. He did not identify the statute but merely referred to "the act of Congress which authorizes importation." *Ibid.*, 448.

affirmed the exercise of police power rather than regulation of interstate commerce by the state.[57] In the future, however, the decision was frequently cited to support state commerce power when Congress had not acted.[58]

By 1837 when Taney became Chief Justice, the scene had changed. The slavery issue had grown to alarming proportions, thus causing some members of the bench to be wary of national interference with that institution under color of commercial regulation. Industrialization, a transportation revolution, the rise of an urban working class, the rapid extension of the frontiers of America brought many economic and social problems. The states found it necessary to adopt measures relative to these conditions, while Congress rarely acted. Taney and some of his Jacksonian associates were willing to approve the expansion of state power. This wing of the new Court was interested in the application of judicial rules to an actual situation. On the other hand, Justices Story, McLean, and Wayne preferred to compartmentize powers as state or national, police or commercial, with no overlapping. In many instances they would use dormant national power to prohibit suspicious innovations by the states. Well aware of the shifting currents, Webster wrote, "The present judges, I fear, are quite too much inclined, to find apologies for irregular & dangerous acts of State legislation."[59]

At its first term, the Taney Court decided *New York* v. *Miln* (1837) in favor of the state. New York had required masters of vessels to report data about, and give bonds for, arriving alien passengers. Justice Philip P. Barbour wrote the Court's opinion, approving the act not as a regulation of commerce but of police.[60] This reflected the justices' continued inability to agree concerning state commerce power. Smith Thompson, originally assigned to write the majority opinion, had the support of two other judges for his view that New York was properly regulating commerce. But since he could not speak for a majority of the seven justices, Thompson filed a concurring

---

[57] 2 Peters 245, 250–52 (1829).

[58] An example is Taney's opinion in the *License Cases,* 5 Howard 583–84 (1847).

[59] Webster to Fletcher Webster, Feb. 7, 1847, *WS,* XVI, 470.

[60] 11 Peters 102, 130–42.

opinion on that basis.[61] In a sharp dissent Story declared the law regulated commerce and collided with Congressional power, which, he said, was exclusive according to *Gibbons* v. *Ogden*.[62]

Webster had not participated in the *Brown, Willson,* and *Miln* cases, but in the 1840's he was counsel in others involving the yet unsettled problem. In some cases an implicit question was the relationship of the commerce power and slavery. Several states restricted the entrance of free Negroes, even sailors in harbor, and such legislation might be inconsistent with an expanded Congressional power over commerce. Justice Johnson had so ruled in his South Carolina circuit decision of 1823. Or might not Congress enact laws limiting or prohibiting the important interstate slave trade? The abolitionists warmly advocated such a policy, and many Southerners deeply feared it.

These fears were unfounded, for the Supreme Court gave little indication of impairing the slavery interest. An example of this judicial caution is *Groves* v. *Slaughter* (1841),[63] involving a Mississippi constitutional provision that prohibited the introduction of slaves into the state for sale. There arose a controversy whether this article of the state constitution was self-executing, in the absence of legislative action, and whether it conflicted with the Congressional commerce power. The arguments of counsel and the several opinions of the judges are more significant than historians have usually recognized.

Webster represented Slaughter in opposition to the state restriction. After an extensive argument that the Mississippi constitution was not self-acting, he turned to an analysis of state and national commerce powers:

> The Constitution confers on Congress the right to regulate commerce. The extent and effect of this grant of power has often been dis-

[61] *Ibid.,* 143–53; Carl B. Swisher, *Roger B. Taney* (New York, 1936), 394–96.

[62] 11 Peters 153–61. "In this opinion," he concluded, "I have the consolation to know, that I had the entire concurrence, upon the same grounds, of that great constitutional jurist, the late Mr. Chief Justice Marshall. Having heard the former arguments, his deliberate opinion was, that the act of New York was unconstitutional; and that the present case fell directly within the principles established in the case of Gibbons v. Ogden, 9 Wheat. R. 1, and Brown v. The State of Maryland, 12 Wheat. R. 419." See also Story's *Commentaries on the Constitution of the United States* (3 vols., Boston, 1833), II, sec. 1057–69.

[63] 15 Peters 449.

cussed in this Court; but all questions upon it are now fully settled. In the case of *Gibbons* v. *Ogden* it was decided that it extends to all commerce between state and state. It was held that the whole subject of commercial regulation was taken from the states, and placed in the hands of Congress.

This must be so, or the whole provision would be inoperative. Nothing, which is a regulation of commerce, can be affected by state laws. Regulation is in what it is considered best to leave free, and exempt from rule. Freedom of regulation, is regulation. Not declaring how action shall take place, allows the action to be performed.[64]

Webster claimed more from the steamboat-monopoly precedent than that decision justified. Certainly in 1841 the question of exclusive or concurrent commerce power was not "fully settled" in favor of exclusive national authority. But the idea of "freedom of regulation" offered substantial comfort to the slave states, because this represented, in Webster's mind, a limitation on Congress as well. Slaveholding was a property right, he declared, which the Constitution recognized. Therefore while Congress could not "interpose" against interstate traffic in slaves, it had the duty to protect "this right of property in the intercourse between states."[65] The lawyer would assign "the peculiar institution" to a unique and preferred position, compared to other subjects of commerce. As long as some states recognized this kind of property, transportation of slaves across state lines would be immune from unfriendly legislation by both national and state governments.[66]

Walter Jones and Henry Clay were Webster's associates, opposing Henry D. Gilpin and Robert J. Walker. Jones directed his attention entirely to an interpretation of the Mississippi constitution and sought to demonstrate that it was inapplicable without appropriate legislation.[67] In a brief part of his rambling, declamatory argument, Clay maintained exclusive national power,

[64] *Ibid.*, 494.   [65] *Ibid.*, 494–96.

[66] At least some Southerners did not understand Webster's position on this subject, because at this time, early 1841, Senator Alfred Cuthbert of Georgia and others were attacking him for upholding the power of Congress to prohibit the interstate slave trade. Cuthbert cited a memorial regarding the Missouri question in 1819 that Webster and other Bostonians had prepared. The Senator from Georgia would have profited by hearing Webster's more recent views in the Mississippi case. See *Cong. Globe,* 26 Cong., 2 sess., 199, 218, 328–32. The Washington *National Intelligencer* and the Washington *Globe* in early April, 1841, were engaged in an angry controversy concerning Webster's ideas about the matter.

[67] 15 Peters 477–81.

but only to sustain this branch of interstate commerce and give it "continued existence."[68] Gilpin and Walker replied that even if the state were regulating interstate commerce (which they denied) "in matters which are the legitimate objects of legislation by the states, they may exercise a power as well as the general government."[69]

The justices spread out in a confusing array of positions in deciding the case. Delivering the opinion of the Court, Thompson limited himself to the narrow question of whether or not the Mississippi constitution was self-executing. He held that it was not and thus had not made the importation of slaves illegal.[70] Thompson voiced his disapproval of broadening the controversy unnecessarily by concluding that "this view of the case makes it unnecessary to inquire whether this article in the constitution of Mississippi is repugnant to the Constitution of the United States; and, indeed, such inquiry is not properly in the case, as the decision has been placed entirely upon the construction of the constitution of Mississippi."[71] Some of Thompson's associates were not so restrained.

McLean was anxious to have his say. Admitting that the constitutional question concerning the commerce clause was "not necessary to a decision of the case," he discussed it anyway. *Gibbons* v. *Ogden,* he said, had ruled that the commerce power "is exclusively vested in Congress"; still, the transfer or sale of slaves was unlike other commerce. Slaves were considered persons as well as property, and consequently the "power over slavery belongs to the states respectively." Upholding each state's right "to guard its citizens against the inconveniences and dangers of a slave population," McLean plainly accommodated his doctrinaire interpretation of the commerce clause to his antislavery convictions. In doing so, he would deprive Congress of a broad area of power.[72]

---

68 *Ibid.,* 481–89.

69 *Ibid.,* 468. Gilpin's argument is in *ibid.,* 456–76. Walker spoke for four days, and his argument was so lengthy that it was relegated to an appendix in the reports. *Ibid.,* 496; Washington *Globe,* Mar. 27, 1841.

70 15 Peters 496–503.

71 *Ibid.,* 503. It will be remembered that Thompson had not wished to decide the *Miln* case on narrow grounds.

72 *Ibid.,* 503–08. McLean neglected to state his position with regard to the decision in the case. He later took pride, more than was his due, in saying that his

Taney concurred with the majority in the decision[73] but felt compelled to rebuke McLean. The Court had never applied the mere constitutional grant of Congressional power over commerce to invalidate state laws, the Chief Justice insisted.

> The point in dispute, therefore, would seem to be but little more than an abstract question which the Court may never be called upon to decide [he said]; and perhaps, like other abstract questions, it is destined, on that very account, to be more frequently and earnestly discussed. But until some case shall bring it here for decision, and until some practical purpose is to be answered by deciding it, I do not propose to engage in the discussion, nor to express an opinion.[74]

Nevertheless with respect to the regulation of the interstate slave trade, Taney resolutely declared that the states had exclusive power and that Congress had none.

Baldwin was the only justice who fully accepted Webster's argument on the commerce clause.[75] He was unwilling to remain silent, though he also acknowledged that this was a "collateral" question. Mississippi had regulated commerce rather than used its police power, he thought, and had thus exceeded its authority. This did not mean that Congress could prohibit or restrict interstate transportation in slaves. Some states classified slaves as property, he observed, and in those places "the owners are protected from any violations of the rights of property by Congress, under the fifth amendment of the Constitution."[76] With regard to slavery, then, the commerce clause was entirely "conservative in character," to protect against discriminatory treatment by the slave states.[77]

All seven justices sitting in this case thought that Congress could not restrict or prohibit the interstate slave trade. Six of them (all except Baldwin), for various reasons, would leave this subject entirely to the discretion of the states. Among

---

fellow judges followed "the lead of my opinion" and held that the "commercial power of Congress did not extend to the slave trade among the States; that Congress had no power over the subject, and that it belonged exclusively to the respective States." Washington *National Era*, Jan. 25, 1849.

[73] 15 Peters 508–10.   [74] *Ibid.*, 510.
[75] *Ibid.*, 510–17.   [76] *Ibid.*, 515.

[77] Webster, Clay, and Baldwin were developing a formula of substantive due process of law, subsequently so significant in constitutional law. See Corwin, *The Commerce Power versus States Rights*, 66–73.

these six were three (Story, McLean, and Wayne) clearly favoring exclusive national power over other branches of inter-state commerce. On the much narrower question decided in this case, a majority of four upheld the contract of sale that Web-ster's client Slaughter had made. Counsel and court had debated the issue between the exclusive and the concurrent formulas with inconclusive results, except to exempt slavery from the applica-tion of either formula.[78]

Four years later Webster argued another case, *Thurlow* v. *Massachusetts,* renewing the forensic dialogue. He repre-sented Samuel Thurlow, who appealed a conviction under a Massachusetts law requiring licenses for the sale of spirituous liquors in quantities less than twenty-eight gallons and thus virtually prohibiting liquor sales altogether. Because of absences the Court continued the case, and Webster reargued it in 1847 in conjunction with similar appeals from Rhode Island and New Hampshire. The three of them, known as the *License Cases,*[79] attracted great attention. During Webster's first argument, a correspondent said that there was "a crowded audience of both sexes to hear him speak; the first overflow of the court-room that has occurred during the present term."[80]

The lawyer was all the more effective since he expressed his own deep-felt convictions. On January 17, 1839, he had written to Governor Edward Everett, "I sincerely hope the license law may be repealed. We are attacked about here from all quarters, and by all sorts of weapons; of which the most annoy-ing are laughter and ridicule."[81] To uphold these temperance laws would strengthen extremists in the slave states, he feared, by encouraging excessive state power. "Everything may be said agt them [the license laws]," he declared, "which Massachusetts says agt So. Carolina."[82]

Webster organized his argument primarily around the

[78] Swisher, *Taney,* 400, has a useful chart of the justices' views.
[79] 5 Howard 504. *Thurlow* v. *Massachusetts, Fletcher* v. *Rhode Island,* and *Pierce* v. *New Hampshire.*
[80] Washington *National Intelligencer* (tri-weekly ed.), Feb. 1, 1845. The New York *Tribune,* Jan. 31, 1845, reported that the courtroom "presented quite an array of beauty and intellect, compared to the usual auditory there assembled."
[81] *WS,* XVIII, 43.
[82] Webster to John P. Healey, Feb. 18, 1845, *ibid.,* XVI, 432.

original-package formula of *Brown* v. *Maryland*.[83] The consequence of the state's policy, he observed, was to prohibit the sale
and consumption of spirits in spite of the fact that the tariff acts
of the United States authorized the importation of liquor. "If
retail is stopped," he continued, "wholesale must stop also. If
consumption is stopped, so must imports be stopped." Consumption succeeds retailing which succeeds importation. This
chain, linked to Congressional legislation, the states must not
break. The reasoning had merit, but it went further than Marshall had gone in *Brown* v. *Maryland*. Thurlow, Webster's
client, was not himself the importer, as Brown had been. He was
a retailer purchasing imports, and he had "broken" the package
into smaller quantities for sale to the consumer.[84] Although
logic may have been on Webster's side, conclusive precedent
was not.

Notwithstanding emphasis upon the conflict between the
license law and the tariff acts, Webster also advanced the
doctrine of exclusive power. This measure, he argued, infringed
upon Congressional authority to admit foreign articles for sale
in the domestic market. He even implied that national power
was plenary as well as exclusive, that it included intrastate as
well as interstate commerce, and that nothing was left to local
decision unless state police power (always anemic as Webster
defined it and inadmissible in this case) could operate.[85]

A word about the phraseology of the Constitution, (Art. I, Section
8) [he said]. "Among the States" Congress shall have power "to regulate
commerce with foreign nations and among the several States and with the
Indian tribes." Among the States does not mean among the sovereignties
of the States, but among the people of the States. "*Several* States" here

[83] The following description of Webster's argument is based upon an account
of it in the New York *Tribune,* Feb. 3, 1845. This is a fuller report than can be
found in 5 Howard 505–14, 538–39.

[84] In fact, the record did not show that Thurlow had purchased the liquor
directly from the importer.

[85] He challenged the credibility of the opposing counsel's statistics and arguments that attempted to prove a connection between intemperance and social evils.
Thus he contended that the statute was not a police measure. Chief Justice Lemuel
Shaw in the Massachusetts Supreme Court had upheld the laws as valid police
regulations; and in doing so, he contributed to the development of the whole doctrine of the police power. Leonard W. Levy, *The Law of the Commonwealth and
Chief Justice Shaw* (Cambridge, 1956), 233–37.

means *all* the States. I would not dwell on this exposition of words, but would recommend it to some writer on verbal criticism.

In looking back, one now thinks it strange that New York should have insisted on making her lakes and rivers and harbors a *mare clausum* to other States. Yet it had the sanction of such men as Spencer. The Chief Justice [Marshall] in his decision on this case [*Gibbons* v. *Ogden*], cut the smallest pattern possible for the work he had to do. He might have given the principle a wider application.[86]

Webster's associates were Rufus Choate and Benjamin F. Hallett. In the first argument of *Thurlow* v. *Massachusetts* Choate contributed little that is noteworthy except his majestic oratory, embellished with classical references and quotations.[87] Hallett, Thurlow's counsel in the state court, did not come to Washington for the case but filed a well-drafted brief (printed in the fifth volume of Howard's Reports). Always adept in using the assistance of others, Webster probably profited from a study of that brief. Hallett's principal point was that the state statute was not a police regulation, as it purported to be. In its actual administration, it prohibited the importation and sale of a whole class of goods which were not defective or injurious. The real objective, Hallett insisted, was to regulate commerce.[88]

To maintain that the legislation was not a genuine police-power measure was a stronger position than the one taken in *Fletcher* v. *Rhode Island* by John Whipple, who unwisely conceded that this license law had such a character. Whipple gave up too much ground, because some justices, McLean for example, would approve a state act if they could classify it under the police power. All that remained was the remote possibility of convincing the Taney wing of the Court that there was a conflict between the laws of Congress and of Rhode Island. Whipple did not contend, as Webster had, that the state was regulating commerce. As a result he abandoned the original-package

---

[86] Webster's suggested course of "verbal criticism" is followed in Crosskey, *Politics and the Constitution,* I, 50–136 and ff. The beliefs of both Webster and Justice Wayne that the *Gibbons* case had upheld exclusive national power were expressed in their speeches at Savannah, May 26, 1847. *WS,* IV, 97, 100.

[87] New York *Tribune,* Jan. 31, 1845; Claude M. Fuess, *Rufus Choate: The Wizard of the Law* (New York, 1928), 161–62.

[88] 5 Howard 514–19.

formula altogether instead of attempting to relate it to the present question.[89]

John P. Hale, representing the plaintiffs in error in the New Hampshire case, did not make these mistakes. He argued that the state had abused its power to protect the public health and morals; and because the power was abused, it interfered with interstate commerce.[90] New Hampshire had here prohibited the sale in the "original package" of a barrel of gin purchased in another state. In this respect, Hale had a less difficult case than Webster's. On the other hand, he did not have a Federal statute, such as Webster had, upon which to rely. He asked the Court to apply Marshall's dictum in *Brown* v. *Maryland,* "We suppose the principles laid down in this case to apply equally to importations from a sister State."[91] In *Pierce* v. *New Hampshire,* however, the chief obstacle to equating the fields of foreign and interstate commerce was the fact that in the former Congress had acted and in the latter it had not.

Counsel for the states in the *License Cases* justified the legislation on the ground of the police power. They asserted that *New York* v. *Miln* was a controlling precedent and that furthermore Marshall had conceded the state's power to protect public health and morals in both the *Gibbons* and the *Brown* cases. Webster's opponent, John Davis, sought to establish a causal relationship of excessive drinking with pauperism and crime. Massachusetts could move against these social evils, he said, even though national and state powers touched each other, for in a federal system of government the two sovereignties might act coincidentally unless their policies were plainly incompatible. And if the states were not regulating commerce, the original-package doctrine was inapplicable.[92]

As Webster feared, the Court approved all three license laws.[93] The decision was unanimous, but six justices in nine

---

[89] *Ibid.,* 540–50.   [90] *Ibid.,* 557–64.

[91] 12 Wheaton 449 (1827).

[92] Davis's argument is summarized in 5 Howard 519–38. Arguments by the attorneys for Rhode Island and New Hampshire are in *ibid.,* 550–54, 564–72.

[93] A month before the decision Webster observed that "nobody can tell what will be done with the *License laws,* so great is the difference of opinion on all these subjects on the Bench. My own opinion is; that the License laws will be sustained. . . ." Webster to Fletcher Webster, Feb., 1847, *WS,* XVI, 490. The letter is mistakenly dated January, 1848, by the editor.

opinions arrived at their conclusions by different paths.[94] Chief Justice Taney accepted the original-package rule as a "just and safe one."[95] The rule, Taney believed, upheld the Massachusetts and Rhode Island laws because they regulated retailing of ardent spirits as distinguished from their introduction as imports. In other words, the package had been broken, and national authority ceased. But in the New Hampshire case the Chief Justice did not apply the original-package formula, since Congress had not acted on the subject. Finding that the state was indeed regulating commerce, he thought "that the mere grant of power to the general government cannot, upon any just principles of construction, be construed to be an absolute prohibition to the exercise of any power over the same subject by the States."[96] He rejected the artificial distinction of the powers to regulate commerce and to protect health or safety. He was interested in the effects, not the purposes, of legislation, and in both instances the state was simply exercising its sovereignty, "the power to govern men and things within the limits of its dominion."[97]

Taney opposed the exclusive-power theory, and so did four of his associates. Yet they could not unite upon a common line of reasoning in these cases. Justices John Catron and Samuel Nelson were with Taney,[98] but the intractable states' righter, Peter V. Daniel, would limit Congressional power much more severely.[99] Levi Woodbury would not admit that the states were actually regulating commerce, though significantly, and suggestive of the later *Cooley* compromise, he defended their power to do so where local conditions warranted it.[100] Justice John McLean accepted the doctrine of exclusive national power. But he would uphold the license laws by classifying them as regulations of police.[101]

[94] Apparently all nine justices sat in the cases at the 1847 term.

[95] Taney recalled that he had argued *Brown* v. *Maryland* in behalf of the state, but "further and more mature reflection" had convinced him that Marshall's rule was "just and safe." 5 Howard 575. His opinion is in *ibid.*, 573–86.

[96] *Ibid.*, 579.   [97] *Ibid.*, 583.

[98] *Ibid.*, 597–609, 618.   [99] *Ibid.*, 611–18.

[100] *Ibid.*, 618–31. See especially pp. 624–26.

[101] 5 Howard 586–97. McLean would limit the original package rule to *foreign* commerce, thus making it inapplicable to *interstate* commerce, such as in the New Hampshire case. Grier concurred with McLean that the laws were regulations of police but expressed no opinion on the question of exclusive or concurrent commerce power. Wayne and McKinley were silent.

As troublesome as the *License Cases* were, the Court was experiencing more difficulty with the *Passenger Cases*[102] on the docket at this very time. Encouraged by the decision in *New York v. Miln* (1837), New York and Massachusetts enacted additional legislation to tax alien passengers arriving at their ports. The question of the constitutionality of these laws attracted much interest owing to the social and economic importance of immigration. Supporters of the measures thought that they were necessary in order to protect Eastern cities from the burden of foreign paupers and other undesirables. Opponents held that the states were unjustifiably regulating foreign commerce, often to the disadvantage of Western states anxious to receive immigrants. *Smith v. Turner* and *Norris v. Boston,* known as the *Passenger Cases,* were lengthily and ably argued. Webster, David B. Ogden, Rufus Choate, and J. Prescott Hall represented the plaintiffs in error, while John Van Buren, Willis Hall, John Davis, and George Ashmun were counsel for the states. At four successive terms the justices heard arguments before arriving at a decision in February 1849.[103] Webster, the only lawyer to appear at each term, worked resolutely to win these cases.

Webster concentrated upon the commerce clause. Reminiscent of his suggestion in the *Gibbons* case of exclusive national power over the "higher branches," his argument was that "the [Massachusetts] act in question is a regulation of commerce of the strictest and most important class, and that Congress possesses the exclusive power of making such a regulation."[104] The state was not really exercising its police power but interfering with the commerce of the United States by taxing it. And, he continued optimistically but erroneously, "This court has decided that Congress possesses the exclusive power to regulate commerce."[105] Making the now familiar appeal to history, he said

---

102 7 Howard 283 (1849).

103 *Ibid.,* 287–88 lists the times of argument and names of counsel.

104 In the Supreme Court Reports, *ibid.,* 288–89, only a short statement of the points advanced by Webster is given. A fuller account is in the Washington *National Era,* Mar. 4, 1847. A summary of another argument by Webster is in *WS,* XV, 403–04, taken from contemporary newspapers.

105 Washington *National Era,* Mar. 4, 1847. Webster cited *Groves* v. *Slaughter,* 15 Peters 504 (1841), which did not support his argument in the slightest.

that a look at circumstances during the 1780's showed that the framers of the Constitution intended Congress as the sole depository of the commerce power. This authority extended over persons as well as things in commerce, over ship masters as well as their vessels. If states assumed power, the national interest would suffer, for Eastern cities were the distributing agents of other parts of the Union. "Unaided by the rest of the Union," exclaimed Webster, "New York would be as nothing, a huge deformity, a *caput mortuum,* and nothing more."[106]

In addition to the commerce clause, Webster advanced other reasons why the statutes were invalid. The passenger laws, he said, were "repugnant to the actual regulations and legally manifested will of Congress." National legislation encouraged "the importation of all foreigners free, untaxed," a policy that the states were defeating. Specifically, he cited the customs statute of 1799 requiring reports of passengers and cargoes on ships arriving from foreign ports.[107] He saw the likelihood of conflict if two sovereignties acted on the same subject; however, he did not convincingly show that such conflict did exist in this situation. Another portion of the Constitution he relied upon was the prohibition of state imposts on imports. New York and Massachusetts were levying a passenger *tax* "in fraud of that prohibition."[108]

Despite the earlier opinions in *Groves* v. *Slaughter* indicating the contrary, Webster thought that some justices might be sensitive to the connection between the *Passenger Cases* and slavery, particularly the Southern restrictions on Negro seamen. To quiet such misgivings, he reportedly acknowledged that slavery was a "peculiar institution, the existence of which was recognized by the constitution of the United States. There it was placed by those who framed its existence, and he

106 *WS,* XV, 403.

107 Washington *National Era,* Mar. 4, 1847. The customs act of 1799 also provided that the personal baggage of passengers be exempted from duties. *U. S. Statutes at Large,* I, 661. Another national law, of February 25, 1799, required Federal officers to cooperate with the states in executing health and quarantine measures, but the states were prohibited from collecting tonnage and impost duties. *Ibid.,* 619. Webster said that Congress was currently considering legislation to remove the evils against which the states complained.

108 7 Howard 289.

did not wish to disturb it, nor should he lift his finger to do so. It belonged not to him, but to those alone who had power over it."[109]

Those present in the packed courtroom praised the power and eloquence of Webster's arguments.[110] Indeed he had made an extraordinary effort, which for the orator was considerable. In his own mind he felt satisfaction with his labors.

In my poor judgment [he wrote] the decision will be more important to the country, than any decision since that in the steamboat cause. That was one of my earliest arguments of a constitutional question. This will probably be and I am content it should be my last. I am willing to confess to the vanity of thinking that my efforts in these two cases have done something towards explaining and upholding the just powers of the government of the United States, on the great subject of commerce. The last, though by far the most laborious and persevering, has been made under great discouragements and evil auspices. Whatever I may think of the ability of my argument, and I do not think highly of it, I yet feel pleasure in reflecting that I have held on and held out to the end. But no more of self-praise.[111]

The other lawyers arguing against the passenger laws covered about the same ground that Webster had. All three of them maintained that at least with respect to foreign immigration, which was a branch of commerce, Congressional power was exclusive. They casually referred to Federal statutes, especially the tariff of 1842, but stressed an idea advanced by Webster in *Gibbons* v. *Ogden:* the silence of the national legislature had decreed its will that the entry of aliens be free from state hindrances. In order to distinguish these cases from *New York* v. *Miln,* they emphasized that the states were levying *taxes* upon commerce for revenue and were not exercising their police power.[112] This point seems to have had effect on several justices.

In defending the state laws John Davis and Willis Hall attempted to show that these were not actually regulations of commerce. They said that by the police power New York and

109 *WS,* XV, 404.

110 Washington *National Intelligencer* (tri-weekly ed.), Dec. 28, 1847, and Dec. 23, 1848; Warren, *Sup. Ct. in U. S. Hist.,* II, 449.

111 Webster to R. M. Blatchford, Feb. 3, 1849, *WS,* XVIII, 294–95.

112 7 Howard 290–314, 379–92.

Massachusetts were seeking relief from the burdens of the alien poor, were using revenues from the taxes to care for paupers, and were not interfering with any Federal law or treaty nor with any constitutional provision.[113] Hall made a telling attack upon the "silence-of-Congress" theory. That rule, he charged, would be "oppressive in the extreme, and impossible. . . . Oppressive, because it requires men to obey laws which they cannot know; impossible, because the courts cannot apply it."[114]

The arguments were full, touching upon every point that might possibly relate to the cases.[115] In fact, they were so full that the restless Webster yearned to escape the courtroom for his beloved Marshfield. "Mr. John Davis," he wrote, "has occupied this whole day [December 21, 1848], and he has either not finished, or else, like the angel to whom enraptured Adam listened, though he has finished, he 'seems still speaking.' "[116]

John Van Buren, son of the ex-President, took an advanced position in support of the New York law. Relying upon *Federalist 32* and judicial precedents, he spoke for full concurrent power by the states. And in the absence of specific Congressional action concerning alien admissions, a subject really reserved to the states, the passenger statute was valid.[117] According to the newspaper reports, Van Buren's argument was well organized and "ingenious."[118] Deploring earlier tendencies toward an alarming consolidation of political power to the states' disadvantage, he implied that the Taney Court was remedying the errors of the Marshall Court. "Fortunately," he continued, "it [consolidation of power] is known in the present day, only by its colossal bones, scattered through the reports of the early decisions of this Court. Its march was arrested—its

113 7 Howard 289–90, 315–79. For one of Davis's arguments, see also Washington *National Era,* Feb. 25, 1847.

114 7 Howard 361.

115 Other constitutional provisions that were explored included Article I, section 10 (prohibition of State imposts on imports) and Article I, section 9, paragraph 1 (the slave-trade clause). United States treaties, Congressional powers and laws concerning tariffs and naturalization, and state internal taxation were also discussed.

116 Webster to George Ticknor, Dec. 21, 1848, *WS,* XVI, 509.

117 7 Howard 366–79.

118 New York *Tribune,* Dec. 24, 1847.

life terminated in *New York* v. *Miln.* The noble ground there assumed has since been maintained, particularly in the Excise [License] cases." He commended the justices for their recent decisions, "indicating that just, liberal and popular impulses pervade this Bench." This aroused Webster's anger. The next day he responded, "The decisions referred to were not fossil remains, but pillars, grand, strong and perpetual; and as to the Court being influenced by popular impulses, that was a left-handed compliment which he would not pay to any Court for which he entertained any considerable degree of respect. It looked like barnburning."[119]

Webster was mildly hopeful of victory, more so than he had been in the *License Cases.* In February 1847 he thought that there was at least an "even chance" that the Court would pronounce the passenger acts unconstitutional despite the "predispositions" of the justices to uphold "dangerous" state legislation.[120] In December he remarked, "I have no doubt, whatever, that the law is with us; but where the Court may be, I know not."[121] A year later, shortly before the decision, he complained, "I argued my cause well enough, & if I were not always unlucky, now adays, in such cases, I should think I saw a glimmering of success. But tho' we shall get 4 Judges, I fear we may not a 5th."[122]

He did get the fifth judge (McKinley); and on February 7, 1849, in a five-to-four division the Court invalidated the statutes. McLean reiterated his view that the power of Congress to regulate commerce was exclusive. The fact that the states were levying a tax convinced him that they were unconstitutionally invading the area of national power and had not adopted a legitimate police measure. He believed that the two sovereignties could not share the commerce power, for it would be degrading to the states, as well as unsound practice, to say that they might act until Congress did.[123] Wayne attempted to summarize what the five justices of the majority, each writing an opinion, meant to decide. In doing so, however, he stated

119 *Ibid.,* Dec. 28, 1847.
120 Webster to Fletcher Webster, Feb. 7, 1847, *WS,* XVI, 470.
121 Webster to Fletcher Webster, Dec. 7, 1847, *ibid.,* 488.
122 Webster to Fletcher Webster, Dec. 26, 1848, *ibid.,* 509.
123 7 Howard 393–410.

his own approval of the exclusive-power doctrine, which *Gibbons v. Ogden* had clearly established, he said.[124] Catron and Grier avoided this point but undoubtedly did not agree with Wayne and McLean. They cited treaties and laws of the United States with which the passenger acts conflicted, thus attaching little practical importance to the question of exclusive or concurrent power since the national power had not lain dormant.[125]

McKinley wrote a puzzling opinion in which he said that he concurred with both McLean and Catron (in spite of the differences suggested above). Nevertheless, the "controlling influence" on his views was Article I, section 9, paragraph 1 of the Constitution. This provision forbade Congressional legislation on "the migration or importation of such persons as any of the States now existing shall think proper to admit" prior to 1808, and therefore by implication it delegated such power after that date. Though the clause had seemed merely to apply to the slave trade, McKinley thought the word "migration" referred to alien immigrants. If so, immigration was susceptible only of national regulation.[126]

As one of the four justices in the minority, Taney believed that the states had exclusive jurisdiction to admit or reject immigrants, a matter beyond the commerce power of Congress. But if admission of aliens should be considered an aspect of commerce, he adhered to his previously declared position that "the grant of a general authority to regulate commerce is not, therefore, a prohibition to the States to make any regulations concerning it within their own territorial limits, not in conflict with the regulations of Congress." He found no national statutes with which the state acts conflicted.[127] Nelson concurred with Taney.[128] Daniel also supported state concurrent power but denied that these laws were really regulations of commerce. He agreed with Taney that the precedent of *New York* v. *Miln* was control-

---

124 *Ibid.*, 410–29; Washington *National Intelligencer* (tri-weekly ed.), Feb. 10, 1849. Wayne clashed with Taney as to the application of *New York* v. *Miln* and charged that Barbour's opinion in that case had been unjustified in saying that persons were not subjects of commerce. He and Baldwin had apparently not agreed to such a ruling during the judges' conference. 7 Howard 429–37, 487–90; Alexander A. Lawrence, *James Moore Wayne, Southern Unionist* (Chapel Hill, 1943), 99–100; Swisher, *Taney*, 404–05.

125 7 Howard 437–52, 455–64.   126 *Ibid.*, 452–55.
127 *Ibid.*, 464–92.   128 *Ibid.*, 518.

ling.[129] Opposing political centralization by judicial construction, the Virginian exclaimed in alarm, "This would be fulfilling almost to the letter the account in the Tale of the Tub, of Jack, Peter, and Martin engaged in the interpretation of their father's will."[130]

Woodbury's dissent is interesting because it foreshadowed the compromise between the exclusive and the concurrent theories that the Court soon accepted.[131] Though classifying the state acts as municipal or police legislation, Woodbury asserted that at least parts of commerce do not require a "uniform rule by Congress."[132] The states had extensively regulated these parts in the past, he observed, and could validly regulate them in the future. He said, "So far as reasons exist to make the exercise of the commercial power exclusive, as on matters of exterior, general, and uniform cognizance, the construction may be proper to render it exclusive, but no further, as the exclusiveness depends in this case wholly on the reasons, and not on any express prohibition, and hence cannot extend beyond the reasons themselves."[133]

Three years later in *Cooley* v. *Board of Wardens* (1852), a majority of the Court arrived at a formula for balancing the claims of state and national powers.[134] Webster did not argue this case but must have found the formula quite acceptable. Five justices took the same position, unusual for the Taney period, upholding a Pennsylvania statute regulating pilotage of vessels engaged in interstate and foreign commerce. Justice Benjamin R. Curtis delivered an opinion that rejected both the exclusive and concurrent doctrines. He held that the state was validly regulating a part of interstate commerce and therefore did not evade the question by labeling the act an exercise of the police power.[135]

129 *Ibid.*, 494–515.   130 *Ibid.*, 518.
131 *Ibid.*, 518–72.   132 *Ibid.*, 546.
133 *Ibid.*, 559. Webster was soon worried about state acts to circumvent the Court's decision by imposing "optional" taxes on ship masters. Webster to Fletcher Webster, Feb. 1, 1850, *WS*, XVI, 532. Ultimately this approach was disapproved in *Henderson* v. *New York*, 92 U. S. 259 (1876).
134 12 Howard 299 (1852).
135 *Ibid.*, 311–21. Note that in his *Gibbons* argument years earlier, Webster had conceded to the states the power to regulate pilotage, but as an exercise of the police power.

Either absolutely to affirm [he continued] or deny that the nature of this power requires exclusive legislation by Congress is to lose sight of the nature of the *subjects* of this power, and to assert concerning all of them, what is really applicable but to a part. Whatever subjects of this power are in their nature national, or admit only of one uniform system, or plan of regulation, may justly be said to be of such a nature as to require exclusive legislation by Congress.[136]

Curtis did not specify which subjects demanded uniform, national supervision or which were open to state regulation owing to the diversity of local conditions. Drawing the boundaries might be the function of Congress. For example, in this case, a Federal law of 1789 affirmed state pilotage regulations. But the Court in the following years was disposed to reserve to itself the responsibility for classifying the subjects. On this occasion Curtis confined his attention to the subject of pilotage, which, he declared, "is local and not national; and it is likely to be the best provided for, not by one system, or plan of regulations, but by as many as the legislative discretion of the several states should deem applicable to the local peculiarities of the ports within their limits."[137]

In these early commerce cases Webster exerted a strong influence upon the direction of constitutional history. First, he consistently argued the anti-state side, in a day when the "negative implications" of the commerce clause were more important than the seldom used delegation of national power.[138] Second, although he failed to win a complete victory for the doctrine of exclusive national power, he lost very little to the states. For many years, owing to judicial conservatism, the states found difficulty in regulating any aspect of interstate commerce; indeed not until the 1930's did the Court approve a genuine state concurrent power.[139] Third, Webster himself first suggested the *Cooley* formula of partially concurrent power. He was more willing, however, to concede something to the states in *Gibbons* v. *Ogden* (exclusive national power only over

[136] *Ibid.*, 319. Italics added.
[137] *Ibid.*
[138] John B. Sholley, "The Negative Implications of the Commerce Clause," *University of Chicago Law Review*, III (June, 1936), 556–96.
[139] See Justice Rutledge's discussion in *Prudential Insurance Co.* v. *Benjamin*, 328 U. S. 408, 412–20 (1946) and Chief Justice Stone's opinion in *Southern Pacific Co.* v. *Arizona*, 325 U. S. 761, 763–84 (1945).

the "higher branches") than in the later *Passenger Cases.* Fourth, he developed a concept very similar to the future rule of "silence of Congress." In the late nineteenth century the fact that Congress was silent about a subject of commerce was often proof enough to conservative judges that the state legislatures could not act. Fifth, he put forward the idea of "freedom of commerce," best expressed in *Groves* v. *Slaughter,* whereby neither Congress nor the states could restrict some portions of interstate commerce. This meant that the power to facilitate commerce would be greater than the power to limit it.

Webster's position was not faultless. Like Marshall, he believed that governmental powers, once defined and distributed, were immutable because they rested upon the universal principles of natural law as well as upon the Constitution. Rarely could Marshall and Webster reconcile themselves to a power being available to both state and nation.[140] The "nature of the power," an expression they often used, did not permit its division. So the wall of separation between the two sovereignties must be unassailable. But for a long time most of the Congressional commerce power that Marshall and Webster nourished so carefully remained dormant, while the Court sometimes forbade the states from acting on problems that required action. In countering this tendency, Taney approved a kind of federalism in American government profoundly disturbing to Webster but useful to this day. Taney's mode of reasoning was more pragmatic than Webster's, but the lawyer's objectives were not at all abstract. As an economic conservative, he disliked tampering with property interests by any government. He disliked it so much he would even use the commerce clause to protect property in slaves.

[140] An exception was *Sturges* v. *Crowninshield,* 4 Wheaton 122 (1819), but Marshall still found a way to invalidate a state insolvency law on the basis of the contract clause.

IX

CONSTITUTIONAL LAWYER
IN AMERICAN POLITICS

No one studying the life of Webster can overlook the connection between his law practice and his political career. Four terms in the House (1813–17 and 1823–27), subsequent service in the Senate until 1850, appointments to the State Department under Tyler and Fillmore kept him in public office almost continuously. Although a good many contemporaries were also active both at the Supreme Court bar and on the political scene, none matched Webster. Henry Clay, for example, came into Court much less frequently; others, like John Sergeant, were secondary political figures. As one looks at this unique dual career, he discovers some interesting relationships between the two sides of Webster's life at the capital.

At times professional commitments and political interests seemed larger than even a man of Webster's energy could manage. During momentous legislative debates, on internal improvements in 1824 and nullification in 1830 and slavery in 1850, he argued cases in Court. Often this division of labor meant he could not fill either responsibility as well as he wished. By the late 1830's he wavered between resigning from the Senate and giving up legal practice. As a matter of fact he took few cases at this time, though an added reason was his rising disinterest, rather dissatisfaction, as Taney's Court made new departures.[1] Within a few years he resumed the pace, mainly because he needed the income; and in the late forties while Senatorial obligations mounted, he handled many of his most important cases.

Despite obvious handicaps, his activities in law and politics were usually compatible, indeed complementary. Attorneys such as Webster, debating great constitutional issues in Congress, discussed them confidently in ground-breaking arguments in Court. States' rights, land policy, public finance, bankruptcy, slavery were judicial as well as legislative questions; and judges listened to counsel attentively on these subjects. In *Groves* v. *Slaughter* (1841) Webster and the other attorneys spoke exhaustively about Congressional power over interstate slave trade at the very time the topic precipitated long debate in the Senate.[2] Similarly in Congress Webster applied to political controversies doctrines to which he had contributed as a lawyer. His admirers listened as if they were hearing a definitive lecture by the Defender of the Constitution. Even rivals and opponents showed respect for his knowledge, if not his judgment.

Involvement with Congressional proposals and legislation concerning the judiciary nicely illustrates the relationship of his two careers. For years after Webster entered Congress, he and his colleagues considered how to reform the system of Federal circuit courts, then increasingly inadequate for a growing country. The West had just one of the nation's seven circuit courts, and this court sat in only three of the nine states beyond the mountains.[3] Inasmuch as each justice of the Supreme Court presided over a circuit, multiplying or redrawing the circuits might also affect that tribunal at the capital by changes in the number or duties of its members. Presidents Madison, Monroe, John Quincy Adams, and Jackson recommended action; but from 1816 until 1837 (when it passed a judiciary act for this purpose), Congress extensively and heatedly discussed the matter without positive results.[4]

[1] Webster to Samuel Jaudon, Jan 13, 1839, *WS*, XVIII, 42.
[2] *Congressional Globe*, 26 Cong., 2 sess., 199, 218, 329–32.
[3] Ohio, Kentucky, and Tennessee. There were nine transmontane states by 1820.
[4] Article III of the Constitution empowers Congress to determine the number of judges and the appellate jurisdiction of the Supreme Court. It also authorizes Congress to create and modify the system of lower Federal courts.

Extreme dissatisfaction in some quarters with the Court's decisions deepened the difficulty of improvements. From an early time Jefferson and his followers had opposed a broad judicial power that might expand national authority at the expense of state sovereignty or individual rights. Whenever the Court decided a case in such a way as to stimulate this lingering sentiment, proposals to limit its power came forward. *Cohens* v. *Virginia* (1821), asserting the Court's appellate jurisdiction in cases decided by state tribunals, greatly irritated the defenders of states' rights. And *Green* v. *Biddle,* decided in preliminary fashion in 1821 and finally in 1823, further aroused their wrath. The *Green* decision invalidated Kentucky's statutes giving credit for improvements to occupants of lands successfully claimed by others. The Court made liberal awards of land to Virginia citizens on the basis of the contract clause and thus convinced people in Kentucky and elsewhere that their liberty was seriously endangered.[5] Congressmen from the aggrieved states urged antidotes: allocation of appellate jurisdiction to the Senate over cases involving the validity of state laws; requirement of more than a mere majority of Supreme Court justices to strike down a state statute; repeal of that section of the Federal judiciary act authorizing appeals to the Court from state decisions. All efforts, whether for legislation or constitutional amendment, failed, but they died hard. Whenever Congress considered any other question concerning judicial reform, the states' rights advocates sought to attach their amendments to the pending bills.[6]

In the House responsibility to study and report on these topics belonged to the Judiciary Committee, on which Webster served during his four years as a representative from New Hampshire. At his last session, beginning in December, 1816, he sponsored a proposal drafted by Justice Story that would have

[5] 8 Wheaton 1 (1823). The Court held that Kentucky "occupancy" laws violated the compact between Virginia and Kentucky, a contract within the meaning of the Constitution, Article I, section 10. Kentucky and other Western states persisted in enforcing such legislation; and, in time, the Supreme Court acknowledged their power to do this. Paul W. Gates, "Tenants of the Log Cabin," *Mississippi Valley Historical Review,* XLIX (June, 1962), 3–31.

[6] Charles Warren, *The Supreme Court in United States History* (3 vols., Boston, 1923), II, 112–28; Albert J. Beveridge, *The Life of John Marshall* (4 vols., Boston, 1916–19), IV, 340–96; Webster to Joseph Story, Jan. 14, 1822, *WS,* XVII, 320.

expanded the jurisdiction of the Federal courts: the bill would have conferred all the original jurisdiction permissible under the Constitution but then exercised by the states (this would have principally involved civil cases arising under the national Constitution and laws).[7] Out of the committee came also a general judiciary bill for reorganizing the circuit system, but this broader bill, with Webster's measure incorporated, failed. On the whole, Webster was not dissatisfied, because he disliked permitting President Madison to fill new judgeships it would have created.[8]

When he returned to the House in December, 1823, he rejoined the committee, this time as chairman, and remained four years until he moved over to the Senate. Doubtless he had not expected the chairmanship, because the previous chairman, William Plumer, Jr., was still in the House; but Plumer in a show of deference to his legal attainments had urged Speaker Henry Clay to name Webster.[9] The new chairman performed his duties skillfully. Though his measures failed, the truth was he faced heavy handicaps of politics and opinion.

Active he certainly was. He framed a bill to remodel the circuit system by extending it to Western states. Here he had three possible courses. First, in order to man two or three new circuits, add more justices to the Supreme Court, then composed of seven members. Objections were that the Court would be too large and that, as the nation grew, Congress eventually would have to stop enlarging the Court. Second, increase the circuits and relieve Supreme Court justices of circuit travel. But did not circuit duty give justices experience on the local level? Third, assign new Western judges only to circuit duty and not to the Supreme Court. But would the West accept such an arrangement, which would make their judges unequal to Easterners?

As he pondered these questions, Webster sought advice from Jeremiah Mason and Joseph Story, the two men whose legal knowledge he most admired. Mason responded by recom-

---

[7] No doubt Story was moved to submit the proposal because of the Court's clash with the Virginia judges in *Martin* v. *Hunter's Lessee,* 1 Wheaton 304 (1816). William W. Story (ed.), *Life and Letters of Joseph Story* (2 vols., Boston, 1851), I, 293–96.

[8] Webster to Story, Dec. 19, 1816, *WS,* XVI, 36–37; *Annals of Congress,* 14 Cong., 2 sess., 190, 206–07, 1056–57.

[9] William Plumer, Jr., "Reminiscences of Daniel Webster," *WS,* XVII, 549. See also Webster to Plumer, Feb. 15, 1824, *ibid.,* XVI, 81.

mending a partial-circuit plan of two new Western judges to serve on circuit but not on the Supreme Court.[10] Unreconstructed Federalist that he was, Mason really preferred to revive the short-lived system established by his party in the statute of 1801, separating the Court from circuits. Likelihood of passing such a bill was slight in view of the partisanship associated with this last-minute act of the Adams administration.[11] As for Story, with unusual detachment the Justice seemed to have no strong preference for any of the three lines of reform. The time would come, he thought, when the volume of judicial business would make circuit travel by justices impossible, but meanwhile an addition of two members to the Court would satisfy him, for it would bring on men having information about different bodies of local law.[12] By mid February, 1824, Webster was ready to report his bill to the House—a partial-circuit plan much as Mason had advised. He believed that excusing all justices from circuit travel would deprive the Court of essential contact with the profession and the people, but he proposed to add four Western judges for circuit duty only. He wished also to expedite cases on the clogged Supreme Court docket by lengthening the annual terms. Occupied with other matters, the House did not show interest in the bill, considering it briefly in May but not voting on it.[13] More important to several representatives were ways to reduce the Court's powers; consequently resolutions reappeared to deny appellate jurisdiction over cases determined by state courts and to require more than a majority of the justices to invalidate state statutes. Webster easily checked these moves, though he did not secure passage of his own bill.[14]

The House still seemed unprepared to act on the judiciary bill the next session, the short session ending March 4, 1825, when attention centered on the undecided presidential election

[10] Webster to Mason, Dec. 22, 1823, ibid., XVI, 78; Mason to Webster, Dec. 29, 1823, Webster Papers (New Hampshire Historical Society).

[11] The law had been repealed by the first Congress of Jefferson's administration in 1802, and since then the justices had been traveling the circuit.

[12] Webster to Story, Dec. 26, 1823, and Jan. 4, 1824, WS, XVII, 339–40, 412–13; Story to Webster, Jan. 4 and 10, 1824, Story (ed.), Story, I, 435–39.

[13] Webster to Mason, Feb. 15, 1824, WS, XVI, 81; Annals of Cong., 18 Cong., 1 sess., 1701–02, 2617.

[14] Webster to Story, Apr. 10 and May 4, 1824, WS, XVII, 349–50; Annals of Cong., 18 Cong., 1 sess., 915–16, 1291, 2514–41, 2618–19.

of the previous autumn. The House was busy with selecting a president from the three leading candidates, none with a majority of the Electoral College. Webster did not even call his measure up for debate.[15] Again critics of the Court, led by the Kentucky delegation, discoursed on ways to diminish judicial power; but the time for legislation of this kind had passed. The Senate approved in principle a bill to increase the Court to nine and create two more Western circuits with new justices. The bill returned to committee for drawing circuit boundaries and did not come back to the floor in time for final disposition.[16]

Possibly another reason why Webster did not then press for his bill was his preoccupation with another proposal, one to amend the Federal criminal code. The law of 1790 left large gaps in Federal jurisdiction over crimes on the high seas, within harbors, and in areas under direct national authority such as forts and arsenals. As counsel in *U.S.* v. *Bevans* (1818) Webster had successfully argued that the act of 1790 did not give the United States circuit courts cognizance over murders on naval vessels in harbors.[17] Justice Story had disliked that decision and still more the Court's earlier holding in *U.S.* v. *Hudson* (1812) that there was no Federal common law in criminal cases.[18] Ever since 1816 Story had been asking Webster and other Congressmen to authorize circuit courts to administer the common law in criminal cases by "legal construction."[19] When these attempts failed, the judge drew a criminal code, largely borrowed from England, and Webster guided it through Congress in this 1825 session.[20] Story's code, derived from old English law, carried heavy penalties for many crimes. Murder, arson, rape, forceful and violent theft upon the seas, and other

15 *Register of Debates,* 18 Cong., 2 sess., 369–71; Webster's draft of reply to Speaker Henry Clay on judiciary bill, [Jan., 1825], "Miscellaneous Bound," XX (Massachusetts Historical Society). As an Adams supporter, Webster would naturally have preferred to wait until the new administration commenced before creating judicial positions for presidential appointment.

16 *Register of Debates,* 18 Cong., 2 sess., 527–36, 582–89, 603–20, 630. Martin Van Buren urged the Senate to postpone the bill and was probably responsible for the fact that his committee did not report the bill back with circuit boundaries.

17 3 Wheaton 336.

18 7 Cranch 32. Thus crimes against the United States were punishable only under statutes of Congress.

19 Story (ed.), *Story,* I, 297–300.

20 Story to Webster, Jan 4, 1824, *ibid.,* 437; Story to John Berrien, Feb. 8, 1842, *ibid.,* II, 402.

acts were subject to capital punishment. Several legislators, especially the learned Edward Livingston, objected to the code's severity; however, Webster managed to retain most of the original provisions. On one important point he had to give way. The code applied to offenses within Federal admiralty jurisdiction, but Webster accepted an amendment to exempt areas already under state cognizance. Since the boundaries of American admiralty law were being probed in the courts and would later extend well beyond traditional limits, states' rights representatives gained a good deal from this amendment.[21] Story was not satisfied, for to assure the bill's passage he had selected only a minor part of the whole English code. Nonetheless, the act was more adequate than he thought, because state courts were competent to handle many classes of cases he called "dispunishable" under Federal law.[22]

When the first Congressional session of the new Adams administration opened in December, 1825, Webster then began a major effort to pass another judiciary bill. On the sixteenth he conferred with the President, who talked about the problem at some length and even mentioned Postmaster General John McLean of Ohio and Senator Hugh White of Tennessee as possible appointees for new places on the bench.[23] Within a week Webster reported a new bill, altered to suit his colleagues in committee. Instead of the partial-circuit plan the bill would establish new Western circuits manned by additional Supreme Court justices; and instead of two more justices, which Webster and Adams preferred, there would be three.[24]

An involved hassle followed. Soon after New Year's Day, 1826, the House debated the bill and continued through much of January. At the outset Webster spoke for his measure. The West, he said, deserved a judicial system equal to the East's,

---

21 *Register of Debates,* 18 Cong., 2 sess., 150–58, 165–68, 335–41, 348–55, 363–65, 713. States' rights fears were further quieted at this very time by Story's opinion in the *Steam-Boat Thomas Jefferson,* 10 Wheaton 428 (1825), holding that admiralty jurisdiction was limited by the extent of the ebb and flow of the tide. But later this rule was abandoned. See above, Chapter III.

22 Story to John M. Berrien, Feb. 8 and July 23, 1842, Story (ed.), *Story,* II, 402–06. This would of course not include cases of crimes on the high seas.

23 Charles F. Adams (ed.), *Memoirs of John Quincy Adams* (12 vols., Philadelphia, 1874–77), VII, 83–84.

24 Webster to Story, Dec. 31, 1825, *WS,* XVII, 400; Webster to Ezekiel Webster, Jan. 29, 1826, *ibid.,* 401.

but for many years litigation had overburdened the courts there while Congress futilely discussed relief. Other proposals had failed to pass; and so Webster contended that though this bill was not the kind he would wish above all others, it was the only kind a majority of Congress would accept. In this speech he avoided a doctrinaire position and seemed interested in passing some sort of legislation rather than insisting upon a particular plan. He did speak unequivocally in favor of circuit travel by Supreme Court justices. There were several advantages to the judges, he believed—contact with local usages and circumstances, constant employment when the Court at Washington did not sit, and experience in special branches of the law such as equity and admiralty.[25]

One by one, Representatives gained the floor for long speeches on the bill and on the role of the judiciary in government generally. Westerners to a man cried for reform on the ground of equal justice to their section. Still rankled by *Green v. Biddle,* Kentuckians may have hoped that increasing the Court would reverse that ruling. But Webster drew support for his bill from all parts of the country; and, as a whole, attitudes toward the Court were respectful or even adulatory. A concrete argument for more Western judges came from John C. Wright of Ohio, who presented a statistical table indicating population, litigation, and geographical extent of existing and proposed circuits. Several other Congressmen also showed that they had given much thought to the question.[26]

The opposition sharpened their poleaxes and went after the Webster bill. Charles F. Mercer of Virginia led the onslaught. Suspecting that the West's purpose was to pack the Court to reverse *Green* v. *Biddle* and thereby deprive his state of its rights, Mercer declared the Court should be smaller but certainly no larger. He wished to relieve justices of circuit duty entirely. This was the only way, he insisted, to clear the enormous backlog on the docket, for the few days the present bill would add to the annual term could not possibly suffice.[27] The argument now seems convincing, but politicians of the 1820's re-

[25] Speech of Jan. 4, 1826, *ibid.*, V, 150–63.
[26] *Register of Debates,* 19 Cong., 1 sess., 883–932, 940–1014, 1020–1148.
[27] *Ibid.*, 892–909, 1125–39.

membered the partisan Federalist act of 1801 too well to accept it. Nor were sensible suggestions to increase responsibilities of district judges received with enthusiasm.[28]

Against each assault Webster stood fast and had a sizeable majority with him. In time it became obvious he did not need to compromise. He defeated motions to amend, postpone, and return the bill to committee. January 25 he closed debate with a set speech defending the original proposals in every particular.[29] The bill passed the House by a margin of more than two to one.[30]

Webster's counterpart in the Senate, chairman of the Judiciary Committee, was the redoubtable Martin Van Buren, who sponsored a bill similar to the one approved by the Senate the previous session and to the House measure just passed. For a week in early April Senators had their say about the judicial system.[31] In zeal and amplitude none surpassed John Rowan of Kentucky, who warned of the Court's dangerous tendencies to consolidate national power and ignore the just rights of Western farmers. Again Rowan offered an amendment to require seven of ten justices to invalidate a state law. But when his motion failed, he lent support to the pending bill to create new circuits.[32] Van Buren, supple politician that he was, expressed sympathy with Rowan's strictures but counseled against amendments that might defeat the general bill.[33] The rank and file dutifully followed Van Buren, and the bill passed.[34]

Then trouble flared, for one difference between the House and Senate bills, which first seemed inconsequential, inflated to an insurmountable obstacle. In drawing circuit boundaries the Senate committee had included Kentucky and Ohio in one circuit and Indiana, Illinois, and Missouri in another; the

[28] The district courts were almost entirely admiralty tribunals. The district judge also sat with a Supreme Court justice on circuit for his district.

[29] WS, V, 165–77.

[30] Register of Debates, 19 Cong., 1 sess., 1148–49.

[31] Ibid., 13–16, 30, 409–83, 497–571.   [32] Ibid., 423–63.

[33] Van Buren declared that ideally he would like to see the contract clause "expunged" from the Constitution.

[34] Register of Debates, 19 Cong., 1 sess., 571. The vote was thirty-one to eight. Among those voting against the bill were John M. Berrien, John M. Clayton, Nathaniel Macon, and John Randolph. Levi Woodbury opposed it but abstained from voting.

House had combined Kentucky with Missouri, Ohio with Indiana and Illinois.[35] When Van Buren reported his bill, he professed no interest either way. It was a matter of local preference, he said. Yet he subsequently became unyielding and moved that the Senate "adhere" to its plan of distributing circuits. Privately he charged that President Adams and Representative Webster were anxious to appoint Postmaster General John McLean of Ohio to the Court, a move supposedly impossible if Kentucky and Ohio were in the same circuit.[36] On the Senate floor he made only a brief, veiled allusion to a "scramble for office." His colleagues not only adopted his motion to "adhere" to their version of the bill but took the unusual step of refusing to discuss the question with the House in conference.[37]

Webster felt sorely disappointed. Sentiment in his own committee compelled him to recommend that the House not surrender to the Senate, though personally he inclined to go far toward accommodation. The outcome was an impasse preventing any legislation, and thus expired the last serious effort toward reform for several years.[38] Occasional gestures were made, but eleven years were to elapse before Congress enacted a statute for two Supreme Court justices and two more Western circuits. After 1826 Webster showed less interest in the whole problem and even in the 1837 session voted for the act without comment.

It is not easy to explain this puzzling behavior in the two houses, each passing similar bills, both adhering to their positions, one refusing even to talk about minor differences. The fact that Adams wished to appoint McLean to the Court may have been a barrier, yet in April, at the time of the Senate bill's passage, Adams appointed Robert Trimble of Kentucky to a

[35] Another difference was the Senate requirement that the new Western judges must reside in the circuits to which they were assigned.

[36] Van Buren to Benjamin F. Butler, May 15, 1826, Van Buren Papers, cited in Warren, *Sup. Ct. in U.S. Hist.*, II, 143 n. 1.

There would have already been a justice, the newly nominated Robert Trimble, residing in the proposed Kentucky-Ohio circuit.

[37] *Register of Debates*, 19 Cong., 1 sess., 671, 688, 691.

[38] *Ibid.*, 2303, 2514–19, 2581–86, 2601–05, 2627–28, 2631–32, 2638–48, 2658; Webster to Story, May 8, 1826, *WS*, XVII, 405; Webster to Edward Cutts, May 9, 1826, *ibid.*, XVI, 132; Webster to Story, May 13, 1826, Story Papers (Massachusetts Historical Society); *Senate Document No. 89*, 19 Cong., 1 sess.; *House Report No. 207*, 19 Cong., 1 sess.

vacancy on the bench.[39] If Adams had been as inflexibly determined upon the McLean appointment as Van Buren alleged,
he could have chosen McLean instead of Trimble, and it would
have made no difference how the circuits were drawn. Actually
disagreement between the houses remained unresolved because
Van Buren and his followers were simply in no mood to compromise anything with Adams or Adams's spokesman in the
House, Webster. Van Buren and many others in Congress were
already looking ahead to the next presidential election.[40]

Throughout his many years as lawyer and politician, a
fundamental of Webster's constitutional thought was his great
confidence in Congress. The national legislative power was broad,
he believed, and must be so either positively to enact laws or
negatively to limit the states. Concerning the first of these purposes his reasoning was Hamiltonian, best exemplified in *Mc-
Culloch* v. *Maryland*. The Constitution, Article I, section 8,
delegating Congressional powers, must be loosely construed; an
enumerated power implied others; some authority inhered in all
governments; the "necessary and proper" clause justified means
to attain legitimate ends. Of all his cases few tested the constitutionality of national legislation,[41] largely because Congress
did not then exercise its powers fully. Still, many cases did involve Congressional power as a prohibition on state power over
the same subject, the issue in *Gibbons* v. *Ogden* where he and
Marshall stretched the meaning of the Federal Coasting Act
beyond credibility in rejecting state statutes. With regard to
bankruptcy, Webster in *Ogden* v. *Saunders* insisted that Con-

[39] This was a vacancy created by the death of Justice Thomas Todd and is
to be differentiated from the new places that would have been provided by the
judiciary bill.

[40] It must be admitted that, in the earlier stages, Van Buren had gone a long
way toward judicial reform by sponsoring a measure which would have empowered
Adams to appoint three new justices. Still he could not antagonize the West by
doing less.

[41] An exception was *American Insurance Co.* v. *Canter,* 1 Peters 511 (1828),
in which Webster successfully argued for extensive Congressional power to govern
the territories. Marshall adopted the lawyer's contention that Congress was limited
neither by Article III nor by the Bill of Rights in establishing courts in the Florida
Territory.

There were some instances, of course, when Webster, like all politicians,
was inconsistent. For example, he opposed a national conscription bill in 1814 on
constitutional grounds.

gressional power was exclusive even though the Court had earlier ruled to the contrary and he had been unable to obtain a bankruptcy act from Congress at that time.

No doubt one good reason for Webster's confidence in Congress was his long service in that body, simplistic though this notion may appear. Familiarity with its characteristics and workings probably allayed what otherwise would have been reservations about legislative power in the mind of a person so prone to talk in terms of judicial supremacy. Especially after he moved over to the Senate, membership in a chamber always conscious of its rectitude and wisdom surely influenced Webster's perspective upon government.

He also trusted Congress because it could encourage business enterprise. To promote rapid economic growth, Congress must release the vast energy of America by stimulative measures. Though he was not consistent on individual issues, Webster never wavered in his concern for rights of property. Not only must government protect these rights, but it must provide a climate in which people could use property fruitfully. Once the country put capital to work, everyone—entrepreneur, stockholder, laborer, consumer—would benefit.[42]

Central to this theme was Webster's position on banking and currency. On either economic or constitutional grounds Congress could, and must, determine that the National Bank was necessary to serve as an efficient fiscal agent of the government, to provide credit, and to supply a sound currency. Despite the Jacksonian complaint that the Bank possessed dangerous control over the economy by manipulating its paper note issues, Webster saw no need for fear. Workingman, businessman, and banker had an identical interest in an expanding system of money and credit. The Democratic alternative of a government subtreasury, he declared, made money scarce and therefore hurt capital and labor alike.

42 On the political and economic ideas of Webster and the Federalist-Whig leadership during the early nineteenth century, see Louis Hartz, *The Liberal Tradition in America: An Interpretation of American Political Thought since the Revolution* (New York, 1955), 89–113; Joseph Dorfman, *The Economic Mind in American Civilization, 1606–1865* (2 vols., New York, 1946), II, 566–74, 606, 613, 617, 621, 635; Richard N. Current, *Daniel Webster and the Rise of National Conservatism* (Boston, 1955).

The same held true of a protective tariff. Although early in his Congressional years as a spokesman of commercial interests he opposed such a policy, after the mid twenties he became the staunch friend of high duties. Now he countered the Calhounite argument of unconstitutionality with unreserved defense of Congressional power. Again constitutional and political elements in his thinking coalesced: constitutionally Congress could regulate commerce; economically and politically it had an obligation of doing so by laying a high tariff for the growth of domestic manufactures.

Webster believed that Congress had substantial, yet not complete, power over slavery, and in 1820, 1832, and 1850— moments when the politics of slavery became animated—he never doubted Congressional power to exclude slavery from the West. In 1820 he assumed high moral ground as well in opposing admission of Missouri as a slave state, while in 1850 he counseled moderation and compromise. Congress, he said, must not exercise its clear power to prohibit slavery in the territories, because the Union was imperiled and because Nature anyway would make slavery in New Mexico impractical. On other aspects of slavery he was constitutionally and politically conservative. In *Groves* v. *Slaughter* he opposed the power of Congress to restrict the interstate slave trade, and on many occasions in Court and in Congress he absolutely denied national power over slavery in existing states.

The best illustration of the relation of Webster's constitutional and political ideas is his celebrated "Reply to Hayne," dramatically delivered in the Senate on January 26 and 27, 1830. During most of that session there was an extended debate, precipitated by Samuel A. Foot's resolutions to restrict sale of public lands. Senators soon turned their attention to the tariff, sectionalism, and the nature of the Union. Robert Y. Hayne of South Carolina supported a policy of low land prices and contended that the East opposed such a policy generous to the West because it feared for its labor supply. The South, having interests similar to the West's according to Hayne, also suffered Eastern exploitation by a protective tariff which cheapened Southern exports and made imports more expensive. Hayne restated familiar theories of Vice President John C. Calhoun that a protective tariff was unconstitutional and that individual states, as sovereign members of the loose compact formed in 1787, could nullify such national legislation.

Then came Webster's reply. After a prolonged defense of his section, his state, and himself, he examined the Calhoun-Hayne doctrine of nullification.[43] The Union, he said, was not a compact of sovereign states. It had been established by the people just as the states had been created by them. It was a government for the welfare of the people and always answerable directly to them, but in no sense was it an agent of the several states. On questions of constitutional power, he declared, the states could not and should not judge. The people had chosen to safeguard their rights and liberties by other means, by plain words of the Constitution delegating limited powers to Congress and prohibiting other powers, by holding national legislators and officers to compliance with the Constitution through frequent elections, and by remedy of constitutional amendment in case of injustice. There was also the ever-present right of revolution, extralegal and extraconstitutional, in extreme circumstances; such was the meaning of Madison's Virginia Resolutions of 1798, upon which Hayne and Calhoun relied, so Webster asserted. But this was something different from state nullification. Besides, on practical grounds, if the "South Carolina doctrine" were accepted, the Constitution would have one meaning to that state, another to Pennsylvania, others to the rest of the twenty-four states. So frail a Union, the Senator declared, could never survive. Naturally Webster placed great confidence in the Supreme Court as interpreter of the Constitution. He did not say as much about this interesting point as he might have, but the outline of his views is clear. Two provisions of the Constitution seemed conclusive evidence that the people intended the Court to have "ultimate jurisdiction to fix and ascertain the interpretation" of the Constitution. Article VI provides that the Federal Constitution and laws are the "supreme law of the land," state constitutions or laws to the contrary notwithstanding. Article III provides Federal judicial power for all cases in law and equity arising under the Constitution and the laws of the United States. "These two provisions cover the whole

---

[43] The whole speech is in *Register of Debates*, 21 Cong., 1 sess., 59–82.

ground. They are, in truth, the keystone of the arch!" As further proof, he added that the first Congress in 1789 had adopted a judiciary act (section twenty-five) to bring "all questions of constitutional power to the final decision of the Supreme Court."

In these debates of the 1830 session, and later when Calhoun returned to the Senate floor, exponents of nationalism and states' rights spun out their positions to the fullest dimensions.[44] The South Carolinians saw the Union as a compact of sovereign states, denied there was any such thing as the people of the United States (only people of a state), rejected the judiciary as arbiter in questions political and nonjusticiable.[45] The states' power of nullification was the next step in this reasoning. As everyone knows, Webster insisted that the government had a direct relation to the people and that the people wisely had entrusted to the Supreme Court the responsibility of identifying boundary lines between the partially sovereign states and the partially sovereign government of the republic.[46]

Webster's famous speeches on this famous topic merely conveyed the thought and even repeated the language of judicial opinions in *McCulloch* v. *Maryland, Cohens* v. *Virginia, Gibbons* v. *Ogden,* and other cases. Unfailingly the ideas were nationalistic: a government made by the people for their benefit and answerable to them; supremacy of the nation over the states; and the unity of the country for war and peace and commerce. No wonder Marshall and Story so admired the Senator's forensic expositions. Still they, more than anyone, understood that he was not merely echoing the Court's decisions, for these ideas went back beyond the decisions. The judges had drawn from arguments of counsel—of a Pinkney, a Wirt, a Webster—and they in turn had expressed at the bar political and legal ideas deeply rooted in American history.[47]

44 Calhoun resigned as Vice President.

45 See, for example, Hayne's response to Webster on January 27, 1830. *Register of Debates,* 21 Cong., 1 sess., 87–88.

46 Webster was more realistic than some later commentators concerning the political function of the Court. See, for instance, Warren, *Sup. Ct. in U.S. Hist.,* II, 183, who looks upon the Court's work as primarily deciding law cases of individual rights and only incidentally questions of politics.

47 Despite his emphasis upon the role of counsel when he discusses various cases, Beveridge gives the impression that in Congress Webster was merely repeat-

A review of Webster's practice in the Supreme Court demonstrates some ways in which he influenced constitutional history. Nearly all of them, in one sense or another, related to expansion of national power. He and his associates effectively advocated a loose-constructionist standard of constitutional interpretation that opened broad areas, legislative and judicial, to Federal jurisdiction. In Webster's day Congress seldom exercised authority to the extent permissible by this standard; yet when it did, such as to charter a bank or regulate commerce, power was available. More often the national courts used jurisdiction they had identified as their own; however, they did so not at the expense of Congress but of the states. The commerce and contract clauses restricted, though they did not absolutely prohibit, many things state legislatures could do; and growth of judicial power on the national level frequently meant diminution on the state level.

As much as anyone, Webster helped fashion this formidable judicial instrument. Before he came to Washington, the Supreme Court had laid down the doctrine that it could invalidate state and Federal statutes if they conflicted with the Constitution, but the extent and uses of the power were uncertain. Term after term in Webster's time they became clearer. With the development of the contract clause to protect economic rights, the Court's function assumed larger importance. And to distinguish between Congressional commerce power and the states' police power also demanded close scrutiny. Even the Taney Court, with its frequent profession of self-restraint, assumed an added burden when it undertook to classify subjects of commerce not requiring a uniform rule. Notwithstanding his sharp criticism of the Jacksonian bench, Webster was satisfied, by and large, with this continuing growth of judicial power. Still, limits were found, such as the Court's refusal to determine "political questions." Oddly, Webster was one of those who advanced this doctrine—in the *Massachusetts Boundary* case, when the majority did not accept his argument against jurisdiction, and then in *Luther* v. *Borden,* when they did.

He was in the foreground too in adapting the ancient

---

ing Marshall's language and borrowing ideas originated by the Chief Justice. *Marshall,* IV, 553–54.

law to needs of a young republic and in helping to create a national system in some branches of law. Over the years in hundreds of cases which have now fallen into oblivion, the justices borrowed, revised, or rejected precedents of the common law. Webster and his fellows litigated land titles, wills, trusts, contracts, and torts within this legal framework handed down from the past. They built briefs on Coke, Blackstone, and the English reports as much as on American cases, so that the result was an adjustment of the old law to new circumstances. Although in *Wheaton* v. *Peters* Webster failed to secure common law copyright protection, his brief and Story's opinion in *Swift* v. *Tyson,* declaring the existence of a Federal commercial common law, established a precedent that endured for a century. So also was English admiralty and maritime law modified: in the first years of the New Englander's practice, he and Pinkney and other attorneys assisted in formulating rules concerning prizes, piracy, and neutrality. Late in life, in the *Lexington* case, he called for substantial change in the jurisdictional boundaries of American admiralty law; and this view, expounded by counsel and adopted by the bench in several cases, extended Federal jurisdiction well beyond its former limits.

Webster's constitutional nationalism had an economic purpose. Both Congress and the state legislatures, he thought, should provide a favorable environment for growth of enterprise. Since the national government could accomplish this only partially, much remained for the states to do. State legislatures must not put up political and legal barriers to banking, transportation, and industry; and so constitutional limitations upon state power were necessary. They must encourage business, even by special privilege or irrevocable monopoly in corporate charters. Here Webster disagreed with such Jacksonians as Taney. He felt this policy safe and desirable, while Taney believed it would stifle economic freedom and expansion to the detriment of the public interest.[48] Time and again the issue recurred in cases involving vested rights. In *Dartmouth College* v. *Woodward* the Court construed the contract clause as a shield for corporate

[48] Webster's thinking was naturally influenced by the evolving economic policies of his own state. See Oscar and Mary F. Handlin, *Commonwealth: A Study of the Role of Government in the American Economy: Massachusetts, 1774–1861* (New York, 1947), 53–92, 113–172.

charters against state legislation. To Webster and all those connected with the case, this did not seem at the moment to be as
important as Marshall's holding the College a *private* corporation immune from state regulation. Standards for identifying a
corporation as public or private would remain vague for many
years. But in the next three decades bench and bar thoroughly
explored the scope of the contract clause. Webster and Marshall
intensely disliked the decision in *Ogden* v. *Saunders* that only
retrospective state statutes violated the Constitution. If they
had had their way, their view of the contract clause would have
become an early substantive due process doctrine. Furthermore,
the Taney Court reduced the possible coverage of the clause
by reading corporate charters narrowly (*Charles River Bridge*
case) and permitting an almost unlimited use of state power of
eminent domain (*West River Bridge* case). Nonetheless, by
1850, vested rights were secure, more secure than Webster and
Story had feared they might be at the hands of Democratic
judges.

After the *Dartmouth College* decision additional questions concerning the legal status of corporations appeared. With
the rise of this kind of business organization the questions multi-
plied and became urgent. In the *Osborn* case Webster won a
great victory for the National Bank when Marshall ruled that
the Federal courts were open to it. In succeeding terms the Court
extended the same valuable privilege to almost all corporations
operating across state lines. Webster did not prevail in his bold
argument that corporations should enjoy the full standing of
citizens under the privileges and immunities clause, but by the
Alabama Bank decision Taney conceded a good deal when he
invoked the common law doctrine of comity in behalf of out-of-
state corporations.

The practical consequences of the commerce cases were
also large. If Webster's version of exclusive Congressional
power had become the law of the land, much of the economy
would have gone unregulated. National power, whatever its
breadth, did not become a positive force for a long time to come.
True, the states had their police power, but by itself this would
not suffice. The Court's compromise between the national exclusive and state concurrent theories more nearly corresponded

to Webster's position than Taney's—after all, Webster had suggested the compromise as an alternative—and provided ample shelter for business enterprise until Congress at last decided to regulate.

Webster, the leading lawyer of his generation, was one of the most important in the nation's history. Few of his contemporaries denied his pre-eminence in the profession, and few would now dispute it. There were more learned, more industrious attorneys in his time and afterward, but none surpassed him in his sure grasp of fundamentals, his powerful capacity to organize, and his remarkable eloquence. And none equalled him in the way he influenced the development of such a wide variety of significant legal rules and ideas. The effects upon American society were profound.

APPENDIX

List of Webster's Cases

This is a chronological list of the cases argued by Webster in the Supreme Court. It will be noticed that some cases were argued and decided at more than one term. The citations are to the names of the reporters, preceded by the volume numbers and followed by the page numbers. Cases argued on constitutional grounds are preceded by one asterisk; those argued and *decided* on constitutional grounds are preceded by two asterisks.

The St. Lawrence. 8 Cranch 434 (1814) ; 9 Cranch 120 (1815).
The Grotius. 8 Cranch 456 (1814) ; 9 Cranch 368 (1815).
**Town of Pawlet v. Clark. 9 Cranch 292 (1815).
The Mary. 2 Wheaton 123 (1817).
The Ariadne. 2 Wheaton 143 (1817).
The George. 2 Wheaton 278 (1817).
The Argo. 2 Wheaton 287 (1817).
Inglee v. Coolidge. 2 Wheaton 363 (1817).
*U.S. v. Bevans. 3 Wheaton 336 (1818).
The Divina Pastora. 4 Wheaton 52 (1819).
U.S. v. Rice. 4 Wheaton 246 (1819).
Brown v. Gilman. 4 Wheaton 255 (1819).
**McCulloch v. Maryland. 4 Wheaton 316 (1819).
**Dartmouth College v. Woodward. 4 Wheaton 518 (1819).
Bell v. Bullard. Court divided and no decision. See front page of 5 Wheaton (1820). Argued in 1819.
The London Packet. 5 Wheaton 132 (1820).
U.S. v. Smith. 5 Wheaton 153 (1820).
U.S. v. Pirates. 5 Wheaton 184 (1820).
U.S. v. Holmes. 5 Wheaton 412 (1820).

The Bello Corrunes. 6 Wheaton 152 (1821).

Cohens *v.* Virginia. 6 Wheaton 430 (1821). Second hearing on the merits.

Sullivan *v.* Fulton Steamboat Co. 6 Wheaton 450 (1821).

Hughes *v.* Blake. 6 Wheaton 453 (1821).

Prevost *v.* Gratz. 6 Wheaton 481 (1821).

Otis *v.* Walter. 6 Wheaton 583 (1821).

Ricard *v.* Williams. 7 Wheaton 59 (1822).

Brown *v.* Jackson. 7 Wheaton 218 (1822).

The Santissima Trinidad. 7 Wheaton 283 (1822).

Greeley *v.* U.S. 8 Wheaton 257 (1823).

The Experiment. 8 Wheaton 261 (1823).

Spring *v.* South Carolina Insurance Co. 8 Wheaton 268 (1823).

**Society for the Propagation of the Gospel in Foreign Parts *v.* New Haven. 8 Wheaton 464 (1823).

*Johnson *v.* McIntosh. 8 Wheaton 543 (1823).

Gracie *v.* Palmer. 8 Wheaton 605 (1823).

Childress *v.* Emory. 8 Wheaton 642 (1823).

**Gibbons *v.* Ogden. 9 Wheaton 1 (1824).

Kirk *v.* Smith. 9 Wheaton 241 (1824).

Two Hundred Chests of Tea. 9 Wheaton 430 (1824).

Renner *v.* Bank of Columbia. 9 Wheaton 581 (1824).

**Osborn *v.* Bank of the U.S. 9 Wheaton 738 (1824).

Wright *v.* Denn. 10 Wheaton 204 (1825).

U.S. *v.* Morris. 10 Wheaton 246 (1825).

Keplinger *v.* DeYoung. 10 Wheaton 358 (1825).

De Wolf *v.* Johnson. 10 Wheaton 367 (1825).

Sixty Pipes of Brandy. 10 Wheaton 421 (1825).

The Marianna Flora. 11 Wheaton 1 (1826).

Etting *v.* Bank of the U.S. 11 Wheaton 59 (1826).

Harding *v.* Handy. 11 Wheaton 103 (1826).

Cassell *v.* Carroll. 11 Wheaton 134 (1826).

Otis *v.* Walter. 11 Wheaton 192 (1826).

Hinde's Lessee *v.* Longworth. 11 Wheaton 199 (1826).

Perkins *v.* Hart. 11 Wheaton 237 (1826).

Armstrong *v.* Toler. 11 Wheaton 258 (1826).

Chirac *v.* Reinicker. 11 Wheaton 280 (1826).

Finley *v.* Bank of the U.S. 11 Wheaton 304 (1826).

Fowle *v.* Alexandria. 11 Wheaton 320 (1826).

Williams *v.* Bank of the U.S. 11 Wheaton 414 (1826).

U.S. *v.* Tappan. 11 Wheaton 419 (1826).

Mills *v.* Bank of the U.S. 11 Wheaton 431 (1826).

Carnochan *v.* Christie. 11 Wheaton 446 (1826).

Clark *v.* Washington. 12 Wheaton 40 (1827).

Bank of the U.S. *v.* Dandridge. 12 Wheaton 64 (1827).

Postmaster General *v.* Early. 12 Wheaton 136 (1827).

Jackson *v.* Chew. 12 Wheaton 153 (1827).

U.S. *v.* Tillotson. 12 Wheaton 180 (1827).

**Ogden *v.* Saunders. 12 Wheaton 213 (1827).

*Mason *v.* Haile. 12 Wheaton 370 (1827).

Columbian Insurance Co. *v.* Catlett. 12 Wheaton 383 (1827).

General Interest Insurance Co. *v.* Ruggles. 12 Wheaton 408 (1827).

U.S. *v.* 350 Chests of Tea. 12 Wheaton 486 (1827).

Potter *v.* Gardner. 12 Wheaton 498 (1827).

M'Gill *v.* Bank of the U.S. 12 Wheaton 511 (1827).

Henderson *v.* Poindexter's Lessee. 12 Wheaton 530 (1827).

McLemore *v.* Powell. 12 Wheaton 554 (1827).

U.S. *v.* Barker. 12 Wheaton 559 (1827).

Chotard *v.* Pope. 12 Wheaton 586 (1827).

Hunt *v.* Ronsmaniere's Administrators. 1 Peters 1 (1828).

U.S. *v.* Saline Bank of Virginia. 1 Peters 100 (1828).

Findlay *v.* Hinde. 1 Peters 241 (1828).

Konig *v.* Bayard. 1 Peters 250 (1828).

Schimmelpennich *v.* Bayard. 1 Peters 264 (1828).

Conrad *v.* Atlantic Insurance Co. 1 Peters 386 (1828).

D'Wolf *v.* Rabaud. 1 Peters 476 (1828).

**American Insurance Co. *v.* Canter. 1 Peters 511 (1828); 2 Peters 554
(1829); 3 Peters 307 (1830).

Pennock *v.* Dialogue. 2 Peters 1 (1829).

**Foster *v.* Neilson. 2 Peters 253 (1829).

*Wilkinson *v.* Leland. 2 Peters 627 (1829). Also Leland *v.* Wilkinson.
6 Peters 317 (1832).

Beach *v.* Viles. 2 Peters 675 (1829).

Thornton *v.* Bank of Washington. 3 Peters 36 (1830).

Bell *v.* Cunningham. 3 Peters 69 (1830).

Inglis *v.* Trustees of Sailor's Snug Harbor. 3 Peters 99 (1830).

Harris *v.* Dennie. 3 Peters 292 (1830).

Finlay *v.* King's Lessee. 3 Peters 346 (1830).

Parsons *v.* Armor. 3 Peters 413 (1830).

Parsons *v.* Bedford. 3 Peters 433 (1830).

Carver *v.* Jackson. 4 Peters 1 (1830).

Wilcox *v.* Executors of Plummer. 4 Peters 172 (1830).

Van Ness *v.* Washington. 4 Peters 232 (1830).

Conard *v.* Nicoll. 4 Peters 291 (1830).

*Society for the Propagation of the Gospel in Foreign Parts *v.* Pawlet. 4 Peters 480 (1830).

Ex parte Crane. 5 Peters 190 (1831).

Bradstreet *v.* Huntington. 5 Peters 402 (1831).

Bank of the U.S. *v.* Martin. 5 Peters 479 (1831).

Winship *v.* Bank of the U.S. 5 Peters 529 (1831).

Edmondston *v.* Drake. 5 Peters 624 (1831).

Potter *v.* Gardner. 5 Peters 718 (1831).

Kirkman *v.* Hamilton. 6 Peters 20 (1832).

Spring *v.* Gray's Executors. 6 Peters 151 (1832).

Grant *v.* Raymond. 6 Peters 218 (1832).

Bank of the U.S. *v.* Hatch. 6 Peters 250 (1832).

Cincinnati *v.* White's Lessee. 6 Peters 431 (1832).

U.S. *v.* Arredondo. 6 Peters 691 (1832).

Binney *v.* Chesapeake & Ohio Canal Co. 8 Peters 201 (1834).

King *v.* Mitchell. 8 Peters 326 (1834).

Carrington *v.* Merchant's Insurance Co. 8 Peters 495 (1834).

Hazard's Administrator *v.* New England Marine Insurance Co. 8 Peters 557 (1834).

Wheaton *v.* Peters. 8 Peters 591 (1834).

New Orleans *v.* Armas and Cucullu. 9 Peters 223 (1835).

Piatt *v.* Vattier. 9 Peters 405 (1835).

Harrison *v.* Nixon. 9 Peters 483 (1835).

Chesapeake and Ohio Canal Co. *v.* Knapp. 9 Peters 541 (1835).

Mitchel *v.* U.S. 9 Peters 711 (1835); 15 Peters 52 (1841).

Crowell *v.* Randell. 10 Peters 368 (1836).

*New Orleans *v.* U.S. 10 Peters 662 (1836).

Veazie *v.* Wadleigh. 11 Peters 55 (1837).

Allen *v.* Hammond. 11 Peters 63 (1837).

U.S. *v.* Leffler. 11 Peters 86 (1837).

**Charles River Bridge *v.* Warren Bridge. 11 Peters 420 (1837).

Wilson's Heirs *v.* Life and Fire Insurance Co. of New York. 12 Peters 140 (1838).

Smith *v.* Richards. 13 Peters 26 (1839).

Andrews *v.* Pond. 13 Peters 65 (1839).

Ocean Insurance Co. *v.* Polleys. 13 Peters 157 (1839).

*Wilcox *v.* Jackson. 13 Peters 498 (1839).

*Bank of the U.S. *v.* Primrose. 13 Peters 519 (1839). One of the Alabama Bank cases.

Lattimer *v.* Poteet. 14 Peters 4 (1840).

Carr *v.* Duval. 14 Peters 77 (1840).

Peters *v.* Warren Insurance Co. 14 Peters 99 (1840).

Sprigg *v.* Bank of Mt. Pleasant. 14 Peters 201 (1840).

Lessee of Pollard's Heir's *v.* Kibbe. 14 Peters 353 (1840).

*Groves *v.* Slaughter. 15 Peters 449 (1841).

Swift *v.* Tyson. 16 Peters 1 (1842). Webster argued case at first hearing in 1840.

Minor *v.* Tillotson. 1 Howard 287 (1843); 2 Howard 392 (1844).

Vidal *v.* Girard's Executors. 2 Howard 127 (1844).

Foxcroft *v.* Mallett. 4 Howard 353 (1846).

Rhode Island *v.* Massachusetts. 12 Peters 657 (1838); 13 Peters 23 (1839); 14 Peters 210 (1840); 15 Peters 233 (1841); 4 Howard 591 (1846).

Wilson *v.* Rousseau. 4 Howard 646 (1846).

Miner's Bank *v.* U.S. 5 Howard 213 (1846).

**Thurlow *v.* Massachusetts. 5 Howard 504 (1847). One of the License cases.

Mathewson *v.* Clarke. 6 Howard 122 (1848). Also Clarke *v.* Mathewson. 12 Peters 164 (1838).

Curtis *v.* Innerarity. 6 Howard 146 (1848).

**Planters' Bank of Mississippi *v.* Sharp. 6 Howard 301 (1848).

New Jersey Steam Navigation Co. *v.* Merchants' Bank of Boston. 6 Howard 344 (1848). Known as the Lexington case.

**West River Bridge Co. *v.* Dix. 6 Howard 507 (1848).

**Luther *v.* Borden. 7 Howard 1 (1849).

**Smith *v.* Turner and Norris *v.* Boston. 7 Howard 283 (1849). Known as the Passenger cases.

Veazie *v.* Williams. 8 Howard 134 (1850).

Reed *v.* Proprietors of Locks and Canals. 8 Howard 274 (1850).

Le Roy *v.* Beard. 8 Howard 451 (1850).

Williamson *v.* Berry. 8 Howard 495 (1850).

Mills *v.* St. Clair County. 8 Howard 569 (1850).

Kennedy *v.* Georgia State Bank. 8 Howard 586 (1850).

Wilson *v.* Simpson. 9 Howard 109 (1850).

Fleming *v.* Page. 9 Howard 603 (1850).

Barnard *v.* Adams. 10 Howard 270 (1851).

Gayler *v.* Wilder. 10 Howard 477 (1851).

Van Rensselaer *v.* Kearney. 11 Howard 297 (1851).

Gaines *v.* Relf. 12 Howard 472 (1852).

Glenn *v.* U.S. 13 Howard 250 (1852).

BIBLIOGRAPHY

A Note on Sources

One of the principal sources for a study of Webster as a lawyer in the Supreme Court is the set of official reports of cases, published successively by Cranch, Wheaton, Peters, and Howard. These volumes state the facts from the records, indicate the proceedings in the lower courts, and summarize counsel's arguments or list their points and citations. For these years many arguments are reported in detail, though occasionally little or nothing concerning the lawyers' positions is included. In some instances one can find fuller reports in contemporary newspapers, books, and pamphlets. The Clerk's manuscript files of the records for this early period, now located in the National Archives, do not contain the attorneys' briefs in cases prior to the 1850's.

Other judicial reports must also be consulted. The set of *Federal Cases* is a valuable selection of cases decided in the United States circuit and district courts. Frequently one must go to the reports of the state courts, especially those of Massachusetts, New Hampshire, and New York. The comprehensive set of *English Reports* is indispensable, since arguments and opinions of that day heavily relied upon English precedents.

The standard, very usable edition of Webster's works is James M. McIntyre (ed.), *The Writings and Speeches of Daniel Webster* (18 vols., Boston: Little, Brown, 1903). Volumes 10, 11, and 15 include quite a number of legal arguments, while volumes 16, 17, and 18 contain letters written by and to Webster. Other volumes print some of his speeches relevant to the subject. Additional correspondence is in Claude H. Van Tyne (ed.), *The Letters of Daniel Webster* (New York: McClure, Phillips, 1902).

The most comprehensive collection of Webster manuscripts is held by the New Hampshire Historical Society. There are twenty volumes of mounted letters and five boxes of loose materials, some of which have not been published. The Library of Congress has another collection of Webster papers in thirteen volumes and three boxes of miscellaneous acquisitions. Many Webster manuscripts are located in the Dartmouth College Archives. Most of these concern the College controversy and cases from 1816 to 1819: correspondence, copies of briefs of counsel, and related material. The Houghton Library at Harvard University has a box of correspondence, mainly letters from Webster to Franklin Haven, president of the Merchants' Bank of Boston, during the years 1837 to 1852.

There are pertinent items in several collections of papers of Webster's contemporaries. The New Hampshire State Library has an enormous file of letters and journals of William Plumer, the New Hampshire governor during the Dartmouth College controversy. A helpful calendar of these papers, prepared by Lynn W. Turner, guides the researcher to the numerous letters concerning the College case. At the Library of Congress a smaller Plumer collection yields other informative material. Further light is thrown on the history of the case in the Papers of Timothy Farrar, Jr., at the New Hampshire Historical Society's library. The Boston Public Library has the original draft of Rufus Choate's eulogy of Webster, which gave a version of the lawyer's peroration in his Supreme Court argument. In the extensive Papers of Joseph Story at the Massachusetts Historical Society are unpublished items showing the long-lasting friendship of Webster and Story. Other letters of interest are in the Story Papers at the Library of Congress. One can find a few relevant pieces among the Edward Everett Papers at the Massachusetts Historical Society. Webster wrote to Everett often during the last twenty-five years of his life, but most of the letters concern politics and other matters. The Papers of William Wirt at the Library of Congress, particularly his letterbooks, contain some useful information. Occasional items can be uncovered in the Papers of James Kent and of Benjamin R. Curtis (both at the Library of Congress) and of Charles Sumner (at Harvard). A significant source relating to the Charles River Bridge case is the manuscript notes by Simon Greenleaf on the arguments of counsel at the Harvard Law Library.

Of course public documents can be profitably consulted. The legislative history and provisions of statutes involved in the cases are derivable from the *Annals of Congress, Register of Debates, Congressional Globe,* and the *Statutes at Large.* Webster's speeches and work in Congress concerning the Supreme Court can also be studied in these references and in the various reports of Congressional committees.

Newspapers of the time reported and commented upon cases of general interest. Oftentimes they carried fuller accounts of the arguments of the attorneys than those found in the official reports. Papers particularly valuable for this topic are the *National Intelligencer* (the semi-weekly edition was used), the *Globe,* and the *National Era*—all of Washington, D.C.—and the *Tribune,* the *Courier and Enquirer,* and the *Herald* of New York.

A Selected List of References

The number of books, pamphlets, articles, and other printed materials touching upon the subject is very large. In the course of writing this monograph, nearly all of the references on the Supreme Court during the early nineteenth century and on Webster have been examined. It would be tedious and confusing to list them all here. Below is a carefully selected bibliography of only those items that are especially significant. There are others, fully cited in the notes, which furnished information of secondary importance.

Adams, Charles F. (ed.), *Memoirs of John Quincy Adams, Comprising Portions of His Diary from 1795–1848.* Philadelphia: Lippincott, 1874–77. 12 vols.

Baker, Elizabeth F., *Henry Wheaton, 1785–1848.* Philadelphia: University of Pennsylvania Press, 1937.

Bauer, Elizabeth K., *Commentaries on the Constitution, 1790–1860.* New York: Columbia University Press, 1952.

Beveridge, Albert J., *The Life of John Marshall.* Boston: Houghton Mifflin, 1916–19. 4 vols.

Binney, Charles C., *The Life of Horace Binney.* Philadelphia: Lippincott, 1903.

Binney, Horace, *Bushrod Washington.* Philadelphia: Sherman, 1858.

Black, John W., "Webster's Peroration in the Dartmouth College Case," *Quarterly Journal of Speech,* XXIII (Dec., 1937), 635–42.

Blackstone, William, *Commentaries on the Laws of England.* New York: Dean, 1836. 2 vols.

Brennan, Joseph, *Social Conditions in Industrial Rhode Island: 1820–1860.* Washington: Catholic University, 1940.

Burnette, Lawrence, Jr., "Peter V. Daniel: Agrarian Justice," *Virginia Magazine of History and Biography,* LXII (1954), 289–305.

Catterall, Ralph C. H., *The Second Bank of the United States.* Chicago: University of Chicago Press, 1903.

Caldwell, Russell L., "The Influence of the Federal Bar upon the Interpretation of the Constitution by the Supreme Court under John Marshall." Ph.D. Dissertation, University of Southern California, 1948.

Chase, Frederick, and Lord, John K., *A History of Dartmouth College.* Cambridge: Wilson, 1891–1913. 2 vols.

Corwin, Edward S. (ed.), "The Constitution of the United States of America, Analysis and Interpretation, Annotations of Cases Decided by the Supreme Court of the United States to June 30, 1952," 82 Cong., 2 sess., *Senate Document No. 170.* Washington: Government Printing Office, 1953.

Corwin, Edward S., *The Commerce Power versus States Rights.* Princeton: Princeton University Press, 1936.

Corwin, Edward S., "The Doctrine of Due Process of Law before the Civil War," *Harvard Law Review,* XXIV (1911), 366–85, 460–79.

Crosskey, William W., *Politics and the Constitution in the History of the United States.* Chicago: University of Chicago Press, 1953. 2 vols.

Current, Richard N., *Daniel Webster and the Rise of the National Conservatism.* Boston: Little, Brown, 1955.

Curtis, George T., *Life of Daniel Webster.* New York: Appleton, 1870. 2 vols.

Dodd, Edwin M., *American Business Corporations until 1860 with Special Reference to Massachusetts.* Cambridge: Harvard University Press, 1954.

Douglas, William O., "Bankruptcy," *Encyclopaedia of the Social Sciences,* II, 449–54.

Farrar, Timothy, *Report of the Case of the Trustees of Dartmouth College against William H. Woodward.* Portsmouth, N.H.: Foster, 1819.

Frankfurter, Felix, *The Commerce Clause under Marshall, Taney and Waite.* Chapel Hill: University of North Carolina Press, 1937.

Freize, Jacob, *Facts Involved in the Rhode Island Controversy with Some Views upon the Rights of Both Parties.* Boston: Mussey, 1842.

Fuess, Claude M., *Rufus Choate: The Wizard of the Law.* New York: Minton, Balch, 1928.

Fuess, Claude M., *Daniel Webster.* Boston: Little, Brown, 1930. 2 vols.

Gass, Edmund C., "The Constitutional Opinion of Justice John Catron," *East Tennessee Historical Society's Publication;* No. 8 (1936), 54–73.

Grant, J. A. C., "The 'Higher Law' Background of the Law of Eminent Domain," *Wisconsin Law Review,* VI (Feb., 1931), 67–85.

Hagan, Horace H., "The Dartmouth College Case," *Georgetown Law Journal,* XIX (May, 1931), 411–26.

Hagan, Horace, *Eight Great American Lawyers.* Oklahoma City: Harlow, 1923.

Haines, Charles G., *The Role of the Supreme Court in American Government and Politics, 1789–1835.* Berkeley: University of California Press, 1944.

Haines, Charles G., and Sherwood, Foster H., *The Role of the Supreme Court in American Government and Politics, 1835–1864.* Berkeley: University of California Press, 1957.

Hale, Robert L., "The Supreme Court and the Contract Clause," *Harvard Law Review,* LVII (1944), 512–57, 621–74, 852–92.

Hammond, Bray, *Banks and Politics in America: From the Revolution to the Civil War.* Princeton: Princeton University Press, 1957.

Harvey, Peter, *Reminiscences and Anecdotes of Daniel Webster.* Boston: Little, Brown, 1878.

Hellerich, Mahlen H., "The Luther Cases in the Lower Courts," *Rhode Island History,* XI (April, 1952), 33–45.

Henderson, Gerald C., *The Position of Foreign Corporations in American Constitutional Law.* Cambridge: Harvard University Press, 1918.

Hill, Clement H., "The Dartmouth College Case," *American Law Review,* VIII (Jan., 1874), 189–239.

Hillard, George S., *Memoir and Correspondence of Jeremiah Mason.* Cambridge: Riverside Press, 1873.

Hunting, Warren B., *The Obligation of Contracts Clause of the United States Constitution.* Baltimore: Johns Hopkins Press, 1919.

Konkle, Burton A., *Joseph Hopkinson, 1770–1842.* Philadelphia: University of Pennsylvania Press, 1931.

Isaacs, Nathan, "John Marshall on Contracts: A Study in Early American Juristic Theory," *Virginia Law Review,* VII (Mar., 1921), 413–28.

Jones, W. Melville (ed.), *Chief Justice John Marshall: A Reappraisal.* Ithaca: Cornell University Press, 1956.

Kennedy, John P., *Memoirs of the Life of William Wirt.* Philadelphia: Lippincott, 1860.

Kent, James, *Commentaries on American Law.* Boston: Little, Brown, 1884. 4 vols.

Lawrence, Alexander A., *James Moore Wayne, Southern Unionist.* Chapel Hill: University of North Carolina Press, 1943.

Lawson, John D. (ed.), *American State Trials.* Report of the Knapp trials of 1830, Vol. VII (1917), 395–670.

Lenhoff, Arthur, "Development of the Concept of Eminent Domain," *Columbia Law Review,* XLII (April, 1942), 598–638.

Levy, Leonard W., *The Law of the Commonwealth and Chief Justice Shaw.* Cambridge: Harvard University Press, 1956.

Lewis, William D. (ed.), *Great American Lawyers: A History of the Legal Profession in America.* Philadelphia: Winston, 1907–09. 8 vols.

Lyman, Samuel P., *The Public and Private Life of Daniel Webster.* Philadelphia: Keystone, 1890.

McGovney, Dudley O., "A Supreme Court Fiction: Corporations in the Diverse Citizenship Jurisdiction of the Federal Courts," *Harvard Law Review,* LVI (1943), 853–98, 1090–1124, 1225–60.

Meigs, William M., *The Life of Charles Jared Ingersoll.* Philadelphia: Lippincott, 1900.

Miller, Howard S., *The Legal Foundations of American Philanthropy, 1776–1844.* Madison: State Historical Society of Wisconsin, 1961.

Morgan, Donald G., *Justice William Johnson: The First Dissenter.* Columbia: University of South Carolina Press, 1954.

Mowry, Arthur M., *The Dorr War; or, The Constitutional Struggle in Rhode Island.* Providence: Preston & Rounds, 1901.

Myers, Gustavus, *History of the Supreme Court of the United States.* Chicago: Kerr, 1918.

Newmyer, R. Kent, "A Note on the Whig Politics of Justice Joseph Story," *Mississippi Valley Historical Review,* XLVIII (Dec., 1961), 480–91.

Nichols, Philip, *The Law of Eminent Domain.* Albany: Bender, 1917. 2 vols.

Niles' Weekly Register. Baltimore, 1811–49.

North, William G., "The Political Background of the Dartmouth College Case," *New England Quarterly,* XVIII (June, 1945), 181–203.

Oster, John E., *The Political and Economic Doctrines of John Marshall.* New York: Neale, 1914.

Pinkney, William, *The Life of William Pinkney.* New York: Appleton, 1853.

Plumer, William, Jr., *Life of William Plumer.* Boston: Phillips, Sampson, 1856.

Porter, Kenneth W., *John Jacob Astor: Business Man.* Cambridge: Harvard University Press, 1931. 2 vols.

Post, Charles G., Jr., *The Supreme Court and Political Questions.* Baltimore: Johns Hopkins Press, 1936.

Pound, Roscoe, *The Spirit of the Common Law.* Boston: Marshall Jones, 1921.

Powell, Thomas R., *Vagaries and Varieties in Constitutional Interpretation.* New York: Columbia University Press, 1956.

Quincy, Josiah, *Figures of the Past.* Boston: Little, Brown, 1926.

Ribble, Frederick D. G., *State and National Power over Commerce.* New York: Columbia University Press, 1937.

Richardson, Leon B., *History of Dartmouth College.* Hanover: Dartmouth College Publications, 1932. 2 vols.

Schaffer, William I., "Daniel Webster—the Lawyer," *Proceedings of the Pennsylvania Bar Association,* XXXVIII (1932), 311–80.

Shirley, John M., *The Dartmouth College Causes and the Supreme Court of the United States.* St. Louis: Jones, 1879.

Sholley, John B., "The Negative Implications of the Commerce Clause," *University of Chicago Law Review,* III (1936), 556–96.

Stern, Robert L., "Problems of Yesteryear—Commerce and Due Process," *Vanderbilt Law Review,* IV (April, 1951), 446–68.

Stern, Robert L., "That Commerce Which Concerns More States Than One," *Harvard Law Review,* XLVII (June, 1934). 1335–66.

Story, Joseph, "Statesmen—Their Rareness and Importance. Daniel Webster," *New England Magazine,* VII (Aug., 1834), 89–104.

[Story, Joseph], *Proceedings of the Massachusetts Historical Society,* Second Series, Vol. XIV (1900–01), 324–60, 399–424. Correspondence of Story, Marshall, Kent, and Webster.

Story, Joseph, *Commentaries on the Constitution of the United States.* Boston: Hilliard, Gray, 1833. 3 vols.

Story, William W. (ed.), *Life and Letters of Joseph Story.* Boston: Little, Brown, 1851. 2 vols.

Story, William W. (ed.), *The Miscellaneous Writings of Joseph Story.* Boston: Little, Brown, 1852.

Strong, Frank R., "John Marshall—Hero or Villain," *Ohio State University Law Journal,* VI (1939–40), 42–62, 158–89.

Swisher, Carl B., *Roger B. Taney.* New York: Macmillan, 1936.

Ticknor, George, "Speeches and Forensic Arguments by Daniel Webster," *American Quarterly Review,* IX (June, 1831), 420–57.

Turner, Lynn W., *William Plumer of New Hampshire, 1759–1850.* Chapel Hill: University of North Carolina Press, 1962.

Tyler, Samuel, *Memoir of Roger Brooke Taney*. Baltimore: John Murphy, 1872.

Van Santvoord, George, *Sketches of the Lives and Judicial Services of the Chief-Justices of the Supreme Court of the United States*. New York: Scribner, 1854.

Warren, Charles, *Bankruptcy in United States History*. Cambridge: Harvard University Press, 1935.

Warren, Charles, *The Supreme Court in United States History*. Boston: Little, Brown, 1923. 3 vols.

Warren, Charles, *History of the Harvard Law School*. New York: Lewis, 1908. 3 vols.

Warren, Charles, *A History of the American Bar*. Boston: Little, Brown, 1911.

Warren, Charles, "An Historical Note on the Dartmouth College Case," *American Law Review*, XLVI (Sept., 1912), 665–75.

Wheaton, Henry, *Some Account of the Life, Writings and Speeches of William Pinkney*. Philadelphia: Carvill, 1826.

Wheeler, Everett P., *Daniel Webster: The Expounder of the Constitution*. New York: Putnam's Sons, 1905.

Wildes, Harry E., *Lonely Midas: The Story of Stephen Girard*. New York: Farrar & Rinehart, 1943.

Wilson, Carroll A., "Familiar 'Small College' Quotations," *The Colophon*, III (new series, 1938), 7–23.

Wise, Henry A., *Seven Decades of the Union*. Philadelphia: Lippincott, 1881.

Wittenberg, Philip, *The Law of Literary Property*. Cleveland: World, 1957.

Woodbury, Charles L. (ed.), *Writings of Levi Woodbury*. Boston: Little, Brown, 1852.

Wright, Benjamin F., Jr., *The Contract Clause of the Constitution*. Cambridge: Harvard University Press, 1938.

Wyllie, Irvin G., "The Search for an American Law of Charity, 1776–1844," *Mississippi Valley Historical Review*, XLVI (Sept., 1959), 203–21.

INDEX

Adams, John Quincy, 166, 233, 236–237
Admiralty cases, 39–52
Alabama Bank Cases, vii, 185–193, 244
Allen, William, 70, 79, 89–90
American Insurance Co. v. *Canter,* vii
Ames, Samuel, 45
Austin, James T., 55–57

B.U.S. v. *Dandridge,* 184–185
B.U.S. v. *Deveaux,* 188, 192
B.U.S. v. *Planters' Bank of Georgia.*
See *Osborn* v. *B.U.S.*
B.U.S. v. *Primrose.* See *Alabama Bank Cases*
Baldwin, Henry: Massachusetts boundary, 55–56; *Charles River Bridge* case, 123; opinion in *U.S.* v. *Arredondo,* 144–145; opinion in *Mitchel* v. *U.S.,* 145; *Girard Will* case, 161, 167; *Groves* v. *Slaughter,* 212
Bank of Augusta v. *Earle.* See *Alabama Bank Cases*
Bank of the United States, 169–194
Bankruptcy cases, 110–118
Bankruptcy legislation, 118–119
Bar of Supreme Court, 27–35
Barbour, Philip P., 130, 208
Bartlett, Ichabod, 7, 74–75
Bell, Samuel, 71, 86
Berrien, John, 144
Biddle, Nicholas, 181
Binney, Horace, 159–167
Blackstone, William, 151
Brandeis, Louis D., 156

Brown, Francis, 68, 70, 90
Brown v. *Maryland,* 207

Calhoun, John C., 239–241
Call, Richard K., 144
Catron, John, 50–52, 217, 223
Charles River Bridge v. *Warren Bridge,* vii, 119–135, 244
Choate, Rufus: lawyer in Boston, 8; Massachusetts boundary, 57; on Webster's *Dartmouth College* peroration, 84; *Goodyear* v. *Day,* 154; *License Cases,* 215; *Passenger Cases,* 218
Circuit courts, 230–237
Clay, Henry: practice in Supreme Court, 30; attorney in *Ogden* v. *Saunders,* 113; bankruptcy legislation, 118–119, *Osborn* v. *B.U.S.,* 179–180; *Groves* v. *Slaughter,* 210–211; mentioned, 31, 227
Clifford, Nathan, 60
Cohens v. *Virginia,* 34, 229
Collamer, Jacob, 137
Cooley v. *Board of Wardens,* 195–196, 224–225
Comity, rule of, 187, 190–191, 193
Commerce clause: and *Alabama Bank Cases,* 193; in *Gibbons* v. *Ogden,* 196–207; in *License Cases,* 214–217; in *Passenger Cases,* 218–224; significance of cases involving, 244–245
Common law, 147–152, 154–156, 242–243

261

Contract clause, 110–141. See also *Dartmouth College* v. *Woodward*
Copyright, 147–153
Corporate charters, 119–141. See also *Dartmouth College* v. *Woodward*
Coxe, Richard S., 53
Criminal code, Federal, 232–233
Crowninshield, Benjamin W., 79
Curtis, Benjamin R., 224–225

Dana, Richard H., 154–155
Dane, Nathan, 47
Daniel, Peter V., 50–52, 136, 138, 223–224
Dartmouth College, 65–67, 108
Dartmouth College v. *Woodward:* in state court, 71–76; arguments in Supreme Court, 80–91; movement for reargument, 89–91; and cognate cases, 91–94, 102–104; propaganda by opposing parties, 94–98; Supreme Court decision, 99–101; printed report of decision, 104–106; historical significance, 106–107; mentioned, vi, 7, 243–244
Dartmouth, Lord, 66
Dartmouth University, 69–70, 104
Davis, John, 124–126, 216, 218, 220–221
Dexter, Samuel, 8
Divina Pastora, 40–41
Dorr Rebellion, 58–59
Due process of law, 82, 119, 212
Dutton, Warren, 123–127, 130
Duval, Gabriel, 123

Eleventh Amendment, 179–181
Eminent domain, 128–133, 136–140
Emmet, Thomas A., 29, 183, 198, 200–204
Etting v. *B.U.S.,* 183–184

Farrar, Timothy, 69, 104–106
Fessenden, Thomas, 154–155
Fletcher v. *Rhode Island.* See *License Cases*
Florida land claims, 143–145
Foreign corporations. See *Alabama Bank Cases*
Foster and Elam v. *Neilson,* 53, 144

Gibbons v. *Ogden,* vi, 196–207
Gilpin, Henry D., 210–211
Girard, Stephen, 156–158, 162–164, 166.

See also *Vidal* v. *Girard's Executors*
Goodrich, Chauncey A., 84
Goodyear, Charles, 153–154
Goodyear v. *Day,* 153–154
Gore, Christopher, 4–5
Green v. *Biddle,* 229
Greene, Richard W., 45, 48–49, 51
Greenleaf, Simon, 124–127
Grier, Robert C., 50, 223
Groves v. *Slaughter,* vii, 209–213, 228

Haines, Charles G., 113
Hale, John P., 216
Hale, Salma, 79, 84–85
Hall, J. Prescott, 218
Hall, Willis, 218, 220–221
Hallett, Benjamin F., 60–61, 215
Hamilton, Alexander, 171, 176, 177
Harper, Robert G., 29–30
Haven, Franklin, 44, 49, 51
Hayne, Robert Y., 239–240
Hill, Isaac, 69, 95
Holmes, John, 78–79, 86
Hopkinson, Joseph: sketch, 29; *Dartmouth College* case, 76–78, 88, 90; *Wheaton* v. *Peters,* 148, 152; *McCulloch* v. *Maryland,* 170, 172–173, 177

Imprisonment for debt, 145–146
Indian land rights, 143
Ingersoll, Charles J., 150, 189–190, 193

Johnson, Reverdy, 30
Johnson v. *McIntosh,* 143
Johnson, William: *Dartmouth College* case, 96–98; opinion in *Ogden* v. *Saunders,* 115–117; bankruptcy legislation, 118; *Charles River Bridge* case, 123; opinion in *Gibbons* v. *Ogden,* 202, 206; Negro seaman case, 206–207
Jones, Walter: sketch, 30; political questions, 53; attorney in *Ogden* v. *Saunders,* 113; *Charles River Bridge* case, 123; *Girard Will* case, 159–160; *McCulloch* v. *Maryland,* 170, 172; *Groves* v. *Slaughter,* 210
Judicial review, 38
Judiciary bills in Congress, 228–237
Jurisdiction of national courts, 240–241

Kenniston trial, 8–9
Kent, James, 13, 96–98, 134–135, 196–197

King, Samuel W., 58–59
Knapp trial, 9

Lexington case, viii, 43–52, 243
License Cases, viii, 213–217
Livingston, Brockholst, 96–98
Livingston, Edward, 113
Livingston v. Van Ingen, 196–197
Louisville, Cincinnati, and Charleston Railroad v. Letson, 192
Luther v. Borden, viii, 58–64, 242

McCulloch, James W., 183–184
McCulloch v. Maryland, vi, 170–178
McKinley, John, 186–187, 193, 222, 223
McLean, John: Massachusetts boundary, 57; Charles River Bridge case, 123; opinion in Charles River Bridge case, 132–133; opinion in Wheaton v. Peters, 150–151; opinion in Groves v. Slaughter, 211–212; License Cases, 217; opinion in Passenger Cases, 222–223; mentioned for Supreme Court appointment, 233, 236–237
McMillan v. McNeill, 112, 118
Mansfield, Lord, 149, 151
Marsh, Charles, 69
Marshall, John: sketch, 18–19; relationship with Webster, 19–20; political questions, 52–53; Dartmouth College opinion, 99–101, 106–107; opinion in Sturges v. Crowninshield, 111–112; opinion in Ogden v. Saunders, 115–117; Charles River Bridge case, 123; opinion in Johnson v. McIntosh, 143; and law of charitable uses, 160, 167; opinion in McCulloch v. Maryland, 175–178; opinion in Osborn v. B.U.S., 180–181; Etting v. B.U.S., 184; B.U.S. v. Dandridge, 184–185; opinion in Gibbons v. Ogden, 202–207
Martin, Luther, 170, 172–173
Mason, Jeremiah, 6–7, 72–73, 184, 230–231
Mason v. Haile, 145–146
Mercer, Charles F., 234
Mitchel v. U.S., 145
Moor's Charity School, 65–67
Morton, Marcus, 122

Nelson, Samuel, 51, 217, 223
Neutrality laws, 40–41
New Jersey Steam Navigation Co. v. Merchants' Bank of Boston. See Lexington case

New York v. Miln, 208–209
Norris v. Boston. See Passenger Cases
Nullification, 239–241

Oakley, Thomas J., 197–198, 200–201, 204
Ogden, David B., 30, 113, 187–189, 191, 193, 218
Ogden v. Saunders, vi, 112–119, 244
Ohio taxation of B.U.S., 178–181
Original-package doctrine, 207, 213–217
Osborn v. B.U.S., vi, 128, 178–181, 244

Paine, Elijah, 148–150
Parish, Elijah, 67
Parker, Isaac, 8, 122–123
Parsons, Theophilus, 8
Passenger Cases, viii, 218–224
Patents, 153–154
Pennock v. Dialogue, 153
Perkins, Cyrus, 90
Peters, Richard, 148, 152
Phillips v. Bury, 81
Pierce v. New Hampshire. See License Cases
Pinkney, William: sketch, 27–28; retained as Dartmouth College counsel, 89–90; McCulloch v. Maryland, 170, 173–178; and McCulloch v. Maryland opinion, 176–178; mentioned, vi, 198
Piracy cases, 41
Planters' Bank of Mississippi v. Sharp, 135–136
Plumer, William, 7, 69–70, 75, 78, 79, 102
Plumer, William, Jr., 230
Police power, 200–208, 214–217
Political questions, doctrine of, 52–64, 242
Privateering cases, 40–41
Privileges and immunities clause, 187–188, 190–192

Raymond, Henry J., 63
Rhode Island v. Massachusetts, 54–58, 242
Richardson, William M., 71, 75–76
Ripley, Eleazar W., 79
Rowan, John, 235

Sampson, William, 113
Santissima Trinidad, 41

Sergeant, John: sketch, 30, *Wheaton* v. *Peters,* 150; *Girard Will* case, 161; *Osborn* v. *B.U.S.,* 179–180, *Alabama Bank Cases,* 187–191; mentioned, 182, 227

Shaw, Lemuel, 8, 121–123

Slavery, 206–207, 209–213

Smith, Jeremiah, 7, 72–74

Smith v. *Turner.* See *Passenger Cases*

Stockton, Robert F., 42

Story, Joseph: relationship with Webster, 13, 20–23; decision in *La Jeune Eugénie,* 42–43; *Lexington* case, 44, 46–47; *Conflict of Laws,* 46–47; on Webster's *Dartmouth College* peroration, 85; views on *Dartmouth College* case, 98; *Dartmouth College* opinion, 100–101; and *Dartmouth College* cognate cases, 102–104; bankruptcy legislation, 118; *Charles River Bridge* case, 123, 124; opinion in *Charles River Bridge* case, 133–134; opinion in *Wilkinson* v. *Leland,* 147; *Wheaton* v. *Peters,* 152–153; opinion in *Pennock* v. *Dialogue,* 153; opinion in *Swift* v. *Tyson,* 156; opinion in *Girard Will* case, 166–167; *B.U.S.* v. *Dandridge,* 185; drafted judiciary bill, 229–230; views on judiciary bill, 230–231; Federal criminal code, 232–233

Stourbridge Canal v. *Wheely,* 131, 134

Sturges v. *Crowninshield,* 110–112, 113, 114, 116, 119

Sullivan, George, 74–75

Sullivan, William, 7

Swift v. *Tyson,* vii, 154–156, 243

Taney, Roger B.: Webster's attitude toward, vii; role as chief justice, 25–27; Massachusetts boundary, 56–58; political questions, 63–64; opinion in *Charles River Bridge* case, 130–132; dissent in *Planters' Bank of Mississippi* v. *Sharp,* 136; Florida land claims, 144; counsel in *Etting* v. *B.U.S.,* 183; opinion in *Alabama Bank Cases,* 190–191, 193; views on state power, 208; opinion in *Groves* v. *Slaughter,* 212; opinion in *License Cases,* 216–217; opinion in *Passenger Cases,* 223

Tariff, 239–240

Taxation, intergovernmental, 171–181

Terrett v. *Taylor,* 82, 147

Thompson, Smith: Massachusetts boundary, 56; opinion in *Ogden* v. *Saunders,* 115; *Charles River Bridge* case, 123, 130; dissent in *U.S.* v. *Arredondo,* 145; opinion in *Mason* v. *Haile,* 146; opinion in *New York* v. *Miln,* 208–209; opinion in *Groves* v. *Slaughter,* 211

Thompson, Thomas W., 2–3, 69

Thurlow v. *Massachusetts.* See *License Cases*

Trimble, Robert, 115, 236–237

Tucker, William J., 109

Tyler, John, 59, 62

U.S. v. *Arredondo,* 144–145

U.S. v. *Bevans,* 39–40, 232

U.S. v. *Fisher,* 177

U.S. v. *Hudson,* 232

U.S. v. *La Jeune Eugénie,* 41–43

U.S. v. *Palmer,* 52–53

Van Buren, John, 218, 221–222

Van Buren, Martin, 235–237

Vidal v. *Girard's Executors,* 156–168

Walker, Robert J., 210–211

Waring v. *Clarke,* 49–51

Washington, Bushrod, 100–101, 115–116

Wayne, James M., 49–51, 130, 222–223

Webster, Daniel: summary of legal career, v–viii; early life, 2–3; legal training, 2–5; legal practice in New Hampshire, 6–7; cases in lower courts, 8–9; qualities as lawyer, 9–15; personal finances, 13–15, 181–182; views on judicial power, 36–38; admiralty cases, 39–52; political questions, 54; *Dartmouth College* case, 68–109; contract clause cases, 110–141; bankruptcy cases, 113–116; bankruptcy legislation, 118–119; and property rights, 142; Florida land claims, 143–145; and copyrights, 147–153; patent cases, 153–154; *Girard Will* case, 156–166; national bank cases, 169–194; commerce clause, 196–226; relationship of legal and political careers, 227–241; views on Congressional powers, 237–239; economic views, 238–239, 243–245; views on slavery, 239–240; reply to Hayne, 240–241

Webster, Ebenezer, 2

Webster, Ezekiel, 4, 6
Webster, Grace Fletcher, 6, 21
West River Bridge v. *Dix*, viii, 136–140, 244
Wheaton, Henry: sketch, 29; attorney in *Ogden* v. *Saunders*, 113; bankruptcy legislation, 118; controversy with Peters, 147–153; reaction to copyright decision, 152–153; mentioned, 105
Wheaton v. *Peters*, vii, 147–153, 243
Wheelock, Eleazar, 65–67, 81, 84, 89, 90, 109
Wheelock, John, 67–70
Whipple, John, 45, 60–61, 146, 215
White, Hugh, 233
White, Joseph, 144
Wilkinson v. *Leland*, 146–147
Willson v. *Blackbird Creek Marsh Co.*, 207–208
Winder, William H., 41

Wirt, William: sketch, 28–29, 33; retained as *Dartmouth College* counsel, 79; and Webster's *Dartmouth College* peroration, 84–85; argument of *Dartmouth College* case, 86–88, 105; attorney in *Ogden* v. *Saunders*, 113; *Charles River Bridge* case, 123; Florida land claims, 144; *Wilkinson* v. *Leland*, 146; *McCulloch* v. *Maryland*, 170; *Etting* v. *B.U.S.*, 183, *B.U.S.* v. *Dandridge*, 184; *Gibbons* v. *Ogden*, 197–198, 201–202
Woodbury, Levi: on admiralty jurisdiction, 50–52; New Hampshire judge, 71–72; opinion in *Planters' Bank of Mississippi* v. *Sharp*, 136; opinion in *West River Bridge* v. *Dix*, 138–139; opinion in *Passenger Cases*, 224
Woodward, William H., 71
Wright, John C., 234